Designing
Sustainability

What is the relationship between design, sustainability, inner values and spirituality? How can we create designs that provide a convincing alternative to unsustainable interpretations of progress, growth, consumerism and commercialism? Building on the arguments first advanced in his widely acclaimed books *Sustainable by Design* and *The Spirit of Design*, Stuart Walker explains how we can achieve the systemic changes needed to address the challenges of sustainability.

Challenging common assumptions about the nature of our contemporary material culture and its relationship to human flourishing, the author introduces approaches to design that draw inspiration from Nature, summon the human imagination and create outcomes which are environmentally responsible and socially just, as well as meaningful and enriching at a personal level.

Offering a unique and original contribution to this vital debate, *Designing Sustainability* is destined to become essential reading for students on courses in design and sustainability and for design practitioners looking for a deeper, more meaningful basis for their work.

Stuart Walker is Professor of Design for Sustainability at Lancaster University and Emeritus Professor, University of Calgary, Canada. He is the author of many award-winning publications and his propositional designs have been exhibited at the Design Museum, London, across Canada and in Europe.

'Quite simply, this is the best book on the key issues that engage us – values, culture, the environment, beliefs, making a better world – that I have ever read. It is utterly original, deeply rooted, supremely pragmatic and splendidly visionary. You will not see anything in our physical, designed, created world in the same way ever again.'

Martin Palmer
Secretary General, *Alliance of Religions and Conservation* (ARC)

'A seminal contribution to the profession of design that begins with the heart and mind of the designer and the values most important to human flourishing. *Designing Sustainability* aims to ground the practice of design in a vision of a civilization worthy of being sustained. The message is timeless.'

David W. Orr
Paul Sears Distinguished Professor of Environmental Studies and Politics, Oberlin College, Ohio
Author of *The Nature of Design* and *Design on the Edge*

'In the bustle of what counts for progress, too often we forget to imbue our objects, places and transactions with the meaning that makes life worthwhile. Joyfully and patiently Stuart Walker shows us how to design spiritual satisfaction into the everyday so that we, and the Earth we inhabit, may be whole again.'

Sara Parkin
Founder Director and Trustee, *Forum of the Future*

'Professor Walker gets to the essence of design for our future, offering a wake-up call for designers and consumers alike. His *Quadruple Bottom Line of Sustainability* turns upside-down the emphasis on design for profit and mass consumerism. He calls for fundamental change and asks us to *"measure our contribution to sustainability not by how much we can do, but by how much we can do without"*. A thought-provoking and contemplative book that should be on every designer's reading list.'

David Constantine MBE
Co-Founder, *Motivation*

'In an age of all-encompassing artifice, *Designing Sustainability* challenges designers to re-think how their discipline understands nature. The originality and import of this book lies in how the author proposes ways of using design as an almost individual means of helping us re-engage transitively and unsentimentally (at deeper levels) with the natural.'

Clive Dilnot
Professor of Design Studies, The New School for Design, New York

Designing Sustainability

Making radical changes in a material world

Stuart Walker

Routledge
Taylor & Francis Group

LONDON AND NEW YORK

First edition published 2014
by Routledge
2 Park Square, Milton Park, Abingdon, Oxon OX14 4RN

and by Routledge
711 Third Avenue, New York, NY 10017

Simultaneously published in the USA and Canada

Routledge is an imprint of the Taylor & Francis Group, an informa business

British Library Cataloguing in Publication Data
A catalogue record for this book is available from the British Library

Library of Congress Cataloging in Publication Data has been requested.

ISBN: 978-0-415-74411-9 (hbk)
ISBN: 978-0-415-74412-6 (pbk)
ISBN: 978-1-315-79732-8 (ebk)

Typeset in Futura
by Saxon Graphics Ltd, Derby

MIX
Paper from
responsible sources
FSC FSC® C013056
www.fsc.org

Printed and bound in Great Britain by
TJ International Ltd, Padstow, Cornwall

To Bill Perks
for his vision and mentorship

Contents

Contents

viii

Figures, Tables
and Plates

Unless otherwise specified, designs, photographs, diagrams and tables are by the author.

Figures

Tables

Plates

Acknowledgements

I would like to thank my students whose questions, conversations and explorations over the years have been so important in shaping the ideas contained in this book. I would also like to recognize the contributions of the many anonymous peer-reviewers who have provided such valuable feedback on earlier versions of these writings; their time and thoughts, given voluntarily, are a critical component of the scholarly enterprise. My appreciation goes to the many authors I have cited – their thoughts and arguments provided the foundation for the design directions explored here. Many thanks to the Social Sciences and Humanities Research Council of Canada and to ImaginationLancaster at Lancaster University for supporting much of the research that led to this book. I am grateful to all those at Routledge who have offered advice and brought this book to publication. Finally, I would like to thank my wife Helen for her astute insights, her editing and her immeasurable support.

Acronyms and Abbreviations

BCE	Before the Common or Christian Era
CE	Common or Christian Era
CO_2e	Equivalent Carbon Dioxide
GDP	Gross Domestic Product
WTO	World Trade Organization

1
Introduction

... brush the sand – and all that you have seen
Has gone, as though the marks had never been.
Such is the solid world we live in here,
A subtle surface which will disappear.

Farid Ud-Din Attar

Designing Sustainability is concerned with creative approaches to design that are rooted in understandings of being human; a type of design that grows out of contemplation, reflection and quietness. These are essential ingredients of the examined life and of spiritual development, and a vital aspect of creativity. Inner values and spiritual wellbeing have long been associated with the natural world. For centuries, in both Eastern and Western traditions, Nature has been seen as a source of spiritual nourishment and something to be honoured and cherished. *Designing Sustainability* refers to ways of designing that emerge from solitude, from thinking deeply about something, from spending time in Nature, being heedful of its rhythms and drawing inspiration from its presence. In this sense, these chapters are implicitly about invoking radical changes; one definition of the term radical being a considerable departure from current norms, and another being related to root principles. Both definitions apply here – the purpose being to summon the human imagination and the creative calling and to reflectively develop design propositions that are in harmony with the natural environment, an ethics of virtue and our spiritual selves.

Such design work will be often out of kilter with current mores and trends. Dominating themes of economic expediency, product proliferation, technological urgency and the 'global race' for growth[1] are hardly compatible with more solitary, introspective modes of being. Similarly, short-term political agendas and ill-considered enthusiasms that direct and constrain academe, and that demand impact, value for money and utilitarian rationales tend to put the cart before the horse. Burdensome requirements for 'real world' impact, bureaucratic compliance, targets, measurable evidence and collective work practices can effectively stultify reflection, imagination, creativity and innovation. Such impositions emphasize rationality, analytical thinking and accountability, but are oblivious to vocation, trust, contemplation, intuition and the numinous.

Yet, despite these passing avidities there remain quieter, more solitary ways of working that still allow us to learn from others and, in turn, to make a contribution. Calmer modes tend to be more conducive to the iterative task of absorbing the considered views of others, drawing connections between seemingly disparate ideas, and generating imaginative concepts. Reading widely, studying creative works, reflecting, writing and sketching – all these are best done alone. Solitude benefits concentration, prevents diffusion of energy on matters unrelated to the task in hand, and can spur creativity and innovation.[2] The creative insights such ways of working may yield will be what they will – they cannot be conjured to serve particular, predetermined, extrinsic ends, whether those be economic, political or something else. Besides, that should not be the concern of academic inquiry, creativity and learning – these things must be pursued for their own sake, as intrinsic goods.

Hence, this form of design is inherently interrogative. It takes us down a path that challenges conventions, probes assumptions and, in a spirit of inquiry, poses possibilities. It is an approach to design that attempts to recognize a wider spectrum of human reality and potential than that offered – for too long – by a constricted but verifiable materialism. Under the harsh but narrow spotlight of abstract rationalization, one and one inevitably and unswervingly make two. The self-evident correctness of the formula bears an intractable logic. One and one make two. We know it. We accept it. We use it. But that does not make it true. In white, windowless corridors, where partiality constructs a quantified reality, one and one always make two. But it is a pale and barren coupling within a manufactured mirage of reality.

Under the warm and wide embrace of a summer sun, one and one almost never make two. In the world we see around us, in the natural world, abstracted rationalizations do not exist. Here we see abundance – where one and one make three, four, five, hundreds and thousands. It is a world aglow with fecundity and fullness. A world of beauty and mundane miracles. This is the real world and, as Papanek once told us, we must design for the real world.[3] This world knows nothing of isolated objects of desire; nothing of materialization detached from provenance or consequence. To design for the real world we have to step back from ingrained conventions and see the world from a broader perspective.

When is a tree? The question might seem bizarre, but it invites us to consider our assumptions about the nature of things. Is a tree the acorn, the sapling, the fully grown oak, or the decaying home of insects and fungi on the forest floor? Is a tree a thing or is it a term we use to signify a particular concentration of growing, maturing, flourishing, dying and decomposing? This is the way of Nature and the way of all material things, whether natural or human-made. We can ask a similar question about our manufactured world. When is an electronic product? Is it the thing we desire, we purchase, we hold in our hand and use? Or is it a mining site with drilling and explosions and machinery, spoil tips, fumes and dangerous conditions? Is it factories and labour exploitation, plastic presentation boxes and shiny novelty surrounded by hyperbole? Or is it discard and landfill, toxicity and leaching? Or is it simply the next model? When we consider trees and products in terms of their provenance and consequence rather than as isolated, static things, we begin to see them in a different light, and it quickly becomes apparent that the tree and the electronic product are fundamentally and inextricably linked – originating from the same source and destined to return to that source after all too brief a period. With apologies to Keats,[4] a thing of beauty is no joy forever ... it is but a firefly flashing in the dark and endless night of eternity.

In this book I attempt to make a contribution to the debate about *designing sustainability* through an interwoven process of thinking and doing, writing and designing. These activities are mutually informative and intimately related, and from them arise, on the one hand, discussions about intentions, priorities, ways of thinking about processes and products, and establishing a basis for designing and, on the other, a series of physical objects. This combination of outputs seems to me the most suitable way of advancing our thinking in design. Design is a discipline that depends on an intimate and thoughtful immersion in the creative process. It calls on the imagination, subjective judgements and a synthesis of ideas through deliberation and practice. Without this critical, practice-based manifestation of ideas through designed artefacts it is, quite simply, not design. Of course, we can and do have excellent critiques of design, and theoretical discussions about design and its products. But it is important to recognize that while theoretical understandings and ideas can inform the creative design process, they themselves are also informed by it. Therefore, to advance the discipline, we have to engage directly in the creating process – a process in which one strives to fuse diverse abstractions into a concrete and aesthetic whole. By engaging in this demanding and frequently frustrating activity we gain understandings and insights, which find their way into the designed artefacts and, on reflection, can find their way too into the developing direction of the theoretical ideas.

In addition, compared to the patently unsustainable direction that much design has been taking for decades, artefacts and imagery that demonstrate alternative,

3

more appropriate directions can have a very positive effect, not least by suggesting a vision of facility and capability and thus reinforcing a sense of self-determination. In a study about imagery related to climate change, for example, O'Neill et al.[5] found that images of energy futures, such as wind farms and solar panels, and products related to lifestyle choices, such as electric cars, tend to support feelings of self-efficacy in the behaviours and practices people undertake in relation to the environment, whereas images of climate change impacts can undermine such feelings by making people feel helpless in the face of such enormous issues.

In Chapter 2, *The Object of Nightingales*, I discuss a basis for design values that is congruent with age-old understandings of human meaning as well as with contemporary notions of sustainability. A critique of naturalistic materialism and its relationship to unsustainable interpretations of progress and growth is followed by a consideration of practical, social and personal meaning and the relationship of these to human values. A basis for meaningful values stemming from the world's wisdom traditions and thence a basis for ethical judgement are related to design decision-making. Some common, but ethically questionable, unsustainable design practices are reviewed – including product transience and distracting modes of use. Ethical, sustainable design decision-making is characterized, which includes notions of moderation, the appropriate place and role of products and the justification for their production in the first place. The result is a basis for product design and production that aligns more closely not only with sustainable principles, but also with deeper, more enduring understandings of human flourishing.

Chapter 3, *Design on a Darkling Plain*, is a practice-based design exploration that looks at the relationship of contemporary products to issues of sustainability and enduring meaning. In particular, the secondary or extrinsic value of products is considered, which includes technological advancement and business development. Instrumental value is also addressed, along with a product's intrinsic value – or lack of it. This leads to a set of general propositions for countering triviality and waste and increasing intrinsic value, and some of these propositions fall under the remit of design. Against this backdrop, product meaning and intrinsic value are explored with special reference to the philosophy of E. F. Schumacher as well as various critiques – from Arnold in the nineteenth century to Orr in the twenty-first – and a case is made for objects of design, rather than art, that have no practical utility but whose function is concerned with what might be referred to as 'inner work'. These arguments and ideas are translated into a series of propositional objects – questions in form – that ask how matters of ultimate concern, which are inherently ineffable, might be appropriately expressed as contemporary, contemplative artefacts.

The creation of *Contemplative Objects*, the subject of Chapter 4, is offered as a means of reflecting upon today's mass-produced version of human-made material culture, and particularly technological products that are ostensibly for human benefit. Through a research methodology that combines critical inquiry

4

with practice-based conceptual design, the assumptions and conventions of our current modes of product development, production, use and disposal are contextualized within the overarching ideology in which they exist. Selected subordinate objects – accessories that serve primary products such as mobile phones, laptops and printers – are stripped of their potentially influential brand identity and other persuasive encumbrances and are included as elements within panel compositions. These aesthetically considered arrangements invite reflection and the seeking of meaning. When accompanied by additional information and arguments, such objects offer a creative, discipline-appropriate means for reflecting upon the practices of product design and the kinds of objects that result from them, as well as alternative directions for a more sustainable future.

In Chapter 5, *Design and Spirituality*, I discuss contemporary calls for including spiritual considerations in our understandings of sustainability. These considerations are contextualized against the backdrop of modernity and the roots of design and manufacturing practices, as well as more recent design developments that focus on social innovation. An exploration of the meaning of spirituality and its relationship to worldviews, human needs and creativity, leads into a reflection on its implications for design. This results in a direction for design that not only brings to the fore ethical and environmental responsibilities, but also enduring notions of human wisdom.

Chapter 6, *The Narrow Door to Sustainability*, begins with a rationale for extending design's ambit beyond materialist and consumerist values in order to address today's pressing sustainability concerns. The contributions and limitations of eco-technologies and service solutions are examined within this context. The case is made that, first, a less consumptive path requires a more fundamental shift in priorities and values, and second, the basis of this shift must be established in deeper understandings of human meaning. The difficulties of including traditional, primarily religious, expressions of inner values in the public realm are identified. However, emerging trans-religious and/or supra-religious forms offer an opportunity for restoring notions of profound meaning and wisdom in our workaday endeavours. This provides a grounding for design development and the creation of a supra-religious spiritually useful artefact, which offers a tangible, creative example of a post-materialist direction for design. In the process, contemporary sustainability concerns are embraced.

In Chapter 7, *A Form of Silence*, I suggest that, to deal more effectively with today's environmental and social challenges, a new attitude or outlook has to be developed. In this endeavour, design can make an important contribution by creating conceptions of material 'goods' that are based on quite different priorities from those that are common in contemporary consumer societies. Design explorations are taken a stage further by developing a foundation for a contemplative object that is non-utilitarian, non-symbolic, supra-religious and, importantly, non-made. It can also be regarded as sustainable, both in terms of the ethos underlying its proposition and in terms of its physicality. After identifying some of the primary obstacles to change, various avenues for effecting change

5

are considered, which can be extrinsic or intrinsic. Intrinsic avenues include the development of a changed outlook and this development is explored in terms of its implications for design. An exemplar object is proposed that expresses something of this new outlook.

Having looked in some detail at values, attitudes and the creation of non-utilitarian, contemplative objects, Chapter 8, *A New Game*, returns the discussion to the functional object. The chapter begins with a consideration of the context and story behind objects, and the relationship of these to meaning and values. As a basis for evolving constructive, positive directions for design development, current preoccupations that drive consumerism, growth and unsustainability are critiqued with respect to ethical understandings, particularly *virtue ethics*. The vital link between the natural environment and our spiritual wellbeing, a link recognized in all societies and cultures, is illustrated through a series of evocative examples. These understandings allow us to contextualize contemporary design and see it from a different perspective. Here I use the Bauhaus chess set, designed by Josef Hartwig in 1923/24, as an epitomic example of the still dominant modernist approach to contemporary design. An alternative, sustainable approach is posited, which yields a propositional object, the *Balanis* chess set. This design is an attempt to respond through form to a larger vision of human reality than that offered by modernist, materialist perspectives. The Hartwig and *Balanis* chess sets, both vehicles for exploring design ideas and directions, serve as tangible demonstrations of contrasting design philosophies and their differences are illustrated and compared. The provenance of the *Balanis* chess set is dealt with in some depth in order to exemplify the origins of meaning and value in design, and their relationship to Nature, locale, process and spiritual wellbeing.

Chapter 9, *Epilogue*, reflects on the attitude that *designing sustainability* requires and nurtures – an attitude that sets aside inquisitiveness and acquisitiveness, and is more accepting, yielding and composed. This supports design directions in which the natural is allowed in and resides with the human-made in balanced accord.

6

2

The Object of Nightingales

design values
for a meaningful
material culture

… such madness is given by the gods to allow us to achieve the
greatest good fortune; and the proof will be disbelieved by the clever,
believed by the wise.

Plato

One evening in 1942, deep inside a wood in the southeast of England, a BBC
sound engineer was recording the song of the nightingale. Coincidentally, this was
also the night of a British bombing raid on Mannheim, and while the sound
engineer was at work 197 bombers flew overhead on their way to Germany. The
recording begins with the song of the nightingale and continues as the drone of
the aircraft slowly increases, becoming a deafening roar as they pass directly
above, before steadily decreasing and eventually fading away; throughout the
recording the nightingale sustains its song.[1, 2] It is a poignant and thought-
provoking piece. The high, trilling notes of the nightingale are natural and
unaffected, and to the human ear, pure, aesthetic and sublime. By contrast, the
ominous cacophony of the bombers is the sound of human-made war
technologies – the manufactured machines of conflict and purposeful destruction.
Significantly, we can clearly identify what the bombers are for; their purpose is
combat, damage and discord. But we cannot say what the nightingale is for; we

cannot think of nightingales in instrumental terms. The nightingale is not a means to some other end, it is an end in itself; it simply *is*.

Robert Louis Stevenson also wrote of the nightingale, suggesting that,

> a remembrance of those fortunate hours in which the bird has sung to us ... fills us with such wonder when we turn the pages of the realist. There, to be sure, we find a picture of life in so far as it consists of mud and of old iron, cheap desires and cheap fears, that which we are ashamed to remember and that which we are careless whether we forget; but of the note of that time-devouring nightingale we hear no news.[3]

The nightingale has a long history of symbolic associations with creativity, the muse, Nature's purity and, in Western spiritual tradition, virtue and goodness.[4] Here, these various symbolic associations come together in a consideration of creative design and its relationship to human values.

I begin with a critique of our current predicament within a dominant ideology of naturalistic materialism, which judging by its outcomes appears to be seriously flawed in terms of its ethical and environmental implications. This widespread ideology, combined with the sophisticated capabilities of scientific and technological advancement, a corporate aspiration of unbridled profit and growth and an undefined, yet largely relativistic ethical position, has created a potent recipe for human exploitation and environmental destruction. I suggest that any meaningful notion of sustainability must be grounded in a firm foundation of those values that are common to all the great wisdom traditions, both religious and non-religious, as well as to contemporary progressive forms of spirituality,[5–9] and that through adherence to such values design can make a tangible, discernible and positive difference to the nature and effects of our material goods.

Naturalistic materialism and human values

Naturalistic materialism is an ideology strongly associated with the post-traditional understandings and philosophies of modernity and late- or post-modernity. These are epitomized by the philosophy of Nietzsche, who so emphatically dismissed traditional beliefs as mere 'idols', along with the moral values that accompanied them.[10] Also known as naturalism, physicalism or simply materialism, naturalistic materialism has become the overarching doctrine of the modern Western world – a world characterized by its emphasis on secularism, rationalism and industrial capitalism. Naturalistic materialism is, nevertheless, a belief system and is no more provable than the traditional beliefs it has tended to depose. As the principal ideology of modernity, its critics have included Thoreau in the nineteenth century,[11] Horkheimer and Adorno in the mid-twentieth century[12] and Schumacher in the latter part of the twentieth century.[13] It is related to forms of modern secular humanism in which human interests and values are based on reason, scientific investigation and experience, and where human fulfilment must be found within the physical world; the physical universe being regarded as the totality of existence, with no place for traditional religious beliefs or notions of ultimate reality, whether theistic or non-theistic.

Thus, naturalistic materialism is an ideology that is linked to the physical sciences;[14] indeed, it is often seen as the only belief system that is compatible with them.[15] It is also an ideology that seeks to mould the natural environment and human society to suit human purposes and is characteristically interventionist, functionalist and grounded in instrumental reason.[16] Scientific investigations and analyses of the physical world lead to understandings of physical principles, and such investigations are regarded as being value-free; being concerned only with the investigation, analysis and understanding of physical phenomena and the physical world.

However, physical principles can be, and frequently are, exploited and utilized for human purposes – and these kinds of activities are *not* value-free. The application of scientific principles to achieve human intention has an instrumental basis and, by the very fact that it is thought to be worth doing, a value judgement is made. Hence, when such applications are developed, either in academia or in corporate research facilities, the question of human values enters the scene. In academia the value may be to demonstrate usefulness and potential functional and/or economic benefit sometime in the future. In the corporate setting the relationship to economic potential will likely be more direct and more immediate. Yet, within the ideology of naturalistic materialism, which as we have seen holds that the value-free physical universe constitutes the whole of existence, the basis for a set of ethical values against which we can gauge the goodness or rightness of these judgements is by no means clear (apart from the claim that such actions are contributing to progress, which in and of itself may be meaningless and without value).[17, 18] Public policy only consolidates such a direction by addressing its decision-making to purely material needs,[19] which become increasingly relative. Within such an ideology, there is a danger that values become based merely on a foundation of ever-shifting societal mores and norms. Here, each incremental change might seem like a small and reasonable step forward but, over time, such steps can, cumulatively, take us down a path that is both socially exploitative and environmentally (and, therefore potentially self-) destructive. In many respects, and despite, or indeed because of, the many and varied material benefits brought about by contemporary technologies, there can be little doubt that this is the road on which we now find ourselves. Traditional sources of meaning and value may have been abandoned, but nothing has replaced them, leading to what Beattie has termed 'valueless' values and a proliferation of meaningless choices.[20] Moreover, there is a certain ambiguity and confusion among some who reject the notion of absolute standards of morality. Arguing for a more pluralistic, and inevitably more relativistic, notion of morality, they also appeal to 'basic moral principles' while offering little justification for such principles or adequately distinguishing them from the 'absolute' moral standards they choose to reject. Apart from this internal contradiction, such a morality confines itself to knowledge and reason,[21]

9

which as we shall see, not only presents a more limited view than that afforded by the world's wisdom traditions, it also opens up the possibility of moralities that are patently immoral; Nietzsche, for example, dismissed traditional 'basic moral principles' such as equality and being kind to one another as mere moral pretensions.[22]

It is important to recognize too that the ideology of naturalistic materialism cannot rule out humanity's traditional understandings of reality. Just because science reports only on findings concerning the physical universe, it does not follow that the physical universe is the totality of existence. Nevertheless, this illogical conclusion is one that has become prevalent. It is a conclusion that is also unscientific; critique, therefore, is not aimed at science but at the scientistic ideology that we have built from its findings.[23] Here, Cottingham usefully distinguishes between notions of naturalistic materialism that are essentially methodological and those that are ontological. Methodologically, naturalistic materialism represents an attempt to explain the totality of existence via physical phenomena, with no reference to notions of a transcendent reality; as such it represents a set of investigative and exploratory aspirations. Ontologically, however, naturalistic materialism claims that the physical, phenomenal universe is the totality of existence – a claim that clearly lies beyond the realm of science.[24] This still-prevalent ontological interpretation, with its ill-defined and questionable value system, is inextricably linked to industrialism and technological conceptions of progress, both of which are precariously dependent on energy resources, especially hydrocarbons. In turn, such developments are catalysts of urbanization, and the promulgation of globalized, growth-based consumer society. It is, therefore, an ideology that not only constricts humanity's notions of meaning and reality, it is also indelibly tied to stripping the planet of its resources at unsustainable rates while simultaneously eradicating the complex interdependencies of biodiversity on which all life depends. However, while it remains a widespread ideology, it is also one that we seem to be slowly freeing ourselves from,[25] with many contemporary theorists regarding moral values as falling outside naturalistic explanation.[26] In moving beyond naturalistic materialism we have the opportunity to reassess our values. This can include the retrieval of understandings that have become increasingly marginalized in 'advanced' societies, but which, for thousands of years, had provided substantive foundations for living that were both meaningful and in balance with the cycles of Nature. Recognizing the significance of these foundations, together with the serious deficits, as well as the benefits, of contemporary approaches will, potentially, allow us to deal more effectively with the social and environmental challenges of our time.

Meaning and its relationship to values

A firmer basis for human values – and their relationship to human endeavour – emerges when we include traditional understandings of meaning. In this regard, there are three incontrovertible elements of the human condition. First, we exist within a natural environment that we utilize to our own ends. Second, human nature is such that we generally choose to live in social groupings. Third, we are individual beings with a distinct sense of selfhood. Corresponding to these three aspects of being human are levels of meaning that can be referred to respectively as *practical meaning*, *social meaning* and *personal* (or inner) *meaning*.[27] This analysis extends Hick's proposition of natural, ethical and religious meanings[28] so as to include not only religion but also contemporary, non-religious or atheistic forms of spirituality; the latter embracing interpretations of humanism that reach beyond the ontological doctrine of naturalistic materialism to acknowledge an ineffable, quasi-transcendent notion of the unity or one-ness of reality.[29] Such interpretations are not far removed from the more humanistic aspects of Buddhism, especially Zen Buddhism.[30] These contemporary forms of spirituality can be entirely secular, or they can include elements of traditional religion, and they often provide a strong basis for inner growth, personal ethics and for addressing today's important environmental and social concerns.[31] Hence, these three major facets of human meaning span physiological aspects of being human, social relationships and personal values and spiritual growth, both religious and atheistic. These, along with their interrelationships, are summarized in Figure 2.1 and can be described as follows.

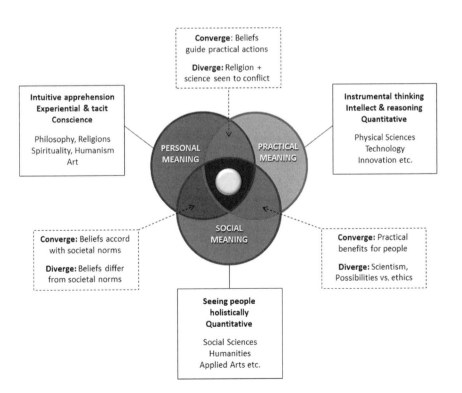

Figure 2.1 *Three facets of human meaning and their interrelationships*

Practical meaning: The natural environment provides us with food, water, shelter, warmth and materials – all of which help satisfy our practical needs and wants. Appropriate interpretation of the natural environment and physical phenomena in order to satisfy these needs and wants, as well as a recognition of the consequences of our actions, give practical meaning to our decisions and actions. Practical meaning is characterized by: that which is sense-based and provable; instrumental thinking; intellect and reasoning; quantitative methods; evidence-based methods; analytical thinking; logic and efficiency. It is perhaps best represented today by disciplines such as the physical sciences, mathematics, engineering, and technology and innovation.

Social meaning: Our interactions and dealings with other people are mediated by concerns such as justice, peace, charity, compassion and the moral compass that informs our social relationships. Our decisions and actions, in relation to ethical principles, moral codes, and social mores and conventions, give social meaning to our lives. Hence, important aspects of social meaning include seeing people as individuals; asking what is good, right and fair, i.e. values/morals; empathy and compassion towards *the other*; and greater emphasis on qualitative rather than quantitative considerations. Social meaning is represented by disciplines such as social sciences, politics, law, philosophy, economics, as well as the applied arts such as design and fashion.

12

Personal meaning: The interior life and addressing perennial questions about *being* itself, life's purpose and ultimate value cannot be pursued through rationalization or proved via empirical methods. These areas of human concern encompass what might be termed the inner search and they can influence our actions in the world. Our attention to these age-old questions can give a personal sense of meaning to our lives through attention to spiritual growth and the development of an inner sense of that which is right and good, i.e. a core sense of ethics and values, which Needleman has referred to as that which is permanent in us, irrespective of sociocultural particularities.[32] The characteristic modes for developing this sense of personal meaning include reflection, intuitive apprehension, direct experience and tacit ways of knowing that lie beyond the capacity of the senses and proof. Such modes transcend thoughts, judgements, knowledge, ideas and concepts and are more concerned with silence, listening and experiencing. They can also include aspects of the active life, especially 'good' works, and fidelity to tradition. Individual striving towards a personal sense of meaning is represented by the world's great theistic and non-theistic religions, philosophies and practices, as well as by contemporary atheistic spiritualities. We could also include certain artistic practices and modes of expression in the fine arts, poetry, music and literature.

The interrelationships among the above categories can be described as follows:

Practical meaning and social meaning: These converge when we develop practical benefits for people in ways that are safe, healthy, just and considered right and good. However, they can diverge when, for example, empirical methods developed in the physical sciences are inappropriately used in the humanities – this leads to scientism and can be dehumanizing. They can also diverge when practical possibilities clash with ethical norms or with diverse ideas of what is right and good.

Social meaning and personal meaning: These converge when personal beliefs, which provide the basis for one's values and ethical judgements, correspond with social conventions, moral codes, laws and societal norms of fairness and justice. They diverge when questions of conscience and liberty of conscience arise, for example when religious or personal beliefs differ from societal norms and existing legislation.

Personal meaning and practical meaning: Personal beliefs, which can include religious faith and/or spiritual convictions, are often a powerful motivator for developing practical solutions. When this occurs, 'higher' or 'inner' ideas find expression through techniques, skills and sense-based modes. Furthermore, the nature of these practical solutions will often differ qualitatively from similar initiatives where such beliefs are not a prime motivator. For example, provision of housing for the poor, when developed by faith groups, will often take a grass-roots approach that involves volunteerism and community and adopts self-build techniques, whereas a non-faith based approach might be the development of a large-scale affordable housing project built by local government. However, personal meaning and practical meaning can frequently diverge because they represent very different ways of encountering the world; personal meaning based on inner conviction and beyond proof contrasts with practical meaning, which is both sense-based and provable. As a consequence, spiritual and religious understandings and scientific understandings are often perceived to be opposed and in conflict – even though, as is clear from the preceding distinctions, this is something of a false dichotomy.

The personal, the social and the practical: The inner life, the social life and the active pragmatic life are, of course, simply different aspects of a single life. They provide us with a basis for doing the right thing and constructing what might be termed a meaningful life, and for making a meaningful contribution to society.

13

Meaning, values and design

We have seen from the above that the inner or reflective life and our sense of personal meaning can provide a basis for our beliefs and worldview – ranging from religious to secular humanist. It is these aspects of meaning-seeking and spiritual growth that have traditionally provided humanity with its understandings of virtue;[33] that is, its notions of what is good, right and true. In turn, this personal sense of ethical values can qualitatively affect our practical actions in the world, as illustrated in Figure 2.2.

Design is, of course, a practical activity which, when linked to mass-production, can have significant and far-reaching consequences. Much contemporary design has become completely bound up with consumerism, transient products and waste – a point raised in the 1970s by Papanek.[34] And because so many of these products are now based on rapidly developing digital technologies, design has become an accessory, first, in endorsing the environmentally unsustainable dogma of progress, which in practice means technological progress and, second, in supporting growth, which in practice means financial growth and the pursuit of ever-increasing profits. An almost pathological quest for the next technological advancement is driven by a desire for competitive advantage to ensure increased sales of mass-produced products which, in turn, create financial growth. These skewed priorities are systemically linked to human exploitation and environmental destruction – a state of affairs that Jackson has termed the 'age of irresponsibility'.[35] This is an inevitable consequence of prioritizing growth in profits within a dominant ideology of naturalistic materialism in which instrumental, material benefits are lauded, ethical values are both vague and relativistic, and higher, more profound notions of human meaning are marginalized.[36]

14

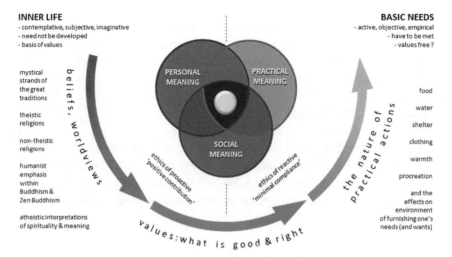

Figure 2.2 Beliefs, values and actions

To reform these practices, and particularly those associated with design decision-making, it becomes necessary to develop a clearer understanding of:

1. a basis for values
2. values for meaningful design decision-making
3. ethically questionable, unsustainable design practices
4. ethical, sustainable design decision-making.

1. A basis for values

If, as discussed, the progress-and-growth system in which contemporary design exists fosters sentiments and decision-making that contribute to social injustice and environmental harm, then to formulate just sentiments and responsible design decision-making we must look to other sources for guidance. To this end, the world's major philosophical and spiritual traditions provide a rich foundation in understandings of virtue. However, it is important to recognize that there is a view within contemporary, economically developed cultures that has become increasingly disdainful and dismissive of these traditions. Here, the most prominent detractors are indicative of a pervasive current that prizes evidence-based research, with its accompanying requirements of facts and proof, over imagination, emotion, empathy and spiritual and cultural traditions. Yet, anthropologist Elizabeth Lindsey calls such traditions humanity's DNA, adding that today, we 'live in a society bloated with data, yet starved for wisdom'.[37] Therefore, as we proceed, it will be important to bear in mind that while it is all too easy to disparage more intuitive ways of knowing with mundane rationalisms,[38] modes of living in which this has occurred are associated with staggering social inequities and unprecedented rates of environmental destruction.

15

It is important, also, to recognize that human values cannot simply be invented, nor can they be based on instinct or reached as a conclusion. Rather, our basic moral principles are grounded in a vast heritage of human experience and understanding, and as such they can be regarded as self-evident precepts and obligatory for their own sake.[39] However, when this foundational heritage becomes marginalized in a world dominated by materialistic understandings, there is a danger that the anchor that holds a value system in place is cut free, allowing values to drift in whatever direction the wind blows. Yet, when we talk of sustainability, these traditions and their teachings are significant because they represent the source of congruence with Nature and of reciprocity with our fellow human beings.

While specific traditions and their cultural practices and accretions are not the concern of this present discussion, it will be worth noting some important features of these traditions, which lead to understandings of human values. We will then consider some of the fundamental values common to all the major traditions, which provide a basis for ethical decision-making.

Spiritual traditions and practices, and human values: Even though the world's major spiritual traditions are very diverse, there are two broad features that are common to them all. First, they all have what might be termed popular practices that serve everyday needs; these include various rituals, ceremonies and rites of passage. Second, there are more dedicated practices, disciplines and methods that are aimed at inner development, insight and transformation. An example from traditional Japanese spirituality is the systematic training method known as *koshinto*.[40] Similar methods are found in all the major traditions – from the *Rule of St. Benedict* and the fifteenth-century writings of Thomas à Kempis in Western Christianity to the *Middle Way* of Buddhism.

Why, one might ask, are such things still relevant? The reason these kinds of teachings, practices and disciplines remain important and are perhaps more relevant than ever is because they are concerned with a desire to reach beyond the ever-changing, frenetic distractions of the busy, active life – beyond the latest gadget, the ceaseless headlines, and the newest trend – to focus on more profound notions of meaning and to apprehend a deeper sense of reality. These traditions are concerned with self-discipline and self-examination, contemplation, silence and the interior life, and insights that extend beyond instrumental thinking and rationalizations. These ways of knowing, we are told, transcend conceptualizations, thoughts, knowledge and words, and can lead to intuitive understandings and at least some apprehension of what has been referred to as the Real,[41] the Ultimate Reality or Ground of Being,[42] the Tao or Way of the Universe, and the interconnectedness and unity of all things.[43] Such insights are experiential and cannot be attained through the senses or through intellectual reasoning. They lie beyond any particular religion or dogma but, whatever the tradition, they have led those who have followed such a path to similar conclusions about values and how we *ought* to live. Even though these values are found through delving deeper into self, fundamentally and somewhat paradoxically, they transcend the ego, the self and selfishness; there are indispensable social as well as environmental (Nature, the universe) dimensions to such traditions. Emerging from these disciplines are teachings that advocate a course between deficiency and excess, as in Aristotle's *Ethics*[44] or the *Analects of Confucius*.[45] Moreover, following this middle course is our ethical obligation – so as to ensure balance and harmony in ourselves, in our dealings with others and with the ways of Nature,[46] and to attain any semblance of earthly happiness. Although there is no logically verifiable connection between these traditions and human values, they have for thousands of years and across all cultures provided the bedrock of ethical behaviour.[47]

A basis for judgement: To follow this path we must have a basis for making right judgements and, as classical Greek philosophy tells us, this is the role of education. True education is concerned with being taught to feel appropriate sentiments – 'to feel joy and grief at the right things', and to 'act according to the right principle', which is that which 'accords with prudence'.[48] Thus, education is about learning to like those things that one *ought* to like, so that one's emotional responses are in line with virtue. Also, we should proceed with consideration and caution in regard to practical matters. In this regard, being frugal and acting with foresight in caring for resources and the economy become essential aspects of right judgement.

If one *ought* to feel joy or grief at the right things, and if there are certain kinds of activities and modes of conduct that one *ought* to engage in, and others to avoid, for one's endeavours to be meaningful and ethical, then this implies that there are some objective standards against which one must judge one's behaviour. This is the principle of objective value.[49] Here, then, we have *subjective emotions*, which in and of themselves are not judgements, *facts*, which are value-free, and *objective value*, the belief that certain attitudes really are right or true while others are wrong or false. By becoming cognizant of these objective standards, via education, our emotional responses to external, factual phenomena have a reference point by which we can make right judgements, and thence act accordingly. For example, certain phenomena require a particular kind of emotional response, such as sympathy, delight or repulsion, and whether or not, as individuals, we are capable of feeling such emotions, knowledge of this requirement through education can guide us to act in a certain way. This recognition of objective value allows our emotional responses to be linked to reason, i.e. our emotional response is reasonable when it aligns with what we *ought* to feel, and unreasonable otherwise.[50]

17

Irrespective of whether we are able to accept the above argument, let us look at the values that these traditions espouse so as to consider their relationship to sustainability. We will then be able to determine if, indeed, they have any relevance for contemporary design and for aligning the nature of our material culture with sustainable principles.

2. Values for meaningful design decision-making

The values and teachings of the various traditions are, of course, wide-ranging and diverse. Therefore, for illustrative purposes, we will focus on some of those that are especially relevant to design and sustainability.

In terms of social considerations, one of the longest-standing and widely accepted precepts found in virtually all cultures across time is the ethic of reciprocity known as the Golden Rule. The call to 'not do to others what you would not want them to do to you', as taught by Confucius[51] is repeated in similar forms in the writings of Plato,[52] Taoism,[53] Hinduism,[54] Buddhism,[55] Judaism,[56] Christianity[57] and Islam.[58] The positive form of this ethic, 'do to others what you would have them do to you', tells us how we *ought* to act towards our fellow human beings.

Clearly, the inordinate economic and social inequities and human exploitation that are so prevalent today, both within and between nations, are incompatible with this ethic. Furthermore, many of these inequities and exploitative practices are directly linked to products and product manufacturing. The social upheavals and poor conditions associated with product manufacturing, waste and pollution in many economically developing countries have received widespread publicity in recent years. However, forms of exploitation are also present in the ways products are designed and marketed, where people's susceptibilities are deliberately manipulated and preyed upon to secure sales, thereby contributing to corporate economic growth. One example of this is 'undercover marketing' where people are unaware that seemingly everyday occurrences are, in fact, staged marketing activities.[59] Another is the common strategy of launching slightly 'improved' versions of essentially the same product at regular intervals, to stimulate desire and imbue notions of perceived obsolescence in relation to the previous model. Such approaches not only contravene the ethic of reciprocity, they are also fundamental to the environmental aspects of sustainability because they drive resource and energy use and generate waste.

Let us now look more specifically at the relationship of material goods to notions of meaning, so as to consider what value *should* be placed on them. The Chinese sage Lao Tzu not only advises against acquiring precious things, but also against putting ourselves in a position where we constantly see desirable things; such things come and go, but attention to them distracts us from what really matters[60] and what really matters is a recognition of the true self in relation to the Tao or the Real. Similarly, Buddhist teaching says that by hankering after transient things we fail to see life as it really is and forget life's true aim.[61] The atheistic existentialist Camus saw the mythic Sisyphus, forever pushing a rock up a mountain, and Kafka's K, attempting to reach The Castle, as two figures whose lives are taken up with the distractions and busyness of worldly affairs. For Camus, it is in the realization of the futility and absurdity of such worldly affairs that meaning is to be found.[62] By contrast, for the Christian existentialist Tillich, meaning is found in the acceptance of and struggle towards the heights, despite the day-to-day busyness and distractions; this, for Tillich, is 'the courage to be'.[63] So we see that, regardless of their nuances and differences, all these and many other traditional and philosophical sources suggest that a preoccupation with and craving for transient, worldly things is fundamentally lacking in meaning and detrimental to the human condition.

If this is indeed the case then the implications for design, and its relationship to sustainability, are critical. Not only is design a discipline that occupies itself with the definition of transient material things but, significantly, it tends to do so in ways that are deliberately intended to distract and arouse feelings of desire, craving and status. Marketing tends to only reinforce such feelings. The result is the constant production of fleeting enticements and contrivances that not only have little relationship to a meaningful life, but which also divert us away from it. In the process, due to the sheer scale of contemporary product production and disposal, design is indirectly contributing to the rapid denudation of resources, the destruction of natural environments and the accumulation of climate-changing emissions.

Clearly this raises significant and pressing issues with respect to design values – if we are to develop a material culture that is both meaningful and aligned with sustainable principles. Here, a meaningful material culture would be one that, in all its facets – its materials, its modes of production, its presence and use, and its ultimate disposal – conforms to, and serves to support, understandings of: human meaning and inner development; social relations and community wellbeing; and environmental stewardship. Therefore, recalling the basis of judgement described earlier, we will now consider some features of ethically questionable, unsustainable design practices, followed by an exploration of more ethical, sustainable design decision-making. However, it is important to note that such distinctions cannot be definitive. It is not so much a case of clear-cut delineations but more a question of emphasis and tone, which can lead to important qualitative differences in the nature of manufactured artefacts.

3. Ethically questionable, unsustainable design practices

If we are to refrain from ethically questionable, unsustainable design practices, we *ought not* to be making design decisions that intentionally try to ensure material goods are:

- **Enticing**: through such commonly accepted practices as unnecessary styling changes, shiny surfaces and aesthetic perfection, and fashionable, exuberant or luxurious enclosures. Such practices stimulate emotions such as craving or vanity that conflict with more profound notions of personal meaning, fulfilment and happiness.
- **Transient**: by engaging in practices that lead to premature product obsolescence – through, for example, unnecessary aesthetic changes or the specification of delicate surfaces and materials that quickly lose their appeal through everyday use and wear.
- **Distracting**: by creating products that allow or encourage opportunities for interruption, endless diversion and amusement, that hinder reflection or are known to contribute to compulsive use behaviours.

Based on the arguments presented here, all the above factors can negatively affect human flourishing while having major detrimental effects on social equity and the natural environment because of their modes of production, use and disposal.

4. Ethical, sustainable design decision-making

To create a material culture that is supportive of higher notions of personal meaning and human potential, as well as being socially and environmentally responsible, we *ought* to be making design decisions that help ensure that our everyday material goods are:

19

- **Moderate:** by consciously avoiding excessive and/or distracting characteristics, features or modes of use. In his housing designs, Irish architect Dominic Stevens demonstrates that moderation need not compromise good design. His sensitively designed homes are modest, low-cost, low-energy buildings that often incorporate reused materials.[64]
- **Relatively unimportant:** by recognizing the place functional goods *should* occupy in human endeavour if they are to comply with our most profound understandings of human meaning, and with ethical behaviours and environmental responsibility. This would mean that everyday products would have to occupy a far less dominant role than is the case today. To be in keeping with such a direction, their design would necessarily be more modest, recognizing their relatively minor place within human endeavours. One way of reducing the importance of possessions is through product-sharing schemes, which already include car sharing and city bike programmes. In their explorations of sustainable living, Manzini and Jégou have developed more radical product sharing ideas, including kitchens, objects and clothing.[65]
- **Useful tools:** by designing products to be functional, reliable and enduring but unassuming.
- **Congruent with meaning:** through their materials, modes of use, aesthetic definitions, symbolic references and non-instrumental characteristics functional goods can, potentially, reinforce ideas of how we ought to act and behaviours that are congruent with environmental, ethical and meaningful ways of living. Conversely, products designed to encourage intense desire or envy would be incompatible with such ideas.
- **Warranted:** the relationship of transient things to obfuscation and distraction from more reflective, moderate modes of being has long been recognized in the major spiritual and philosophical traditions. In the past century these detrimental effects have become combined with the devastating social and environmental repercussions of growth-based globalized mass-production. Therefore, we can no longer simply ask how products might be designed in better, more responsible ways. We must also ask if the design and production of a product is even justified in the first place. Today, the design rationale for a new model of product is usually expressed in instrumental terms – it performs faster, it is thinner, it offers higher resolution. These very mundanities are the currency of aspirational marketing with minor technical and aesthetic changes being linked to success and status. However, the underlying reason for producing yet another new model is invariably the generation of company profits and growth. When the source of our design decisions comes from a philosophical perspective that prioritizes materialism and worldly absorptions, the rationale and justification for design decisions will reflect this emphasis, and the product design itself will be a tangible manifestation of these practical, utilitarian values, with a corresponding

20

lack of emphasis on other factors. Such validations are generally accepted and regarded as enough within the growth-based system in which design and manufacturing reside. However, given the corrosive effects that the global production of transient things, particularly short-lived technological products, can have on personal wellbeing,[66, 67] social justice[68] and environmental stewardship,[69] there is a need to consider not only instrumental but also ethical justifications, as well as justifications that take into account deeper concerns related to spiritual or inner values. We must begin to ask if the production of yet another product is a good and right thing to do, and if the functional benefits or improvements, which are often minor, are warranted – now that we are aware of the cumulative effects of continuously producing, packaging, shipping, using and disposing of millions of such products. These questions are fundamentally related to notions of personal meaning and to sustainability; significant reductions in consumerism are essential for the furtherance of both.

- **Empathetic:** to help ensure that our material productions are more consistent with traditional understandings and ethical principles, we have to develop approaches that are far more empathetic to both people and place. It becomes important to be open to aspects that are often unconsidered or given short shrift in contemporary practice – aspects that can be intuitively apprehended but not necessarily supported by facts or intellectual reasoning. The architect Christopher Day recognizes these important facets of knowing when designing a new building for a particular site. His practice not only involves consensual, participatory methods, but he also spends time at the location being silent, listening, being open to first impressions – refraining from walking, talking, making value judgements or inferences, or even thinking – in order to apprehend something of the essence of the place.[70]

21

There various characteristics of ethical and meaningful design decision-making are summarized in Table 2.1.

Table 2.1 **Characteristics of ethical and meaningful design decision-making**

	Characteristic	Descriptor
Essential	Ethic of reciprocity	Design decisions to reduce production costs: • are in accord with good-quality human work and do not depend on low wages, poor labour conditions or the elimination of jobs through automation. • are in accord with natural systems and do not degrade water quality, air quality or the environment.
To be promoted	Moderation	Intentional avoidance of excessive or diverting features and modes of use.
	Relative unimportance	Recognition of the relatively lowly place functional goods should occupy in our lives to be in accord with notions of human meaning and with ethical and environmental responsibilities.
	Congruence with meaning	Through their materials, use, aesthetics, symbolism and non-instrumental characteristics, products can support ideas of how we ought to act and behaviours congruent with environmental, ethical and meaningful ways of living.
	Warranted	Is the design and manufacture of another product even justified given the corrosive effects that unprecedented levels of globalized production are having on Nature, social wellbeing and personal contentedness?
	Empathy	Product concepts, production, use and disposal methods that are considerate of people and place.
	Usefulness	Products that are functional, reliable and enduring but unassuming.
	Elegance	Through attention to form, proportion, expression and detail, products that grace the world by their presence.
To be avoided	Enticing	Products designed to encourage consumption – through fashionable, colourful 'perfection', as well as branding and marketing that stimulate cravings and feelings of vanity.
	Transient	Practices that encourage perceived obsolescence – via regular model changes and aesthetic updates, use of delicate surfaces that quickly fade, and styles that rapidly become tired and outdated.
	Distracting	Products that encourage diversion or compulsive use behaviours, that interrupt thoughts and hinder reflection.

Conclusions

Not everyone is temperamentally inclined towards the interior quest,[71] and we may or may not be able to accept traditional understandings of inner apprehensions and ways of knowing as a basis for values. Nevertheless, it does seem that these traditions lead to values that are consistent both with human development and with contemporary understandings of social responsibility and environmental care. Crucially, the essential values these traditions advocate are fundamentally at odds with many of today's common practices in design – from built-in obsolescence and products of distraction, to incremental product releases that arouse feelings of dissatisfaction and stimulate consumption and waste.

The unremitting production and marketing of short-lived, unrepairable and often relatively trivial products is associated with gross social disparities and environmental destruction on a massive scale. In addition, according to the world's traditional sources of meaning, it is also destructive to our own wellbeing and happiness. For these reasons the ethical underpinnings of many of our contemporary, widely accepted practices are highly questionable. Morality and creativity have always been closely associated with the meaningful life – but in a globalized system of corporate profit-seeking that is driven by technological advancement and grounded in an ideology of naturalistic materialism with its facts, evidence and proofs, there is a danger that these more intuitive ways of knowing become drowned out by mundane rationalizations that offer only a narrow, meagre notion of human flourishing. To return again to Stevenson, seeking for the nightingale and hearing him – which gives life its enchantment and grace – becomes overshadowed by 'cheap desires and cheap fears [and] that which we are ashamed to remember'.

23

3

Design on a
Darkling Plain
transcending utility
through questions
in form

And we are here as on a darkling plain
Swept with confused alarms of struggle and flight,
Where ignorant armies clash by night.

Matthew Arnold

There are opportunities today for design to employ its creative skills and
knowledge to take the discipline in new, little-explored directions. Doing so will be
of critical importance because the accelerating pace of technological
advancement in recent years, especially in digital technologies, has not only
created a plethora of new products and economic benefits but also an increasing
sense of disquiet. This uneasiness about the pace of change and the impacts of
technological objects, introduced in the previous chapter, is caused by a variety of
factors that can be summarized as follows:

- the environmental repercussions of production and waste;[1, 2]
- the social exploitation often associated with how these goods are made;[3]
- concerns about the personal impacts of using these products, such as
  social isolation and compulsive use behaviours;[4]
- growing concerns about the relationship of these technological objects to
  our spiritual wellbeing[5] and those things that may be important to human

welfare and our relationship to the world but are unsuited to digital media.[6]

These shortcomings are significant and present us with a considerable challenge in relation to sustainability. However, they also offer us an opportunity to explore how we might configure things differently – in ways that offer new layers of meaning that, hitherto, have been largely absent from our construal of design.

In this chapter I will discuss a rather different approach to design for sustainability from that offered by such methods as product life cycle assessment, eco-efficiency and other essentially technocratic paths. These tend to fall within an eco-modernist approach to sustainability, which has been criticized for its techno-economic optimism and for providing only incremental improvements to a fundamentally unsustainable system.[7, 8] As such, it represents a way of thinking that is short term, opportunistic and increasingly outdated; essentially, it seeks to maintain the status quo and fails to explore new, substantively different avenues.[9] Consequently, it does little to acknowledge or contribute to the transformational change and shift in thinking that many are suggesting are needed to effectively respond to the challenges posed by sustainability.[10, 11, 12] Approaches are required that explore alternatives to the current system – a system rooted in the continual, growth-driven production of technological products. In the early stages, such alternatives will necessarily be exploratory and conjectural. New possibilities can be conceived, discussed, combined and taken forward, and over time new directions may emerge.

25

Through reasoned argument and design engagement, this chapter explores one such direction, a direction for *designing sustainability*. Instead of considering artefacts of utility – whether in the form of products or services – which has preoccupied design for a century or more, the focus here is on the creation of artefacts for reflection and inner growth. While this path is more speculative than pragmatic, nevertheless, it serves to raise a number of important questions about our current conceptions of design and its relationship to sustainability.

First, the kind of reflective objects posited here can be stable – they need not be dependent on the use of digital technologies and are therefore not subject to their ever-changing advancement. It is this continuous advancement, so closely associated with the new and the latest, that is a key driver of consumerism, growth, rising energy use and escalating emissions and waste, particularly the growing problem of e-waste.[13, 14] More stable forms of material culture would be compatible with sustainability propositions that argue for a different kind of economic system; a system that recognizes that Western-style capitalism, which has largely excluded the environmental and social costs of doing business, is seriously flawed,[15] and one that fosters steady state or low growth rather than unrestrained growth tied to materials extraction, over-production, energy use and waste.[16, 17]

Second, in the fast pace of modern, connected life, the presence of objects whose purpose is aimed at reflection, inner growth and matters of ultimate concern can offer a salutary reminder of purpose, values and 'things that really matter';[18] this has always been the role of such objects.[19, 20, 21] Use of digital technologies is tending to erode such focused attention, and this can have a detrimental effect on the spiritual self.[22, 23] It is notable that busyness, distraction and a preoccupation with material things and their acquisition, all of which have long been regarded as hindrances to the examined life, come together to produce a powerful combination in digital products. Thus, the design of objects aimed at 'inner work' rather than outer utility can contribute to:

1. the stabilization of material culture and the reduction of consumerism, waste, materials use, energy use, packaging, transportation, etc.;
2. development of a non-growth-based economic system that is more compatible with the environmental and social facets of sustainability;
3. inner development and one's sense of personal meaning, aspects that, in recent years, have become increasingly important to our understandings of sustainability[24, 25, 26] and to critiques of digital futures.[27]

The value of products

It becomes evident that we have to give further consideration to the value of products, to where value lies and to what this signifies. As we will see, in addition to the products themselves, value also tends to be ascribed to the intellectual challenges associated with their technological development, as well as to the entrepreneurial challenges they present, which include the pursuit of business opportunities and business development. Significantly, however, it is these very areas of focus and value that provide a robust explanation for the trivialization of objects in consumer-based societies. Consequently, it also becomes important to explore ways of tackling these shortcomings in our contemporary notions of products, including those that are especially relevant to the designer. Here, the value of objects will be considered with reference to the divergent nature of design problems, as well as to profound notions of human meaning, as discussed in the work of E. F. Schumacher. Several design propositions or questions-in-form have been created as part of this exploration, based on an understanding of design as a question-asking activity rather than a problem-solving activity. These propositional objects, which are representative of ideas and values that are largely absent from contemporary digital products, have no utilitarian purpose but are nevertheless functional in that they offer a focus for what we might call 'inner work'. Furthermore, in setting aside practical application, these objects employ symbolism to refer to dimensions of human life and meaning that have been steadily marginalized during the modern era[28] but which are seen today as key aspects of sustainability.

Therefore, via propositional design practice, these (inescapably specific) manifestations represent attempts to translate ideas about object value into tangible form; ideas that not only transcend utilitarian value but also reach beyond aesthetics and rhetoric. The resulting objects raise questions about the role and place of deeper notions of human meaning in material culture, and their appropriate modes of expression. Hence, these are objects of design inquiry rather than objects of commercial design. Practical utility has been consciously omitted in order to delineate more clearly how other important but non-utilitarian factors, particularly those pertaining to deeper notions of human meaning and ultimate value, might be understood and thence manifested in form.

Where value lies and the trivialization of material culture

Some might view the sustainability-related concerns associated with contemporary products, particularly those based on digital technologies, as a relatively minor issue – an issue associated with a rapidly developing sector, which will be addressed and overcome as the sector matures. This would seem overly optimistic. The way in which technologies have progressed over the course of the past two to three centuries and the values this type of progress represents are indicative of a trajectory that bolsters and reifies a perilously narrow way of thinking and being in the world; one in which practical, outer concerns have come to dominate and where more profound, inner concerns play little or no part.[29] Yet, even such a narrowly scoped vision of advancement could, in principle at least, address some of the more damaging environmental consequences if adequate legislation were to be enacted. Unfortunately, as is all too evident, assiduous lobbying to protect powerful corporate interests along with the short-term agendas and *realpolitik* of contemporary democracies tend to prevent or at least debilitate such measures. However, if it is the case that the so-called environmental crisis should be more accurately spoken of as a spiritual crisis, as Buchanan, among others, has suggested,[30] then the implications for how we design our material culture, and the values we bring to bear, represent a significant creative challenge. It is a challenge that we are generally ill-prepared to tackle for the very reason that the pervasive culture in which design resides – in industry and education – is one that tends to value and prioritize practical, outer concerns over deeper questions of purpose and meaning.

27

The fundamental problem with such an inadequately scoped notion of design and production is that the means are apt to supersede and effectively become the ends. In other words, the processes of product development and business development become the driving forces, and valued for their own sake. As a result, the products themselves and their purpose and real value are only significant in as much as they provide the means to these other ends. Of course, product development and business development can be of enormous benefit and can bring their own rewards, but when they become the *raison d'être* of our approaches to material culture we have a recipe for unconstrained product proliferation and product trivialization – along with the portentous consequences such a direction connotes.

The product development process: Value and satisfaction can be found through problem solving and facing intellectual challenges. Achieving a set of predetermined objectives – for example, to develop a smaller, lighter, faster, higher-resolution mobile device that offers increased versatility of applications, higher speeds and data capacity – calls on ingenuity, problem solving and technical proficiency; solving such 'problems' can be both intriguing and demanding. Setting ambitious objectives can drive a project's development and provide considerable satisfaction and a sense of achievement.

These technical challenges are undoubtedly fascinating and endlessly absorbing – regardless of the potential value of the end result. Value here lies in the intellectual challenge for those involved in the specifics of the technological development – the scientists, engineers, academic researchers and technologists. However, while the development of such products might be enthralling for those immersed in the process, the end use of the product is often trivial and banal.[31] Indeed, the development of technology is frequently pursued with no immediate view to its potential usefulness – it is undertaken as an intellectual pursuit for its own sake and as such can be regarded as worthwhile and of considerable value. However, transforming such a technological advance into a marketable product after the fact is another thing entirely. While such a transformation can help fund the research and development for further technological advances, let us not confuse the value of the intellectual pursuit with the value – or lack of it – of the mass-market products that make use of such technologies. These are two very different things. It may well be that the product that incorporates such a technology is of little real value in our day-to-day lives, but we may be persuaded otherwise through skilful marketing in which incremental 'improvements' or marginal 'benefits' are ascribed disproportionate significance.

The business development process: Value and satisfaction can be found, also, in developing and maintaining a business enterprise. In the process, jobs are created, profits are made and wealth is generated. In turn, such wealth can be used for employee wages, research and development, and business improvement and expansion. This creates wealth for individuals, communities and countries; and business and income taxes help pay for health care, education, social services, infrastructure and security. While all this, too, can be regarded as worthwhile and of considerable value, if the primary purpose of that enterprise becomes growth and profit-seeking, then the material products produced become simply a means to that end and, in themselves, of only secondary importance. The necessity is to produce something, anything that will turn a profit and contribute to growth – even if that thing is trivial and banal.

While gaining profits and growing a business can be worthy elements of entrepreneurship and enterprise, seeking them for their own sake can distort the purpose and legitimacy of industry. Unfortunately it has long been the case that other responsibilities, including good citizenship, and ethical and environmental accountability, have not been taken seriously or effectively incorporated into most

28

business practices.[32] Such developments are due, in part, to the conventions and expectations of investment, dividends and shareholder gain, and the need to constantly demonstrate not just reasonable profits but a continual increase in profits, i.e. continual growth. For the shareholder, such profits are unearned – one does not put in a fair day's work for a fair day's wage. While such speculative forms of profit-seeking have become normalized in contemporary society, they should not be regarded as sacrosanct and immutable, especially if they are a distinctive feature of a system that is proving to be inherently damaging.[33] One of the greatest spiritual leaders of the twentieth century, Mahatma Gandhi, regarded 'wealth without work' and 'commerce without morality' as fundamental social transgressions.[34] It is the circumvention of such principles that drives the unbridled growth agenda of modern economics – an agenda that is inextricably linked not only to social injustices and environmental ruin, but also to the trivialization of our material culture through the proliferation of incremental variations on an outmoded theme. Design has been quite complicit in this trivialization, and in the process it has demeaned the creative gift at the heart of the discipline and diminished its contribution and potential.[35]

Therefore, having considered the values associated with product and business development we will now turn to the products themselves. What value do they have, what benefits do they bring and are these benefits worthy of the costs? The answers are by no means straightforward.

29

Product value: There are many products that clearly offer benefit to individuals and society. Basic tools, for example, allow us to perform important and necessary tasks – from growing food to building houses. And there are more sophisticated products that enable a host of contemporary activities – some of these are work related and ease the task of human labour, some are aesthetic and culturally enriching, while others are aimed at entertainment, diversion and feeding a consumption-dependent economic system.

Many products that aid us in our tasks, from power tools and domestic appliances to computers and modes of transport, we judge to be necessary and beneficial. Nevertheless, and regardless of their usefulness, they are too often created by employing globalized manufacturing processes that are exploitative, and in their making, use and disposal are highly problematic in terms of their broader environmental and social effects.[36] Modes of production and product functionality, maintenance and use, therefore, require constant scrutiny and improvement. In addition to those products that many would agree are useful or even essential, the manufacturing sector is also responsible for myriad novelties, fleeting amusements and gizmos, together with a continual stream of 'updated' gadgets. These products may help drive consumerism, economic growth and the creation of wealth, but their real value as things is highly debatable. Often, it seems we are too enamoured with innovation but give little time to contemplation, and are more concerned with the latest ideas but give little consideration to the wisest ideas.

The continual production of novelty and the proliferation of distracting pursuits are dominant characteristics of 'developed' societies based in consumer capitalism; where innovation, information and newness are all highly valued. Criticism of these overriding preoccupations goes back a long way. Writing in the second half of the nineteenth century at the height of the Industrial Revolution, Arnold saw them as barriers to personal growth and societal development.[37] In the mid-twentieth century, Horkheimer and Adorno gave a blistering critique of 'the culture industry', arguing that industrially produced entertainments and diversions – which they regarded as manipulative, desensitizing rubbish – offered 'freedom from thought' and a substitute for profundity. They regarded such works as impediments to the reflective life, which undermined individuality and debased personality.[38] Later in the twentieth century, Papanek severely criticized the role of design in pandering to such triviality, arguing that Industrial Design had become an inherently harmful profession and that the products of design should be not only socially and environmentally responsible but also of spiritual value.[39, 40] Today, the expanding reach of consumer society, the sheer pace of product production and change, especially in digital products – and through these, increased opportunities to access and be constantly distracted by information, infotainment and pre-packaged amusements – mean that these concerns and criticisms are more pertinent than ever. So, even though we may not be able to draw a definitive line between a necessary product and a trivial novelty or 'new' model, the presence of grey areas should not prevent us from addressing the issues. In light of the potentially ominous cumulative effects, of which today we are only too aware, the continued production of such products is becoming increasingly questionable. Yet it is these very products, which are neither especially useful nor enriching, that have become so critical to business development, job creation and the generation of wealth.

To address these concerns, and expanding on those already included in Table 2.1, it will be necessary to consider:

1. **Responsible resource use:** To be more discerning and more responsible as governments, companies and individuals in regard to the products we wish to produce and use – in terms of their value and contribution as things, irrespective of any secondary benefits they might hold for their developers (e.g. researchers, technologists, etc.) or for business development and wealth creation. If these considerations were to become part and parcel of our thinking, we could foresee a time, for example, when we will need to seek permission to use natural resources and energy – but only for non-trivial, non-wasteful purposes. We might well reach a point where we can no longer afford to indiscriminately produce 'things', use natural resources as if they were free for the taking[41] and burn hydrocarbons and create waste for non-essential purposes. Norms can change very quickly once their effects have become widely understood.

Relatively recently, commonly accepted practices included the discharging of untreated waste into rivers, smoking in public places including aeroplanes and differential pay for women doing the same jobs as men. All these became unacceptable and illegal within one generation.

2. **Product endurance:** To develop ways of applying scientific and technological development that contribute to human wellbeing but do not feed excessive production and consumption. For example, by creating objects that can be valued and kept relevant in the long term, rather than products that are rapidly replaced in the short term.

3. **Services:** To develop ways of generating wealth and jobs that are not so dependent on finite natural resources, short-lived products and growth in production.[42] For example, by supplementing longer lasting products with services and developing service-based communities.[43]

4. **Integrity:** To reduce the negative impacts of production and consumption in a sincere and responsible manner. Here it is important to recognize that, in a globalized production–consumption system, individual countries with developed economies can often claim and demonstrate a stabilization in their carbon dioxide emissions. However, this is only possible because the consumer products used in these countries have been manufactured in developing countries, where emissions have been rising significantly.[44]

5. **Worthwhile products:** To design those objects we can reasonably judge to be worthwhile on their own merits in ways that are more responsible and holistic in their conception. For example, design for maintenance and upgrading rather than disposal and replacement.

6. **New priorities:** To work towards the development of a material culture that expresses a reoriented and more meaningful set of priorities; i.e. priorities that place less emphasis on novelty and superfluity, and take a more conscientious approach to resource use and waste production. The task of envisioning such a material culture represents a valuable role for design in the transformation to a new kind of ecological economic culture.[45]

It will be a considerable undertaking to reform our current systems so that those involved more willingly and more effectively embrace these directions. It will entail business incentives, legislation, international agreements and more. In this, the discipline of design can make important contributions – particularly with respect to points 5 and 6 above. Because design is not a deterministic discipline, it is the designer's role to explore and develop creative possibilities and through such work express ideas about how objects *could* be. But that is not the whole story. In developing and expressing these ideas the designer is also making a series of what he or she considers to be reasonable judgements and, in the process, is therefore also expressing opinions about how products *should* be.[46] Hence, and as will be explored further here, the designer's role is one that inescapably includes ethical, and even spiritual, considerations.

Intrinsic value of objects
and a more consequential notion of design

Many of today's products lack intrinsic value and enduring meaning as things. This is especially true when they are conceived primarily in terms of instrumental benefits that are based on rapidly advancing technologies. This raises the question of how we might imbue things with meanings that surpass mere practical utility.

Many authors agree that when it comes to values there is little credible alternative to those that have come down to us through the ages via the great philosophical and religious traditions. It seems that fundamental human values, ethics and notions of meaning and meaning-seeking transcend any particular philosophy or religion – a fact recognized by those of faith[47] and of none.[48] This foundation of values and routes to personal meaning offers a basis for acting in the world – for human expression and the ways in which our endeavours are constructed and played out. Such matters are of critical importance in our approach to sustainability if it is to mature beyond mechanical measures of eco-efficiency and confront the root causes of our systemically unsustainable endeavours.

E. F. Schumacher, author of the seminal text *Small is Beautiful*[49] and one of the key early figures of contemporary sustainability, fully recognized the importance of transcending the mundane, utilitarian aspects of our activities. He acknowledged the vital role of intrinsic value and more profound notions of inner meaning – within and beyond the necessary, but prosaic, utilitarian aspects of life.[50] He wrote of the importance of inner development, which affects – or should affect – the nature of our outer activities. Those who earnestly strive towards inner development inevitably struggle against outer indulgence, selfishness and acquisitiveness and the activities they foster. Even though they may often fall short, the inner struggle provides direction and, importantly, a basis for judgement. Schumacher offers the example of art – regarding art that aims to stimulate the feelings as entertainment, or to stimulate the will as propaganda. For the creation of what he terms 'great art' neither one is enough. In Schumacher's terms, great art conveys something deeper, or higher – alluding to that which really matters, call it ultimate reality, Truth or, for some, God – by appealing to a human faculty of knowing that transcends (but does not negate) reason. In doing so, it helps nourish our inner, spiritual selves.[51] In this way, 'outer' artefacts (*appearance*) can serve as reminders and objects of focus for 'inner' understanding and development (*experience*); signposts for remembering and turning to the inner work which we each, as individuals, have to do to become full persons. Moreover, it is a task that has always been associated with understandings of truth and goodness. How we should live in the world is an unending negotiation between one's inner development, the path to true freedom, and the outer world, the path of necessity. This constitutes a divergent problem and because of its inherently unsolvable, and therefore angst-ridden, nature we have tended to concentrate our efforts on solvable convergent problems. In doing so, we have limited and constrained our potential as human beings.[52]

By considering sustainability as a series of convergent triple bottom-line problems, the deeper, underlying issues are avoided, and rationalized, analytical methods and instrumental solutions tend to represent convergent approaches to the issue. Moreover, in design we have yet to develop and expansively embrace the particular contribution that the discipline can bring to the sustainability question – namely, experience in dealing with divergent problems, and within this, design's contribution to more profound, inner aspects of being human. To address these shortcomings, we must consider the discipline in new ways. For example, and as has already been intimated in this chapter (see *The value of products* section above), it is common to regard design as a problem-solving activity. But, if the kinds of problems that design deals with are divergent and inherently unsolvable, then it would seem that we have been looking at its purpose and contribution from the wrong angle. Instead of seeing it as a problem-solving activity, we should be seeing it as a question-raising activity. Design outcomes should be regarded not as solutions but more properly as questions that ask us to consider the appropriateness of a particular synthesis of ideas. One proposition might be preferred or judged to be more fitting than another, but this preferred proposition is not a solution in the way that a maths problem yields one correct answer. Moreover, if design asks us to consider appropriateness, we are unavoidably faced with questions that encompass values and priorities.

Buchanan sees such design propositions as 'vehicles of argument and persuasion about the desirable qualities of private and public life', which he calls the '*rhetoric* of products'.[53] Following on from Schumacher's discussion, we see that if products are 'vehicles of argument and persuasion', they are concerned with stimulating the will and therefore fall under the rubric of propaganda. If, in addition, such products serve to stimulate our feelings, they are entertainments. Neither of these acknowledges that deeper, spiritual aspect of ourselves, the development of which is essential to human flourishing and true happiness. Traditionally, in 'outer works' this facet of being human has been addressed through neither rhetoric nor entertainment but through symbolism.

33

Sustainability, inner meaning and symbolism

To develop a more substantial understanding of sustainability, and its implications for the design disciplines, it is necessary to move past rationalistic interpretations that confine themselves to convergent, solvable problems. Addressing sustainability through such means simply maintains a way of apprehending the world that, despite its material advancements, is proving deficient in meaning and destructive in practice.

In cultivating a more comprehensive notion of sustainability we see that, in addition to Schumacher, more recent authors have also highlighted the essential relationships among societal and environmental wellbeing, and inner, personal meaning and spirituality. Orr, for example, links spiritual paucity to social alienation, societal instability and a sense of meaninglessness and hopelessness;[54]

Hawken associates spiritual understandings with planetary care and societal transformation;[55] and others have suggested that unsustainability is fundamentally linked to a loss of spirituality.[56] A critical aspect of such relationships is the reciprocity between our worldly activities and inner, spiritual development. The fruits of the former – tangible outcomes – can either support or hinder spiritual growth. The fruits of the latter – inner development – can inform the priorities embodied in and thus the nature of outer works. Hence, when the inner self is given greater acknowledgement and becomes a more deeply informing aspect of our activities, outer works become more closely aligned with, and even representative of, inner truths.

In addition, because higher notions of meaning are essentially ineffable, lying beyond the realm of describable concepts or categories, they have traditionally been referred to or articulated in outer works through symbolism. Thus, we see in the Hindu sacred text the *Bhagavad Gita* that an external dialogue, apparently between Arjuna and Krishna, is symbolic of every human being's internal striving and questioning about the meaning of life and the contentions that occur between the everyday or outer person and the innermost self; the great battlefield they survey, with armies arrayed before them, being symbolic of this inner conflict or 'struggle for self-mastery'.[57] This struggle is a fundamental theme of all the great traditions, where it is invariably conveyed through symbolism. Needleman, in relating the legend of Solomon's throne, refers to the symbolic representations of inner discord depicted on the steps that lead up to the throne. For example, the lamb and the wolf, respectively, symbolize purity of heart and devouring passions, and the eagle and the peacock represent spiritual heights and earthbound vanities. He points out that the two opposing directions of the Christian cross also symbolize this inner conflict.[58] Nicoll, whose writings were so influential in Schumacher's work, distinguishes between the undeveloped person who seeks understanding only through external, sense-based evidence, and the more fully developed person who seeks inner growth and psychological truth. He suggests that the first is incapable of comprehending the second because the level of understanding is of a lower order, and that a life spent without striving towards inner growth is a life that 'misses the mark', which is the literal meaning of the Greek word translated as 'sin'.[59] Nicoll wrote extensively about the importance of symbolism and interpretation in traditional sacred writings, all of which have literal, outer meanings and symbolic, inner meanings. Literal interpretations might reveal contradictions or suggest malice or objectionable practices – but to interpret them in this way is to miss their inner, symbolic meaning. He also explains that symbolic language is necessary because higher, spiritual meanings cannot be directly conveyed through words, they have to be grasped psychologically.[60] Through dedication and striving, the inner non-literal meanings are absorbed and become clearer at a pace with one's inner development.

Sustainability, symbolism and designing

We can summarize from the foregoing that:

Designing is an activity that is inherently concerned with divergent problems – problems that have no definitive solution. Instead, during the creative design process a range of factors become synthesized. We use these different syntheses to ask questions about appropriateness: *Which of these design propositions is the most appropriate, judged against a wide range of sometimes conflicting considerations?*

Designing sustainability is, therefore, also concerned with divergent problems – so confining our approaches to convergent, solvable problems is to exclude critical factors that are essential to our comprehension of the challenges facing us.

Inner values, spirituality and designing sustainability: Many authoritative voices have suggested that inner development and spirituality must be included in our understandings of sustainability and, by association, our design endeavours that strive towards sustainability. Therefore, the non-utilitarian aspects of product design must reach beyond conventional considerations of aesthetics and products-as-agencies-of-persuasion, to address factors that pertain to more profound notions of being human.

Use of symbolism in designing sustainability: Inner development and spiritual teachings have traditionally been conveyed through symbolism, because these ways of knowing cannot be expressed in ordinary literal terms; rather, they become known through dedication and striving towards inner growth. For this reason, the importance of symbolism in the development and expression of material culture must be acknowledged if our efforts at designing sustainability are to address deeper notions of human meaning.

35

It becomes clear that if design is to more effectively address sustainability it has to transcend utility and conventional function-led, and especially technology-led, approaches. It has to become informed by and imbued with deeper meanings that pertain to inner, spiritual sensibilities. Seeing design in this way expands the remit of the discipline beyond practical functionality, aesthetics and rhetoric. Indeed, within such a remit it becomes entirely possible to develop design propositions that have no practical outer utility whatsoever. Even so, creating objects that have no practical use does not mean that they have no functional purpose. But such objects should not necessarily be categorized as art, or *only* as art, or even as 'great art', to recall the earlier reference to Schumacher. Their functional purpose allows them to be just as readily seen as works of design. In fact, many medieval religious paintings, which today are to be found in galleries and are regarded as art, were originally created not as art works but as functional works of faith –

reminders of and focal points for inner work and spiritual growth.[61] Other examples of such objects include Greek iconography and Buddhist mandalas. In addition to aesthetic experience, all these aim at the inner transformation of the individual. Moreover, to create functional design propositions that attend to this inner aspect of ourselves, prosaic practical utility may have to be omitted, for to include it could detract from or even destroy their purpose.[62, 63]

Design consists of two broad parts – the rational and the non-rational, the cognitive and the intuitive, or the convergent and the divergent. In a culture in which naturalistic materialism, scientific endeavour and technological advancement have become paramount, unsurprisingly design has tended to focus on the rational side, creating objects that offer, or purport to offer, some practical material (outer/worldly) benefit. Our society in general and design in particular have become dominated by such objects. In the process, those other aspects of design – the intuitive, the emotive and the inner have been co-opted to serve outer purposes – to make the objects of design more attractive, more tempting, more saleable, more usable. Employing the intuitive, divergent aspects of creativity and design to serve only these worldly aims is to diminish the discipline and to forego other, deeper possibilities.

The divergent, the intuitive and the non-rational are vital aspects of design because they are vital aspects of being fully human. It is these facets of design that provide the basis for developing a more profound and, potentially, more sustainable notion of material culture. Over the course of the past half century or more, design's allegiance to prosaic outer concerns has contributed to the trivialization and rapid disposability of consumer products, environmental damage, exploitation of labour in developing countries and a crisis of meaning in richer countries.[64, 65] Therefore, it is perhaps time for the design pendulum to swing in the other direction, to explore new possibilities by focusing design's efforts not on practical outer needs and wants but on inner, spiritual needs and nourishment. With this in mind, a number of propositional objects have been developed which attempt to translate the ideas presented here into material form.

Propositional objects

These objects are not offered as solutions but as propositions – questions in form that ask if this or that synthesis of ideas through materials is an appropriate expression for a contemporary 'spiritually useful' object. Notably, the form of expression is symbolic rather than literal, the function being contemplative rather than practical. The purpose of these objects is to provide a focus and visible presence – to remind the user of the inner life, to give pause and offer a locus for reflection.

Somewhat unavoidably, the symbolism for such objects tends to be drawn from the traditions of a particular culture or belief system, rather than being universal (although we will explore trans-cultural, trans-religious possibilities in Chapters 6 and 7). While the vast heritage of the world's major religions and philosophies can be viewed as different paths to essentially the same goal of inner development and becoming a full person, their different geographical and cultural roots have meant that there has been no language, symbolic or otherwise, that has effectively encompassed them all in a way that is very helpful.[66] Consequently, such objects are usually expressed in the symbolism of a specific tradition – here the Judaeo-Christian tradition – or else, as Wittgenstein said, we must remain silent.[67]

The propositional objects presented here employ an aesthetic language of spare, science-related purposefulness to refer to inner ideas via symbolic forms. Figure 3.1, entitled *Babel*, comprises four transparent sample bags. The lower two contain brick and slime (oil and earth), the upper two stone and mortar, thereby symbolically contrasting self-made and timeless notions of 'truth', as conveyed in the story of the Tower of Babel in the Book of Genesis in the Old Testament of the Bible.[68] Figure 3.2, entitled *Cana*, is made up of three glass test tubes containing, from left to right, stone, water and wine, referring to stages of inner development as represented in the story of the Marriage at Cana in the Gospel of John in the New Testament.[69] Finally, Figure 3.3, apart from marks indicating title and date of authorship, is left blank. After Wittgenstein, it is entitled *Whereof one cannot speak*, and represents the ineffable nature of our deeper ideas of meaning. Clearly, such objects have no utilitarian purpose, their functionality lies in their presence as touchstones for the inner self.

We can consider these objects against the four points that emerged from the foregoing discussion. As we have seen, design and design for sustainability deal with divergent issues; given the same starting point, design can yield a broad range of outcomes. Hence, these objects represent but one set of possibilities among many. With respect to inner values, spirituality and design for sustainability, based on a growing recognition of the need to include more profound notions of being human in our understandings of sustainability, these objects set aside pragmatic function and technology-based utility to focus specifically on ideas of inner development and spiritual growth. Finally, in considering their use of symbolism in design for sustainability, the understandings to which these propositional objects refer can be known experientially, but not via intellectual reasoning, facts and cognitive knowledge. Traditionally, in both text and imagery, such understandings have been addressed through symbolism and here, these three compositions draw on the symbolism of a particular spiritual tradition. In doing so, aesthetic sensitivity was a significant factor in their expressive development; aesthetic beauty being an important link to profound experience and spiritual growth.[70] The form of the objects, which are essentially small wooden panels, is in keeping with a long tradition of such artefacts within Christianity – from the wooden icons of Eastern Orthodoxy to the small panel paintings of folk-art traditions in Latin American Catholicism. Here, however, the form of expression represents an attempt to address these issues in a visual language informed by post-traditional sensibilities. Customary figurative forms have not been used because their very familiarity tends to reduce their potency, especially in modern societies that have become increasingly secularized and sometimes antagonistic towards religion. If sustainability is to embrace ideas of spirituality, new forms of expression must be explored that are relevant to and appropriate for our time. Here, this exploration draws on the language of science, the major driving force in contemporary societies, together with the stark, clinical, modernist aesthetic that is such a powerful symbol of contemporary ideas of progress. Hence, imagery related to science and rationalism is used to create forms that refer to spiritual and intuitive apprehension, which seems an appropriate synthesis of the two broad facets of design mentioned earlier (see section above, *Sustainability, symbolism and design*). This combination of traditional spiritual symbolism and post-traditional forms of expression within a unified whole is one way of trying to come to grips with and manifest a more holistic notion of sustainability. By intentionally combining ideas that remain in considerable tension, but which, as we have seen, are essential to our developing understandings of sustainability, these compositions can provide a basis for reflection; particularly reflection on the questions and challenges such tensions raise for design today.

These are what might be termed academic or interrogative artefacts; they represent particular points in a continuing exploration and probing of the nature of design for sustainability. They are not commercial propositions. While attention has been paid to the aesthetic experience offered by these objects, there is no requirement for, nor has there been any attempt to address, considerations such as producibility, marketing or branding and the persuasive 'rhetoric of products' that is associated with their commodification.

Therefore, in attending to the aims set out earlier in this discussion, these objects represent one way for design to more effectively address sustainability. For the purposes of the exploration, utility and conventional function-led and technology-led approaches were set aside, along with forms of expressive rhetoric associated with commercial objectives. Instead, the focus was on notions of human understanding that pertain to inner growth. The objects express these ideas through the use of an aesthetic language that attempts to synthesize contemporary priorities with spiritual traditions as a basis for reflection and, potentially, as a stimulus for further exploration, development and resolutions of *designing sustainability*.

Conclusions

The reader might well ask if such a direction is actually design at all, or if it is art. Faced with the significant challenges posed by sustainability, and the conventional role of design in fostering consumerism[71] it becomes important to ask if we can, or indeed should, think of design in another way. Since the early years of the twentieth century, when Industrial Design emerged as an identifiable discipline,[72] we have tended to think of design in terms of practical, utilitarian benefits, form and aesthetics. However, this itself is rather different from an earlier time when key design concerns were surface application, pattern and ornament.[73] Over the course of the last 100 years or more, utilitarian benefits have been delivered, increasingly, through advanced and continually advancing technologies. As a consequence, the products of design have become ever more short-lived. These temporary objects serve to maintain an economic system that is based firmly on an agenda of progress and growth; an agenda that, as I mentioned at the start of this chapter, many are now challenging because of its relationship to environmental degradation, climate change and the promotion of unsustainable ways of living. This raises questions about the role and contribution of design in envisioning and fostering a more abiding form of material culture. Here, this has been explored through the notion of function being concerned with inner work rather than outer utility linked to transient technologies. A technology-free object aimed at inner work can be appreciated as something other than art. As mentioned earlier, there are precedents for this in religious objects that, though art-like, are not regarded as art within their traditions but as objects that have a function; that function being a focus for contemplation and inner reflection. If such an object is not regarded as art, if it has a function, perhaps we can call it design. Moreover, if in its making it valorizes human skills and creativity, it is relatively stable and therefore enduring, it does not create pollution in its use, and its purpose is aimed at inner growth, then perhaps we can call it 'sustainable' design.

Clearly, if we are to develop a richer, more substantial interpretation of material culture, design has to go beyond the narrow dictates of rationalized, instrumental products constructed from highly refined, synthetic materials and aimed at market-oriented mass-consumption. As a number of key figures in the field have argued, a deeper aspect of being human has to be included in our notions of sustainability, one that recognizes inner growth and spiritual wellbeing. If this more essential significance is to somehow inform and affect the nature of our material culture, designers must bring a rather different sensibility to their work. Such significance cannot be achieved through rationalizations or rigid, literalistic interpretations but through the ambiguities, uncertainties and potency inherent to allusion, symbolism and aesthetic experience. Broadening our notions of design to include facets that are largely absent from commercial design interests could yield a more meaningful and more sustaining version of material culture – through the qualities of its physical 'thingness', and by experiencing the tangible in ways replete with layered associations to the natural environment, culture and timeless notions of human meaning. In doing so, it may be possible to develop a more responsible and more imaginative understanding of design – one capable of overcoming the destructive tendencies on which much contemporary design relies – from abusive labour regimes, to profligate use of natural resources and production of climate-changing emissions.

If it is to become a more consequential, professional discipline, design has to raise its sights above, on the one hand, the exploitative and the polluting and, on the other, its preoccupation with prosaic, transient facade. To do this, the designer has to distinguish true creativity, the imaginative and the meaningful from the surfeit of mundane veneers that have come to characterize the discipline in recent decades. And design has to loosen its adherence to corporate practices that are unsustainable and often dishonourable. To transform our material culture in its design, production, use and post-use to address the environmental and spiritual challenges of our time, it becomes necessary to elevate the discipline and to embrace aspects that cannot be found, no matter how hard we look, through the lens of a microscope or on a balance sheet. Instead, the designer has to draw on other sources and perhaps especially those too-easily-forgotten aspects of human society, culture and tradition that have long been associated with the struggle towards inner development, meaning and becoming fully human.

4
Contemplative Objects

artefacts for
challenging
convention and
stimulating change

Still, they have an intimation, and that's so much to the good. Oran,
however, seems to be a town without intimations; in other words,
completely modern.

Albert Camus

The challenges posed by sustainability require a fundamental shift in our thinking
and in our approaches to the production, use and replacement of products. Such
a shift is advocated by a growing number of thinkers in both academia and
industry,[1, 2] many of whom suggest that change must occur at the local level rather
than as, or primarily as, some large-scale project.[3, 4] These directions not only cast
doubt on an economic model that demands continual growth in productivity, but
also imply a re-positioning of our individual relationships with products, and with
material culture in general. It becomes necessary to more clearly recognize the
indisputable connections between our personal workaday acts of product
acquisition, use and disposal and their damaging consequences. Yet, it is the very
familiarity and routineness of many of these acts that tend to work against such a
recognition. To overcome this, we must make efforts to see contemporary products
in a different light – for what they really are and for what they actually do –
unencumbered by marketing hyperbole. The product compositions created as part

of this practice-based inquiry are one attempt to do this. They invite the viewer to see ubiquitous technological products from a fresh angle, and in so doing to reflect upon them and their effects, as a precursor to building a more benign, more empathetic notion of material culture.

This chapter, therefore, looks at the relationship between prosaic objects and an understanding of sustainability that includes personal meaning along with practical and social meaning, and where economic considerations are acknowledged as a means rather than an end, and of a lower order than the other three.[5]

The approach taken is one in which critical inquiry is pursued in conjunction with the creation of expressive artefacts. Reasoned argument, or rhetorical criticism, based in literature review is developed to investigate, reveal and critique existing norms and ideologies; particularly those that are proving so problematic in relation to our evolving interpretations of the term 'sustainability'. This is combined with interrogative design practice, introduced in the previous chapter, which differs in purpose from pragmatic or commercially oriented practice. Here, creative practice is employed to explore and express ideas arising from the critical inquiry. Reflecting on the resulting artefacts informs and spurs additional practice and further inquiry. In this way, the emerging artefacts become contributing elements in the development of critique; as such, one of their roles is as arguments manifested in tangible form or *demonstrative rhetoric*.[6] However, while this form of academic, propositional design has a rhetorical role, its main purpose

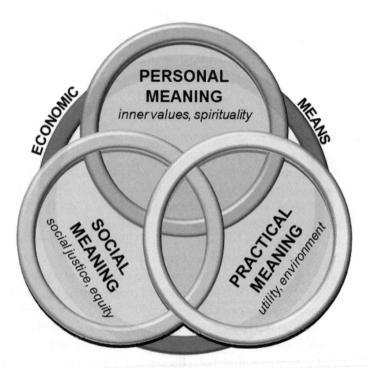

Figure 4.1 *The quadruple bottom line of sustainability*

is to help advance our thinking about the creation and manifestation of a sustainable and meaningful material culture. Hence, the approach is experimental and interrogative and one that combines analysis with synthesis. It represents the necessary practice-based component of design, which is complemented by study and intellectual reasoning. Rational argument that draws variously on cognitive knowledge, empirical evidence and information from other disciplines informs and is informed by aesthetic expression and the subjectivity, reflection and intuition inherent to creative practice. Moreover, arguments and creative practice are advanced with reference to ethical understandings that seek to steer our endeavours in directions that are socially just, environmentally responsible and personally meaningful. In this way, the creative core of design is affirmed within the research process and integrated with other scholarly approaches. This is consistent with a growing recognition among design thinkers that to advance sustainability, our notions of education and knowledge must embrace more than evidence-based research, empirical facts and instrumental methods.[7]

Progress and products

A human-made artefact is symbolic of the worldview held by the society in which it is created. For instance, modernity, the dominant worldview in Western societies for several centuries, can be seen as one in which major emphasis is placed on:

- the scientific method, the natural and social sciences, and empirical evidence as the primary bases of reliable information and significant knowledge;
- progress, interpreted particularly in terms of advancements in knowledge and understanding of and ability to have authority over the natural world;
- the transformation of advances in scientific knowledge into technologies for human benefit;
- the commodification of technologies and their wide distribution – both for human utility and for the creation of wealth, which are seen as activities that have overarching advantages for societies, nations and companies.[8]

Naturally, the artefacts produced by a society that holds such a worldview will possess characteristics that reify these priorities; effectively, the artefact becomes a manifestation and demonstrative endorsement of its values. Consequently, we would expect to see artefacts that, through their purpose, appearance, function, capability and other attributes, are indicative of a particular interpretation of progress. It is notable that within this worldview, 'progress' is not generally taken to mean the ethical or spiritual development of the individual or improvements in the plight of the poor and disenfranchised. It is more often understood as referring to advances in cognitive knowledge, empirical evidence and command of the physical world that are coupled to an instrumental view of Nature's 'resources', which are extracted to serve human purposes through the development of technological products. While it may be argued that this latter interpretation serves the former, such a connection is by no means assured and may, in fact, be

43

countervailing.[9] Within such a worldview we would expect to see artefacts that are, or are claimed to be, based on the latest scientific advancements, that feature the most up-to-date technologies and that have improved functionality and increased capability over earlier models. We would also expect to see external treatments consistent with these ideas, such as immaculate finishes, visual features that speak of multi-functionality, and changing forms and colours, which all serve as outer indicators of these techno-centric notions of progress. And finally, we would expect to see artefacts that are available to large numbers of people, because such objects need to be both available and affordable to many if they are to serve the goal of growth. But here again, the term 'growth' in general use is not taken to mean a rise in social equity and justice, increases in overall education levels or expansion in rainforest preservation. Rather, it refers to economic growth, a significant element of which is based on consumerism, which serves to fuel further technological development, production and consumption.

These developments are completely in accord with the worldview of modernity and facilitated by the economic system that has come to predominate within it. Western-style capitalism has proved extraordinarily adept at promoting technological progress. However, in the pursuit of ever-more profits, it has also created staggering social disparities, squandered natural resources[10, 11] and dismissed as mere superstition profound human insights that, throughout history, have provided a foundation for worldly moderation, social conscience and personal meaning.[12] Ironically, as Eagleton has pointed out, its faith in its own superior rationality is also a type of superstition, which is now threatening to destroy the planet.[13] And even though we have been slowly emerging from modernity for some decades, into a period that has been termed late-modernity or postmodernity, many of its most significant priorities still hold.

These notions of progress are firmly grounded in productivity and manufacturing, which have become increasingly concentrated in Asia. In the foreseeable future, it is unlikely that it will be feasible to recreate such manufacturing, and attendant jobs, on a significant scale in Western countries. Not only is labour less expensive in many Asian countries, but a critical mass of manufacturers has now accumulated that regionally concentrates interdependent, highly flexible and adaptive supply chains, large-scale production capabilities and the vast cohorts of skilled labour needed to assemble contemporary microprocessor-based products.[14] However, rather than lamenting this transfer in production, we should, perhaps, be considering different directions entirely. While Asia currently has a firm hold on product manufacturing – following on from the achievements of the United States in the twentieth century and Britain in the nineteenth – such activities are not only becoming increasingly self-destructive in terms of their cumulative environmental effects but can also be seen as something of a misdirected human absorption in material novelty. For instance, when the head of one of the world's leading electronic products companies attempts to impress the President of the United States by demonstrating a new driving game on a handheld device,[15] it may be time to reconsider our priorities. As mentioned in previous chapters, such absorption hinders reflection and thwarts contentedness.[16, 17] In contrast, inner pursuits not only require far less in terms of material products, the very presence in our lives of such 'goods' is consciously de-emphasized; this has been a common teaching of the world's great spiritual traditions for millennia.[18]

Transcending the status quo

To respond to these concerns, in the light of contemporary notions of sustainability, we should be cautious in proposing new technological solutions and yet more useful material goods, however green their credentials. Doing so would serve to maintain the existing condition, rather than contribute to the more fundamental shift that is needed. It is perhaps more fitting to pause, to think more comprehensively about the products we already produce and their implications, and to develop objects that are about different things entirely; things in which modernity-postmodernity has thus far shown relatively little interest compared to its enthralment with technology. To this end, creating objects that prompt contemplation – first, about deeper aspects of human understanding and inner fulfilment, as explored in Chapter 3, and second, about current technologies themselves – would appear to be more in keeping with a changing worldview and a more essential, systemic shift in priorities and practices. The focus of this chapter is the latter category – objects that invite reflection upon current technologies in the light of sustainability.

45

While sustainability has become a grossly overused and misused term, when correctly employed it refers to a variety of important, interrelated ideas. It is understood here as being composed of four broad elements – i.e. a *quadruple bottom line*. The three primary elements of *practical meaning*, *social meaning* and *personal meaning* were described in Chapter 2. These three are based on fundamental principles of human existence in the world; we live in a physical environment and have functional requirements, we are social creatures, and we seek meaning and purpose in our lives. The fourth element, *economic issues*, is a human construct rather than a premise and is therefore allocated a secondary role; being regarded as a means to an end rather than an end in itself.[19] Such ideas have a long pedigree. Ruskin, for example, expressed similar sentiments. His are among the most significant nineteenth-century critiques of industrial capitalism and the role of economic issues and wealth creation; others include *The Communist Manifesto*,[20] Thoreau's *Walden*[21] and Morris' writings on work and socialism in the 1880s.[22] Ruskin, whose ideas influenced Tolstoy and Gandhi, argued that it is the responsibility of those who create wealth to make it work for the good of all, for society,[23] and not simply to accumulate it, not to use it for luxuries that are unavailable to so many.[24] His main principle was that people should be valued, not wealth and its accrual. He also wrote of the poisonous smoke of industrial chimneys – a proto-environmentalism that alludes to today's concerns over climate change.[25] More recent critiques, particularly those of Habermas, draw attention to the fact that modernity, 'which is still dominant but dead', has resulted in the separation into institutionalized specialisms of cognitive-instrumental, moral-practical and aesthetic-expressive forms of rationality and meaning; and tradition, social conventions and virtues have been eschewed.[26] Habermas suggests that these areas of knowledge and rationality are respectively represented by *science* (where 'truth', or reliable knowledge, derives from information acquired via scientific methods); *morality* (normative rightness); and *art* (authenticity and beauty). One result of this has been a marginalization of religion in civil society,[27, 28] and with it ideas about spiritual practice, inner growth and traditional conceptions of virtue and moral values. Academia has not escaped this bias towards secularization. Generally, inclusion of religious and spiritual matters does not figure highly in many areas of the modern university; their absence is especially marked in the social sciences and a number of disciplines within the humanities, including design.[29]

It is the challenge of *designing sustainability* to overcome these various separations and exclusions and to realize more holistic, integrative approaches that more fully acknowledge the relationships among:

- the attainment of practical meaning in ways that are appropriate to context and circumstance;
- ethical responsibilities including environmental ethics and the effects of environmental impacts on people;
- individual spiritual beliefs and inner growth, which represent traditional sources of virtue, perennial values and profound meaning;
- aesthetic expression and notions of beauty.

In other words, *designing sustainability* demands an approach in which ethical and spiritual considerations, environmental responsibilities and practical requirements become synthesized via the process of designing, and manifested through aesthetic expressions that speak of a deeper kind of beauty, one that transcends mere surface and style. The aim is to develop forms of material culture that, in all aspects of production, use and post-use, are empathetic to both people and place.

Objects for reflection

The aesthetic appeal, branding and advertising hoopla surrounding many of today's consumer products are clearly influential and beguiling. They are perhaps especially effective when applied to products that incorporate progressive technologies, such as smart phones, tablet computers, laptops and a host of other 'next generation' digital objects. The publicity and fabricated excitement, not to say hysteria, that accompanies many of these products make it difficult to see them impartially. This pervasive psychological manipulation through marketing strategies that invariably exaggerate the importance of minor differences is one of the key factors that drive the consumerism machine. Such strategies are not new. They go back to the 1920s with the instigation of built-in obsolescence and the annual model change in the automobile industry – a strategy designed to create dissatisfaction and stimulate sales.[30] It is also the case that we tend to reveal rather imitative behaviours when it comes to our purchasing habits and, consequently, within a pervasive consumption-dominated milieu, if the media as well as our peers seem to be excited about a new product, we will often act in a similar way. There are many examples of such behaviours.[31, 32] Hence, this kind of consumption-focused system is not only associated with environmental damage and social disparity, but also with the calculated creation of dissatisfaction.[33, 34] Furthermore, implicit in the relentless stoking of desire for the novel and the technologically innovative is a concomitant disdain for the recently outmoded. While we might have assumed that we could regard older products with a more neutral eye because they are no longer swathed in media hype and have lost the gloss of newness, this is not the case in contemporary consumer culture. The very fact that such products are functionally or aesthetically outmoded means that they tend to be regarded with certain derision. Consequently, any lessons to be learned from them, such as their all-too-brief use of resources and their contribution to landfill waste, are inevitably less potent.

For these reasons, neither new products nor recently outmoded products provide an appropriate physical presence for reflecting on contemporary, technologically based, material culture and its consequences. However, there is a further category of objects that we can consider for this purpose. As our gaze focuses firmly on the shiny new devices that appear so regularly in the media spotlight, little consideration is given to the accompanying, rather dull accoutrements on which they depend. Yet, these lowly accessories – disposable ink cartridges, batteries, chargers – also speak of our faith in and reliance on technology but, unlike the primary products they serve, these objects are not valued as things. They may be rather reluctantly tolerated because they are needed, but they are not appreciated, treasured or even really seen. These are not possessions as such, but merely instrumental agents, with no other positive contributions to the world, aesthetic or otherwise; indeed, quite the opposite. They are the necessary auxiliaries and consumables on which our glamorized digital devices depend. We acquire them as means, not ends, but we have no real desire to own such objects. Hotels, for example, often have boxes of forgotten phone chargers waiting to be reclaimed. These subsidiary products rarely feature in advertising or promotional materials and they are generally free of what might be termed persuasive aesthetics.

Wittgenstein made the point that when objects are constituents in a state of affairs, they fit together and form a determinate relationship to one another and this determinate relationship forms the structure of the state of affairs.[35] Here, these menial accessories are as integral to the unsustainable nature of our material culture as the principal products themselves, but being free of outer adornments, accompanying rhetoric, sought-after functionality and social cachet, they offer a more effective basis for seeing things as they really are and provide a more appropriate focus for contemplation and reflection.

It is becoming increasingly clear that we have created a state of affairs in which the mass-production, use, discarding and replacement of objects is in serious conflict with the best interests of society, ourselves and the natural environment. It is equally clear that there is a lack of will to take any significant action to reduce consumerism and our production of waste and pollution. In fact, the opposite is true. Governments and corporations alike encourage production and consumption, despite energy-related carbon-dioxide emissions being at an all-time high.[36] It seems that we have become so accustomed to our current form of material culture that we do not readily recognize it for what it really is and for what it represents. Consequently, it is necessary to develop new ways of seeing this state of affairs – ways that are free of the aesthetic refinements, idealizations and techniques of persuasion that obscure our view of reality. Alternative avenues have to be explored that circumvent such influential but unhelpful associations. Here I present one such avenue.

Contemplative objects

Figures 4.2, 4.3 and 4.4 show three panels, respectively entitled *Land*, *Water* and *Air*. All three feature familiar but secondary or ancillary products that have been stripped of their outer garb of brand graphics and arranged within a rectangle of white paper mounted on re-used plywood. Thus, these compositions present nothing but the products themselves within a limiting frame that separates them from their surroundings and their normal context of use.

48

Although they are presented as panel compositions, it is important to recognize that these are not art objects, nor are they design objects. Rather, they are objects *about* design objects. They are academic in purpose, forming part of a continuing inquiry through creative practice. This kind of design work is concerned with reflecting upon, questioning and exploring the evolving potential of the discipline itself. Design has a long history of such practice from De Stijl and the Bauhaus in the 1920s to Alchimia and Memphis in the 1970s and 1980s, to Droog Design in the 1990s. These compositions were created to provide a basis for reflecting on contemporary material culture in relation to sustainability. More particularly, they provide a focus for seeing ubiquitous objects anew, and for considering their role in our own activities and everyday routines.

The very act of displaying objects in this way – allocating them a special place – invites contemplation.[37] Ordinary things are brought to the fore and highlighted. Moreover, through their titles, suggestions are made about their respective relationships to the natural environment, especially in regard to: landfill in the form of e-waste, millions of tonnes of which are discarded around the world annually; water quality and its degradation through the leaching of toxic substances; and air pollution and climate-changing emissions.[38]

Presented as minimal figure–ground aesthetic arrangements, one might judge these compositions to be beautiful. However, the aesthetic gaze demands deeper reflection and the seeking of meaning, which in conjunction with the title of each panel can create a tension between notions of beauty and the wider implications of that which is before us. By this means, the viewer is asked to consider ubiquitous technologies from a fresh perspective – one that is less encumbered by modish allurements and persuasive promotional technique. The aim is to better recognize the inescapable connections between our individual, workaday activities and:

- our dependency on technology and its associated energy use, along with our frequency of need to charge, to plug in, to discard and replace;
- the taken-for-granted side of this dependency in terms of availability and affordability, access to electricity supply and the acceptability of single-use disposable, replaceable products;
- the devastating degradation of the natural environment, which provides the materials for production and absorbs the damaging fallout of use and disposal, together with the deprivation and disfigurement this brings to the world.

Presenting such products in this de-contextualized manner can prompt us to reflect upon our actions and our own use of contemporary technologies. They implicate us personally. Each time we discard an ink cartridge we are wasting hard won, non-renewable hydrocarbon resources and committing them, along with heavy metals and potentially harmful ink compounds, to overflowing landfill sites. Each time we throw away single-use batteries we are washing our hands of toxins that will seep into the soil and the aquifer. And each time we plug in the laptop or phone charger we are, in effect, activating a small CO_2 pump that discharges polluting gases into the atmosphere.

49

These particular artefacts are representative of the vast number and variety of resource- and energy-consuming, polluting artefacts that we readily accept, use and discard today. In doing so, we reinforce the inequities and economic injustices that enable these products, and the primary products they serve, to be both available and affordable. Indeed, their availability and affordability are inextricably linked to their disposable, replaceable forms. Without gross economic disparities, exploitative production practices, wasteful use of resources and scant attention to pollution and emissions, contemporary technological products *simply could not exist in the forms that they do*. If they existed at all, they would have to be conceived as products of permanence and would inevitably be far more expensive. Consequently, we could not afford to replace them so readily, neither the primary products themselves nor their secondary, lacklustre accessories. Hence, they would have to be designed to be upgraded, refilled and effectively maintained.

Connecting our everyday routines and product usage to these larger sustainability issues is a critically necessary step in fully acknowledging the implications of our individual actions. Doing so inevitably raises questions about purpose, right living, individual conscience and one's sense of contentedness and inner peace. These compositions, therefore, touch upon all four elements of the *quadruple bottom line* of sustainability, including notions of personal meaning.

What we hold most dear

Banal as they are, the products featured in these compositions represent and reflect contemporary ideas about meaningful and purposeful human existence. They are symbols of what we hold most dear – physical manifestations of the predominant worldview. In the modern mind, the perennial search for meaning has become a secularized endeavour. Instead of regarding it as an inner search via spiritual growth and sacred tradition, meaning is sought through the ideology of progress,[39, 40] which, as discussed, has become inexorably bound to ever-advancing technological devices and gadgets.

These compositions can be interpreted, therefore, as *retablos* or icons for our time. Mexican *retablos* and *ex votos*, as well as other forms of expression prevalent within religious traditions, portray holy figures, saints, miracles or apparitions. Such artefacts are tangible indicators and focal points for fidelity to that which is regarded as the source of meaning and ultimate good. The panel compositions presented here play a similar role. However, within the progress-based worldview, meaning-seeking is located firmly in the physical, mundane realm rather than the metaphysical or spiritual. As a consequence, human potential and aspiration have become channelled towards the instrumental and the utilitarian. The aim of these compositions is to invite reflection on the inadequacy of such a locus of meaning by linking commonplace products of progress, which we all use in our day-to-day lives, with their broader implications and their cumulative effects on society, the natural environment and our own sense of meaning. They follow on from Chapter 3's consideration of contemplative objects for inner work, which set aside any concern for practical utility. The three compositions presented here employ a similar aesthetic language but in contrast to those earlier propositions, in these panels there is no allusion to spiritual interpretation. Instead, they are representative of the ideology underpinning our consumer-oriented, and evidently unsustainable, material culture. Thus, the predominant ideology of progress is placed alongside more traditional, and arguably more holistic and more profound, notions of being human. The inclusion in these compositions of prosaic utilitarian products can perhaps allow us to see them, and the ideology on which they are founded, from a fresh perspective – for what they really are and for what they actually represent.

Contemplating objects

When our aesthetic gaze is focused on artefacts that have been separated from their surroundings and contained within a frame, we cannot contemplate them in an entirely disinterested manner, as we can Nature. Through the convention of the containing frame, such objects are understood as objects of contemplation – independent of any function they may have had in ordinary life. Furthermore, such objects are a means of communication; Scruton calls them a 'middle term', which serves to communicate between the creator of the framed artefact and the viewer. Such objects have intended messages, but our experience of them cannot be completely divorced from our knowledge of their constituents – not only their function but also their environmental and social connotations. This knowledge will affect our aesthetic experience and consequently our judgement, because our perception of what is beautiful is intimately related to our notions of morality, the spiritual and, for many, the sacred. Traditionally, beauty has been closely associated with virtue, with the deepest spiritual values of being human, and with a sense of reverence for the world.[41] Hence, there is a connecting thread that links our contemplation of these artefacts – singled out from their normal context and presented as objects of significance worthy of our attention and aesthetic gaze – with our judgement of beauty; a judgement that is not disinterested but connected to knowledge of implications and impacts. When accompanied by this knowledge, it becomes difficult if not impossible to see such objects as beautiful. This is because our ideas of beauty are incompatible with the massive scales of environmental degradation, unethical practices and social injustices that have come to be associated with globalized product production practices.

While environmental degradation may be unavoidable when the materials of the earth are extracted for human use, today its sheer scale is unparalleled. This situation is linked to an ideology that values continuous economic growth based on technological development, mass-production, short product use cycles, disposability and replacement. By contrast, more benign approaches, such as product–service combinations that favour upgrade and repair[42] and that value localization for whole or part of the production,[43] could help moderate resource use and environmental damage. This, in turn, would contribute to a reorientation of priorities – away from ever more convenience and the putative benefits of owning the very latest product – towards deeper, more lasting notions of human fulfilment.[44] While we might benefit from their utility, it is also important to recognize that such objects add ugliness, not beauty, to the world. When considered in the round we become aware that, despite their benefits, our current renditions of material culture continually erode the three primary constituents of the *quadruple bottom line*, including our own sense of contentedness and spiritual wellbeing.[45]

The presentation of these objects within an aesthetically considered composition divorces them from their branding, their commodification and their usual context and provides an opportunity to see them anew.[46] The meanings interpreted from such expressions, which draw on the observer's knowledge and experiences, are not precise. The creator may have particular meanings in mind, which they hope to convey, but the viewer also brings their own interpretation, which may be rather different, and which will vary from one person to another. Even so, judgement is not arbitrary. Arriving at a value judgement about the work requires that the object be regarded as significant – as something worthy of our contemplation. Regarding the object in this way invites reflection, the seeking of meaning and the making of a judgement. Information or arguments that accompany such a viewing can affect how we see it and help us arrive at a judgement of value, which will be a function of *our* values. We refer what we see and our emotional, subjective responses to our values, and it is with respect to

51

these values that a judgement is made. For example, we might initially be drawn to a piece, finding the composition intriguing, perhaps beautiful. Closer examination reveals that it is made up of disposable, harmful items, which is reinforced when we read the title of the piece as Land, Water or Air. We can then contemplate the meaning of the piece with this information in mind, and perhaps with additional information about the rationale for its creation – as described here – and arrive at a judgement of value. We might find the piece effective but perhaps we are no longer able to regard it as beautiful because its constituents are associated with the sullying of Nature and/or with socially damaging practices. This contradiction between outer, superficial beauty and the destructive implications of the incorporated components is designed to invite reflection. It is an attempt to create an aesthetic experience that focuses attention on the deficiencies of contemporary material culture, along with the daily routines it facilitates.

Hence, each composition can be understood as an expressive form that does not describe but connects, in the eyes of the viewer, the familiar everyday products of our digitally directed world with their wider implications. The aim is not concerned with moralizing but with recognizing relationships, with seeing things differently. This 'seeing things differently' is critically important if we are to change our conventions and develop more sustainable ways forward. To see things as they really are, in their roundedness, is a sign of maturity because we are being clear to ourselves about our actions, and truthful to ourselves about their implications. Potentially, we can recognize more specifically and proximally that it is these very things, these all too familiar everyday accoutrements of our lives, that are the roots of unsustainability. These small, innocuous-looking elements are the unremarkable, readily discarded and replaced outcomes of a progress-and-growth-based technocracy that is founded on an ideology that remains predominant but is clearly deficient.

Design's eye

For a century or more design, particularly Industrial Design, has been conceived as a service to industry – a way of adding value, increasing sales, improving manufacturability, reducing costs, and providing the aesthetic identity of products, systems or, indeed, a company.[47] Accordingly, it has been an active player in making our production–consumption system what it is today. However, design's eye can be focused elsewhere, and its role can, and arguably should, be construed rather differently if it is to play a significant part in creating a sustainable future.

The design process brings together a wide variety of often disparate factors and considerations and, through visual techniques and aesthetic sensitivity, empirical information and utility, and intuition, emotion and symbolism, integrates and presents them as a creative, coherent and unified whole. The knowledge, skills, techniques and synthetic praxis of design are, therefore, well suited to the complexities and multifarious dimensions of sustainability. However, for design to

Propositional Objects

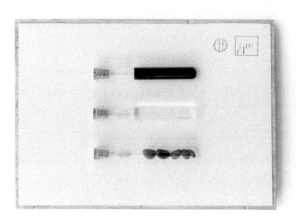

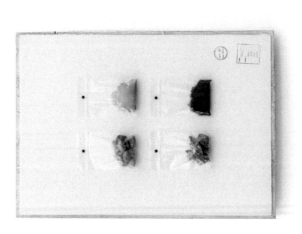

Figure 3.1
Babel
brick, stone, slime, mortar, zip lock bags,
handmade paper on Morecambe Bay driftwood
275 × 395 × 25 mm

Figure 3.2
Cana
stone, water, wine, test tubes, handmade
paper on Morecambe Bay driftwood
275 × 395 × 25 mm

Figure 3.3
Whereof one cannot speak
handmade paper on Morecambe Bay driftwood
275 × 395 × 25 mm

Figure 4.4
Air
used cell phone charger, paper,
recovered plywood
640 × 360 × 50 mm

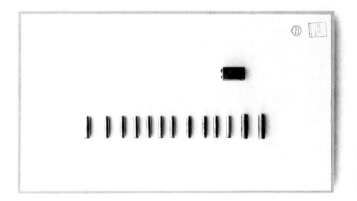

Figure 4.3
Water
used batteries, paper, recovered plywood
640 × 360 × 40 mm

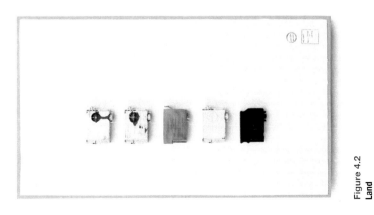

Figure 4.2
Land
used printer cartridges, paper, recovered
plywood
640 × 360 × 35 mm

Figure 6.1
Oriel Triptych: a spiritually useful object
re-used plywood jetsam, leather, glass and flour-based paste
196 × 125 × 36 mm (closed); 196 × 240 × 36 mm (open)

Figure 6.2
Hinge detail
panels hinged with cotton thread bindings

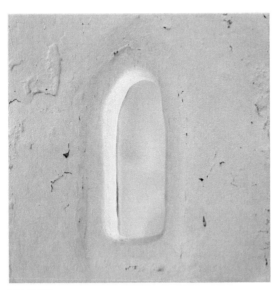

Figure 6.3
Arch detail
with hand-painted, translucent glass

Figure 6.4
Leather frame detail
attached with re-used screws,
to hold glass in place

Figure 7.3
StoneWork

Figure 8.3
Balanis chess set
holm oak with stained flax cord

address this effectively it must turn a critical eye on itself and its own assumptions and conventions. The existing condition and the all-too-familiar accoutrements of daily life have to be seen in a new light and scrutinized with a meaning-seeking gaze. To facilitate such critique, design itself can offer a creative way forward by reconceptualizing how we see familiar things and presenting them within an unfamiliar aesthetic frame. The contemplation of such objects may suggest intimations of something more and, to recall Camus, that would be so much to the good, because without such intimations we will remain, to our detriment, completely modern.

53

5
Design and
Spirituality

creating material
culture for a
wisdom economy

by their very nature rules crowd out virtues

Clifford Longley

In 1854, at the height of the British phase of the Industrial Revolution, Charles Dickens published *Hard Times*. Set in a mill town in the northwest of England, it was a damning critique of utilitarianism, empiricism and the metaphysic of materialism. He titled the first chapter 'The One Thing Needful' – a quote from the New Testament that emphasizes the importance of the spiritual life.[1] Traditionally regarded as 'the best part' of our humanity,[2] Dickens clearly felt it was severely lacking in the developments of his time.

Interestingly, Dickens' insightful commentary on industrial capitalism was accompanied by a presaging of its implications for design – implications that would become more apparent in the century to come. Responding to changes in design education in 1850s England, he wrote 'the school of design was all fact ..., and what you couldn't state in figures, or show to be purchasable in the cheapest market and saleable in the dearest, was not, and never should be'.[3] And in a passage that brings to mind the early twentieth-century paintings of Mondrian, the Red and Blue chair of Rietveld, and designs of the Bauhaus, 'You are not to have, in any object of use or ornament, what would be a contradiction in fact.... You must use,' said the gentleman, 'for all these purposes, combinations and modifications (in primary colours) of mathematical figures which are susceptible to proof and demonstration. This is the new discovery. This is fact. This is taste.'[4]

Essentially, Dickens' critique was of modernity and its developments, and the title of his opening chapter identified the ingredient he felt had been trampled in the rush to progress. It is an ingredient that a number of prominent voices are calling attention to today in response to contemporary, postmodern concerns about sustainability. Nair, for example, contends that, after some 300 years of exploitative growth based on under-pricing resources and externalizing costs, Western-style capitalism has hit a wall. He suggests that we have to go beyond the simplistic mantra of growth and consider more meaningful notions of human progress.[5]

The period of modernity – from about 1500 CE to the mid-twentieth century – saw Western societies focusing their efforts on understanding and commanding the natural environment to an unprecedented extent. This emphasis on scientific investigation, empiricism and technological development resulted in a plethora of benefits, both practical and prosaic. It was also accompanied by a secularization of society, the development of a politics of democracy and a new economic system based in industrial capitalism, whereby the profits of productivity were reinvested for the expansion and growth of production and profits, along with the development of new markets for the manufactured goods. This period witnessed a decline in the place and prominence of institutional religion and of spirituality in general. Secularization naturally meant that the spiritual dimension became a less important aspect of public decision-making, professional practices, education and worldly affairs in general, being instead restricted to the private domain or simply fading away.

In previous chapters I have discussed how the spiritual aspect of our humanity, if developed, has the potential to reorient our practical, worldly endeavours in ways that can have positive social implications, as well as having a moderating influence on acquisitiveness and consumerism, which helps reduce environmental impacts. Both of these are primary elements of utilitarian interpretations of sustainability, i.e. the triple bottom line of economic, ethical and environmental accountability. More importantly, however, the inclusion of spirituality and the personal ethic it can engender in a *quadruple bottom line of sustainability*, as described in Chapter 4, can have a far more substantial, foundational effect; one that goes to the heart of human purpose and fulfilment, and the plight of people and planet. This most profound, meaning-seeking aspect of our humanity is, we are told, the source of inner peace and true happiness, and for this reason it has traditionally been regarded as 'the one thing that is needful' and the 'best' part of us. This chapter considers this notion of *personal meaning* in greater depth. It shows how the major worldviews through human history have respectively emphasized personal meaning, practical meaning and, latterly, social meaning. In addition, it demonstrates that, despite varieties of expression, the essential features of personal meaning are universal. They are also critical for developing a more

55

encompassing interpretation of design for sustainability – one that reorients how we conceive of and produce our material culture.

The demise and nascent return of spirituality

In northern Europe the idea of spirituality became severely demoted as a consequence of the Protestant Reformation. The Reformers rejected the idea of pursuing inner, spiritual development via a separated, more ascetic way of life, instead seeing it as something that should pervade and be part of ordinary, secular life.[6] Consequently, the contemplative traditions – represented by the great medieval mystics such as Hildegard of Bingen and Julian of Norwich, and the prominence of monasticism – went into severe decline. In England the sixteenth century saw the violent eradication of such traditions with the Dissolution of the Monasteries. These ways of life, which had ancient roots, were concerned with inner development, spiritual growth, insight and awareness. As such, their significance was similar to the contemplative traditions of the East, within Sufism, Buddhism, Hinduism and Taoism.

The eighteenth and nineteenth centuries witnessed the development of the reductionist philosophies of Empiricism and Utilitarianism, which favoured quantitative methods and tended to confine notions of legitimate knowledge to sense-based data. This period saw the development of more liberal, pluralistic societies that initially were tolerant of and later became indifferent to religion. As more secular sensibilities developed, the Church declined, and with it, collective, communal expressions of spirituality.[7] With the growth in application of scientific methods, modernity became increasingly associated with cognitive knowledge and the evidence-based research that science can provide. Collectively, these developments led to the rise of the 'modern' worldview, with its pervasive assumption that the physical universe is all that exists.[8] This, however, is a belief system, an act of faith[9] and, as such, it is something that science can neither prove nor disprove because science confines its observations and inferences to the physical world (see discussion of naturalistic materialism in Chapter 2).

The modern worldview virtually expunged the relevance of spirituality from public, and often private, life and had the effect of secularizing society. Remnants of the spiritual life were reduced to a basic code for living that encompassed 'prosperity, peace, [and] mutual benefit', but these were bereft of their roots – roots that had penetrated deeper apprehensions of human meaning.[10] The ideology of naturalistic materialism became so embedded in Western thinking that it came to be taken as self-evident, and other aspects of our humanity – intuition, sense of transcendence, and the spiritual self – became eclipsed. This was the worldview that dominated the twentieth century – a period that produced many technological innovations but also witnessed the rise of industrialized and technological warfare, environmental destruction, and massive global social inequities. As a consequence, views started to change. The authority of the modern worldview began to wane, and the latter half of the twentieth century saw the development of postmodernity.

While it retains many of the ideological biases of modernity, postmodernity has brought to the fore issues of social equity and justice and heralded the emergence of the environmental movement. During the latter half of the twentieth century, the assumptions of modernity were perhaps still too firmly entrenched to also allow redress of the spiritual void at the centre of contemporary life – despite the efforts of a few influential writers.[11, 12] However, by the early years of the twenty-first century, a growing number of voices from a variety of disciplines were suggesting that any serious understanding of sustainability must include spirituality in the mix of essential considerations. These contemporary understandings, while not undermining the value and contribution of science, are nevertheless recognizing its limitations and acknowledging that there are other aspects of our humanness that lie beyond the empirical framework of naturalistic materialism.[13] In the *quadruple bottom of line of sustainability* these other aspects are collectively referred to as *personal meaning*, which includes the spiritual or meaning-seeking path and the ethical perspective and matters of conscience that emerge from it. It is a path that 'determines the ethical, cognitive, and pragmatic value of all human action' and that transcends sociocultural conventions and differences.[14] Such understandings, which became diminished in much modern thought, are represented in all the great philosophical and religious traditions, not so much in the particularities of specific, culturally relevant practices, but more so in the contemplative traditions common to them all.[15]

While some authors broaden the notion of sustainability beyond instrumentalism, eco-efficiency and environmentalism to include practical moral reasoning,[16] many go further by highlighting the importance of the spiritual dimension. Orr argues that spirituality is an indispensable element of the transition to sustainability and that convergent problem-solving through the application of logic and rigorous method is simply unsuited to and incapable of tackling the divergent problems posed by sustainability, which are characterized by competing perspectives.[17] In addition to prosperity, social justice and environment, Inayatullah has also called for spirituality to be encompassed by the term sustainability.[18] Mathews suggests that, for a more sustainable future, the next stage of human societies will be post-materialist and post-religious, but not post-spiritual; one characterized by a more synergistic relationship with Nature that allows for change but is less controlling and dominating than was the case within modernity.[19] In many traditions, including the Abrahamic religions predominant in the Western industrialized nations, the notion of the divine is core to understandings of spirituality. Berry has argued that in order to move towards a spirituality that is more intimate with the natural world it becomes necessary to move from a spirituality of the divine as found in sacred texts to 'a spirituality of the divine as revealed in the world about us.'[20] Van Wieren has considered the relationship between spirituality and ecological restoration, and Porritt has linked sustainability and environmental care to a defence of meaning, a perspective that, as we shall see, is in accord with other explanations of human meaning.[21, 22]

In light of the ecologically damaging consequences of modernity and the shadow of meaninglessness and alienation that has accompanied the materialistic outlook, particularly in the twentieth century, it is perfectly understandable that today we should be considering the importance and implications of spirituality in our conceptions of reality, i.e. our evolving worldview.[23, 24] We can examine this development from three perspectives: in terms of worldviews; in terms of psychological interpretations of human needs; and in terms of human meaning. Taken together, these three angles of vision provide a robust basis for including notions of personal meaning that embrace spirituality and the personal ethic it can foster in our interpretations of sustainability. Moreover, from a design perspective, such an inclusion raises an important challenge to the design community, including design education, as to what it might mean for design endeavours.

Perspectives on spirituality:

Worldviews, human needs and levels of meaning

In terms of our worldviews – our changing conceptual frameworks of reality – these can be expressed as three broad categories: traditional, modernity and postmodernity.[25] The traditional worldview began with the global changes of the Axial Age (c.500 BCE) concerning self-awareness, the spiritual sense and notions of transcendence through such developments as monotheism in the Middle East, which included Zoroastrianism and Judaism, and later Christianity and Islam; the philosophy of reason in Europe, especially through the philosophical developments of figures such as Socrates, Plato and Aristotle; Buddhism and Hinduism in India; and Confucianism and Taoism in China.[26] The unsurpassed contributions of the traditional worldview[27] – irrespective of differences of sociocultural interpretation, practices and language – gave rise to our most profound understandings of human meaning, the spiritual self, and a personal sense of rightness, goodness and truth which forms the basis of a personal ethic and questions of conscience. Within this worldview, continuity with and learning from the past were critically important. It is a view in which spirituality or, in its communal form, religion, figures prominently. And the vista embraces the physical, sense-based world, as well as the inner self, which is usually regarded as being of higher meaning and value. It is a metaphysics that tends toward an integrative approach in which human actions, including the production of mundane goods, strive to be in accord with, and are often imbued with, social and spiritual meanings. However, a preoccupation with material goods is generally considered to be an obstacle to spiritual growth, and in times when the traditional worldview was more dominant there were far greater efforts afforded to projects that recognized the numinous. This included the construction of places for religious practice and the creation of symbolic objects that referenced the inner life, faith and the spiritual self; and as we saw in Chapter 3, symbolism was used to point towards that which is essentially ineffable.

The beginnings of modernity, from about 1500 CE, emerged in northern Europe through developments in science and philosophy. Subsequently, the Industrial Revolution of the eighteenth and nineteenth centuries saw unprecedented advances in science and technology. These changes were accompanied by a progressive secularization of society, the development of a politics of democracy, an increasing command of nature, and an economy based on industrial capitalism. Continuity with and learning from the past became far less relevant, and symbolic dimensions of life were marginalized.[28] The new priorities were efficiency, originality, progress, expansion and growth, and looking to the future.[29]

Modernity resulted in the development of design practices that enabled material goods to be rationalized for efficient, technologically sophisticated mass production. Advancements in science and industry – within a worldview in which meaning was found through progress and growth – led to what has been termed the 'Revolution of Rising Expectations', which was based firmly on material benefits.[30] However, what was not sufficiently recognized was that expansion in the production of material goods, made from metals, hydrocarbons, minerals and organic materials – was inevitably accompanied by degradation of the natural environments that yielded those resources and received them back as waste and pollution. Similarly, a preoccupation with and growth in utilitarian benefits and the diversions they offered was accompanied by a general decline in traditional conceptions of human flourishing and the profound notions of meaning they accorded.

59

Postmodernity emerged during the mid-twentieth century in response to the shortcomings of modernity and what Smith refers to as 'the truncated worldview of the enlightenment', but then, unreasonably, it attempted to suggest that worldviews themselves are misguided, which is something of a contradiction in terms.[31] Despite this, postmodern perspectives, which developed during a period of post-industrialism and rapid globalization, have raised our consciousness of social justice and have advanced human rights to a greater extent than previously.[32] While maintaining much of modernity's ideology of naturalistic materialism, the postmodern era has greater awareness of its shortcomings. Nevertheless, there have been few signs of attenuating production of material goods or effectively tackling the growth–decline problem that is devastating the natural environment. On the contrary, growth and expansion remain the watchwords of business and governments alike, even though the environmental consequences are now widely recognized. However, due at least in part to the relocation of mass-manufacturing centres from the Western economically developed countries to other regions, design began to shift its attention from product or industrial design, which dominated most of the twentieth century, to design related to social issues. Thus, in Europe especially, we saw the emergence during the latter years of the twentieth century and the early years of the twenty-first, of areas such as service design, social marketing and social innovation, and an increased emphasis on participatory design, co-creation, creative communities and so-called 'design thinking' being applied to social and management issues, rather than to the development of material goods.[33] However, these attempts to rebuild and re-engage with the communal vie with the atomizing tendencies of contemporary communication technologies; as Wilson has put it, 'Surfing the net we discover not a common culture, but a million, million separate emptinesses.'[34] Moreover, the extended span of Western, predominantly secular values that has accompanied the globalization of markets and the expansion of transnational corporations has resulted in a fear that values are being threatened in those cultures where traditional worldviews remain dominant. This has led to a rise in fundamentalism, which itself is a postmodern phenomenon.[35] It represents an entrenchment of views and an unwillingness to find conciliation between one's most deeply held beliefs and worldview, and the views and beliefs of others. Fundamentalist stances do not only apply to religion, but can be equally present among those who hold secular, atheistic views.

What becomes clear from this brief characterization of predominant worldviews is that each has prioritized certain aspects of human understanding, which can be summarized as personal meaning during the traditional or pre-modern period, i.e. religious or transcending worldly, material interpretations; practical meaning during the period of modernity (i.e. naturalistic materialism) and social meaning in the current period that we refer to as postmodernity – this nascent period in human development can, perhaps, be nominally identified as a time of emerging post-materialism. None is sufficient in itself to satisfactorily address human needs, aspirations and potential. A more comprehensive, balanced and tolerant view must include the truth that resides within each, as suggested by the dashed lines in Figure 5.1.[36]

Human needs

From a psychological perspective, these worldviews correspond approximately to Maslow's well-known hierarchy of human needs, which in its original form had five broad stages. Modernity's emphasis on understanding and controlling the natural environment and on utilitarian matters corresponds primarily to satisfying the two lower-level stages of physiological needs and safety needs. Postmodernity's emphasis on human rights and issues of social concern and justice corresponds to the two higher-level stages of belongingness and love needs and esteem needs. And the profound insights of the traditional worldview – concerning inner development, spiritual growth and ultimate meaning – correspond to the highest level of human needs, self-actualization. In later developments of this hierarchy, Maslow expanded the higher level needs to include cognitive needs and aesthetic needs, which are prominent aspects in traditional, modern and postmodern worldviews, and self-transcendence needs, most clearly present in the traditional worldview.[37]

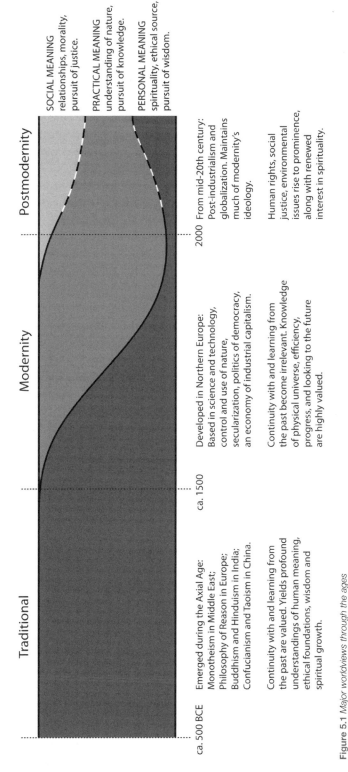

Figure 5.1 *Major worldviews through the ages*

SOCIAL MEANING
relationships, morality,
pursuit of justice.

PRACTICAL MEANING
understanding of nature,
pursuit of knowledge.

PERSONAL MEANING
spirituality, ethical source,
pursuit of wisdom.

Traditional

Modernity

Postmodernity

ca. 500 BCE

Emerged during the Axial Age:
Monotheism in Middle East;
Philosophy of Reason in Europe;
Buddhism and Hinduism in India;
Confucianism and Taoism in China.

Continuity with and learning from
the past are valued. Yields profound
understandings of human meaning,
ethical foundations, wisdom and
spiritual growth.

ca. 1500

Developed in Northern Europe:
Based in science and technology,
control and use of nature,
secularization, politics of democracy,
an economy of industrial capitalism.

Continuity with and learning from
the past become irrelevant. Knowledge
of physical universe, efficiency,
progress, and looking to the future
are highly valued.

2000

From mid-20th century:
Post-industrialism and
globalization. Maintains
much of modernity's
ideology.

Human rights, social
justice, environmental
issues rise to prominence,
along with renewed
interest in spirituality.

Levels of meaning

From a philosophical perspective, the three worldviews indicated also correspond with Hick's levels of meaning consisting of, in order of ascendency, natural, ethical and religious meanings.[38] Together, these levels of meaning encompass (1) how to interpret and respond to the natural world and matters of self-preservation – and, as Eagleton has pointed out, to be meaningful our responses must respect the world's 'grain and texture';[39] (2) social responses and interactions, morality and notions of community; and (3) our responses to an intuitive apprehension of the nature of reality that lies outside analytical or logical comprehension, but which pertains to a sense of ultimate meaning.

These perspectives reveal that modernity, and still to a large degree postmodernity, have tended to confine human efforts to the first rungs of human potential, i.e. to utilitarian needs and benefits. Moreover, the economic system, which stokes progress and growth in these areas, leads to no higher aspiration than the generation and accumulation of capital. Eagleton has likened this state of affairs, which for all its technological prowess preoccupies humanity with lower material concerns, to that of the Stone Age.[40] The heritage of human knowledge down the ages tells us that to thrive and find fulfilment, our efforts must include more than practical considerations and more still than social relationships and matters of social justice. Our highest potential and the ever-present meaning-seeking aspect of our humanity must also be attended to, and this is achieved through dedication to inner development, which can lead to spiritual growth and wisdom. These different aspects of being human are, of course, interdependent, and this interdependence has implications for how we conceive of the purpose and design of our material culture and, indeed, for its fundamental nature and meaning.

The spiritual understanding

The term spirituality stems from the Christian tradition, although its contemporary usage is universal. It refers to a wide range of ideas, experiences and practices considered to be life-enhancing and related to human wellbeing, and which are holistic in that they can affect all aspects of life. It is also closely associated with the imagination, creativity, relationships and ideas of a transcendent reality beyond sense-based evidence and proof. Similarly, it is associated with peace, joy, justice and a unified sense of body, mind and soul. Spirituality is often linked to religion, theism and the divine, but can also be atheistic and entirely secular.[41]

All the great spiritual traditions are concerned with the transformation of the individual: from a self-centred way of encountering the world to an inner realization – an intuitive apprehension – of our place in and connectedness to the whole of reality, and a sense of its goodness and truth. Among the different traditions, this is variously termed Enlightenment, the Way of Virtue and the Tao, and it is seen as a realization of Ultimate Reality, the Ground of Being, the Kingdom or simply the Real. The various traditions are concerned with essentially the same kind of thing – the individual's inner self and a realization, or reaching an inner conviction, that a more profound or higher apprehension of reality is possible – beyond the external, sense-based world that we encounter on a daily basis. All the great traditions recognize that the central, spiritual core of each individual has to be developed through a personal striving via inner work. This development requires self-discipline, contemplation and self-examination, and right actions in the form of selflessness, service and concern for others[42] and, as we saw in Chapter 3, throughout human history certain kinds of material artefacts have been used to help focus our attention on such matters.

Thus, the traditional worldview sees individuals as having an outer, active life and an inner, spiritual, contemplative life.[43, 44] Meaning, fulfilment and attainment of our full potential are to be found in striving to harmonize and find unity between these two overlapping, but often competing or divergent, aspects of ourselves. In the Western tradition, this idea can be depicted as two intersecting fields within a larger ground, as shown in Figure 5.2.

The active life is the life of necessity lived according to traditional ethical teachings, such that the nature of our worldly activities is modulated by notions of goodness and truth. In the traditional worldview, such activities are characterized as selfless actions and service. In both Western and Eastern traditions, this is described as practical goodness, charity, or consecrated action.[45, 46] Such is the good active life.

The overlapping section represents a second phase of the active life, which is enhanced by an understanding of the basis of ethical and spiritual teachings – not just compliance with them. This also represents the first phase of the contemplative life, the inner path of spiritual growth. The individual engages in self-examination

63

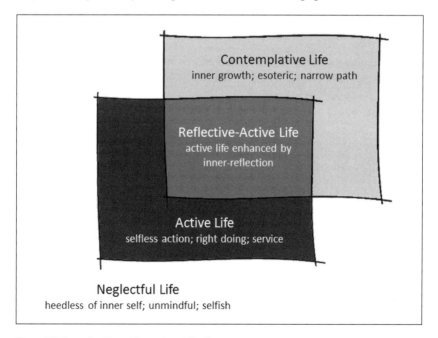

Contemplative Life
inner growth; esoteric; narrow path

Reflective-Active Life
active life enhanced by
inner-reflection

Active Life
selfless action; right doing; service

Neglectful Life
heedless of inner self; unmindful; selfish

Figure 5.2 *The active life and the contemplative life*

and strives for understanding. This intermediate stage – representing a reflective, active life – is traditionally regarded as better than the active life alone.[47]

The upper area represents the second degree of the contemplative life, where the active life is largely (but can never be entirely) eschewed, and one is dedicated to inner growth. It represents the contemplative tradition, which has existed in all cultures for thousands of years, but is for those who are temperamentally inclined to such asceticism. It is a life dedicated to 'the one thing needful' – which as we have seen is traditionally regarded as the 'best' part of us because it can lead to a sense of unity, wholeness and joy, i.e. true happiness.[48]

The ground in which these stages exist represents the life that is uninformed by or unconcerned with such ideas, which is traditionally regarded as neglectful or as missing life's purpose. This is the unreflective life of sensual, worldly pleasure; the unexamined life, which Socrates regarded as not worth living.[49]

These stages of individual development, from neglectfulness to right doing, right thinking and right being, which can lead to inner transformation, are depicted in various symbolic ways within the Christian tradition, as we saw in Chapter 3.[50] Similar ideas are present in all the great traditions. In Islam the 'good' active life, the life of right doing, is one lived according to divine law, *Sharī'ah*, and the contemplative life, the more esoteric, narrower path, is known as *Tarīqah*.[51] Buddhism speaks of the impure path of unmindfulness and of the noble eightfold path, which includes rightness in terms of views, determination, words, action, livelihood, effort and mindfulness, leading to a sense of unity, i.e. *nirvana*.[52] In Hinduism there is the path of ignorance, the path of action – which involves ensuring that worldly activities conform to higher notions of meaning – the path of knowledge of spiritual wisdom and the path of devotion and connection via the inner self that leads to enlightenment.[53, 54] Table 5.1 summarizes these traditional understandings of inner development and their parallels with human needs, with interpretations of human meaning, and with the *quadruple bottom line for sustainability*. While the factors and emphases among these various perspectives are not exactly coincidental – their common feature is the relationship between the outer, active life and development of the inner, spiritual self – traditionally, it is inner development that leads to 'right' action in the world.

An additional consideration here, which may seem paradoxical to the modern mind, is that for contemplative experience and development of the inner self and charity, we are told that knowledge is a hindrance, analysis is pointless, research is inapplicable, methods are irrelevant, techniques are useless and explanation is not possible.[55, 56] Contemplative practices and the insights they can yield are non-intellectual, non-emotional and are not based in reason. Moreover, they do not require the use of logic, nor do they depend on discursive thought.[57, 58] These notions are perhaps easier to grasp if we think of love, because this, too, is not dependent on research, analysis or intellect; in spiritual traditions the word love often refers to charity or unselfish love. Moreover, some traditions (e.g. Zen Buddhism) deliberately seek to confound intellectual reasoning and emotions to

Table 5.1 The quadruple bottom line of sustainability and its parallels with human needs, human meaning and traditions of inner development

Unsustainability heedlessness	Practical Meaning apt response to needs, environment	Social Meaning apt response to other people	Personal Meaning apt response to inner self	QUADRUPLE BOTTOM LINE OF SUSTAINABILITY (Walker, 2011, 187-190)
	Economic Means money as a means to an end; economic equity			
	Physiological, Safety	Belongingness, Love	Self-Actualization, Self-Transcendence	MASLOW'S HIERARCHY OF NEEDS (Huitt, 2007)
	Natural	Ethical	Religious	LEVELS OF MEANING (Hick, 1989, 148-158)
Neglectful Life	Active Life selfless service	Reflective, Active Life	Contemplative Life the narrow path	CHRISTIANITY (Johnston, 2005, 68; Schumacher, 1977, 148)
Ignorance	Right Action	Knowledge of Spiritual Wisdom	Inner Life, Devotion	HINDUISM (Patton, 2008, xiv-xv; Easwaran, 2000, 74-76)
Unmindfulness	Right Doing	Right Thinking	Right Being	BUDDHISM (Mascaro, 1973, 29-32)
Infidelity	Right Living in accord with Divine Law, Shari'ah		Esoteric, Spiritual Way, Tariqah	ISLAM (Nasr, 1966, 93; Quran, 9:23)

foster deeper ways of knowing. The intellect is concerned with *thinking about* something, emotions are concerned with *feelings about* something, but what is needed is *direct experience*.[59, 60, 61]

This brief overview of the meaning of spirituality and the paths of spiritual development clearly demonstrates that traditional spiritual understandings are intimately, indeed critically, related to our worldly activities, the nature and content of those activities, and the approaches we take to pursue them.

Spirituality, contemplation and the creative process

In contrast to much of his earlier work, in 1968 at the age of 75, the Catalan artist Joan Miró created three enormous, very sparse pieces that he called *Painting on white background for the cell of a recluse (I), (II) and (III)*. Each painting bears an erratic but continuous hand-painted black line on a white ground. Miró said of these paintings: 'it took me only a moment to draw this line with my brush. But it took me months, perhaps even years of reflection to form the idea of it.'[62]

The spiritual tradition and creativity are closely connected. Creative activity is pursued through practice, thinking and reflection, and so has many parallels with the contemplative life. It has been widely recognized that true creative endeavour is expressive of similar inner or higher notions of human concern – that the best of the arts point us in the direction of spiritual awareness and truth and that the visual arts have a spiritual dimension.[63, 64] The British artist David Hockney regards all creativity as being about love.[65]

In addition, sudden insight or spontaneous understanding is an intimate part of the disciplined process of contemplative practice and spiritual development. Recognized in both Western and Eastern spiritual traditions, religious and non-religious, it refers to an immediate, direct, albeit fleeting, apprehension of reality that is neither speculative nor contestable.[66, 67, 68] It is also a key feature of creative, practice-based activities. In both cases, such insight is often reached through dedication, self-discipline and persistence. In contrast to systematic, empirical approaches, which are characteristic of much scientific inquiry and technological development, there is no methodology or technique for gaining such insight. Rather, it is the unpredictable, uncertain outcome of an integrated and immersive process of practice, focused thought and contemplation. In fact, methods and techniques are useless – such developments cannot be pursued through reasoning, or discursive or analytical thought, and knowledge can, potentially, be a hindrance.[69, 70]

66

In contrast to this rather risky, indeterminate process, embarking on a definite course of action with a distinct goal, a defined set of objectives and a clear methodology can offer a more secure, safer option, but this can also be a way of avoiding the deeper issues. Setting out on a project in which much time is spent gathering and analyzing data in order to acquire proof or evidence can send us down a path that is very busy, but often quite mechanical in its procedures. This kind of work can be a convenient and dependable substitute for the difficult, often angst-ridden task of surrendering oneself to the process, striving for creative direction and acquiring sudden but elusive insight, which one intuitively senses or knows – but cannot prove – has a rightness to it. This requires that we have faith in, and make a dedicated commitment to non-intellectual, reflective, creative practice.

Architect Christopher Alexander regards that which is permanent in people as a central quality of human life and the human spirit. He suggests that it is also central to timeless ways of creating or, more accurately, generating human-made environments and artefacts. Places, buildings and artefacts that possess this timeless quality – a quality that can be perceived but remains nameless – contribute to a human-made environment that resonates with and nourishes the human spirit.[71] However, this cannot be pre-planned, it results from a process of emergence that is not generalizable but is specific to context.[72] Here we see a relationship between the human spirit and the character and tenor of design. Design that is capable of nourishing people and which is sympathetic to the natural environment becomes fundamentally connected to the 'particularities of place';[73] it cannot be mass produced. Hence, it is related to localization, which Scruton, among others, advocates as essential to addressing the environmental stewardship and social responsibilities inherent to contemporary understandings of sustainability.[74] He regards religious or spiritual practices that focus on that which is present and immediate before us as critical to our notions of the sacred and our love of and care for place. It is this personal relationship that creates a sense of responsibility and overcomes the view that sees the Earth merely as an 'it' – a resource to be used.[75] Scruton's conservatism roots his arguments in local action. Others take a larger-scale or macro view of the links between environmental and spiritual considerations. Some have suggested that widespread spiritual renewal is needed if we are to change from our current, environmentally destructive course.[76] Tucker contends that a macro perspective is needed if we are to revise the ways in which we regard our place within the natural processes of life on Earth, and such a revision raises questions about the relationships between ecology and our notions of the sacred, the spiritual and the religious sense.[77] Berry argues that, as developments in Western civilization led to a view of human domination over the natural world, a sense of the spiritual order and the sacredness of Nature was lost. A critical requirement in establishing a different, more reverential view of the Earth is a rediscovery of its mystique, a new admiration, and a renewed sense of care.[78]

It becomes clear that, whether approached from a local sense of place or from a larger-scale perspective, there is a wide range of authoritative voices that find critically important relationships among human actions, environmental responsibility and stewardship, and our spiritual or religious sense. These relationships are not abstract. They can inform our approaches to economics, as in contemporary critiques of growth within discussions of ecological economics, our ethics and our sense of moral obligation towards the natural environment and, as we shall see in Chapter 8, the development of business strategies that endeavour to conform to sustainability principles.[79] And they can affect how we think about and approach design – as exemplified in architecture by Alexander, Van der Ryn and Day and, in product design, by Papanek and Branzi, among others.[80, 81, 82]

67

Implications for design

In considering these issues in relation to the imaginative, creative process of designing material artefacts, we see that intellectual discussion, analysis and conventional notions of research tend to be less important than direct engagement in the process itself; a process that is pursued through practice, reading, thinking and contemplation. It requires freedom from distractions, preoccupations with 'busy work' and being constantly occupied and active. In fact, it is a process in which it sometimes appears as if nothing is being done. Additionally, within the creative process the designer is often called upon to make aesthetic judgements, which are sense-based. Hence, emotions will naturally and inevitably play a role. Here, it is important to recognize that emotions serve as the connector between the inner self and our external activities and experiences in the world.[83] When designing an artefact, we must be aware of our emotional responses, our feelings about the developing work. And these can be related to ideas of spiritual development in that traditional notions of right action – the personal ethic discussed earlier – can serve as a key source for making appropriate decisions.

To this end, the designer has to try continually to ensure disciplined or mindful critique in order to recognize traits in the emerging work and, if appropriate, redirect it if it seems to be becoming associated with emotional responses that are dissonant with spiritual understandings of right action, right livelihood, right effort, etc. These might include feelings of selfishness, greed, vanity, deceit or prestige – in the designer during the course of design development, or in others if design decisions mean that the work is likely to evoke such emotions. This reflective critique can apply to the design of the artefact itself and to the design of its associated promotional materials for purposes of advertising and marketing. It is just such critique that links personal meaning – comprising spirituality and substantive values – to creative decisions and thence to the nature of our human-made environment.

This relationship between design activity, emotional responses and mindful critique represents the vital link between our inner selves and our actions in the world. A material culture developed to be congruent with spiritual understandings and reflective of the awareness that contemplative practice yields would begin to express a very different ethos from that which is so evident today. It would be driven by an approach that strives to be free of those things that are at variance with inner growth. For example, objects that distract, that offer endless opportunities for diversion, that encourage self-indulgence or stoke feelings of vanity, all of which confuse or contradict 'right thought'. Potentially, our material culture, and the ways in which it is designed and manifested, could be in far greater accord with inner development, thereby enhancing the conditions necessary for its advancement. This points to a material culture that is less concerned with facilitating busyness, utility, accomplishing practical tasks and 'getting on', i.e. less concerned with creating and assisting in the progress of outer, worldly activities. Instead, it suggests a material culture that sets the right kind of environment for correspondence between the inner and outer person, which is the traditional path of wisdom and happiness.[84] This is not to suggest a rejection of technological products and the benefits they can bring. Rather, it is to recognize a significant imbalance in priorities and approaches, in which high rates of scientific and technological progress have been accompanied not only by levels of production, consumerism and waste that are seriously compromising the planet's ecosystems, but also by a reification of materialism, empiricism and rationalism that has worked to the detriment and exclusion of other ways of knowing. In this regard, traditional understandings of practical goodness are critically related to the social and environmental care demanded of us by contemporary ideas of design for sustainability. They create the connection between one's spiritual development and compassion towards others and the world itself.

Clearly, much contemporary design practice contradicts these ideas, frequently aiming instead to foster feelings of acquisitiveness, envy and status. Unlike

68

traditional understandings of the active life, within today's corporate culture the kinds of products being produced are uninformed by and often antithetical to long-established teachings that support just and appropriate ways of living in the world, i.e. that support a 'good' active life of unselfishness, charity and consecrated action.

The priority of the corporation is profit, and its employees are 'legally obliged to set aside their own values' in order to maximize profits for the organization and its shareholders.[85] Strikingly, but like others who have advocated *laissez-faire* economic policies, Milton Friedman saw any other priority, such as wider social responsibility (and one could add environmental care), as a threat to a free society.[86] In recent years, however, some moves have been made to supersede such outmoded views. *Certified B* corporations, for example, build social and environmental responsibilities into the business model, and through their legal frameworks are able to protect themselves against actions from shareholders who may disapprove of such inclusions, which may adversely affect profit maximization.[87] Such developments, however, remain the exception rather than the rule. It is important, also, to recognize that, in addition to the devastating consequences of their economic priorities, the psychological manipulation by corporations through their use of marketing techniques is both powerfully persuasive and ubiquitous. Hence, through their various activities, and often supported by government policies, corporate practices have tended to undermine our most enduring understandings of goodness, right action and ethical values, which emerge from inner development and are exemplified by selfless service, compassion and charity. Bakan has argued that the contemporary corporation is a morally blind institution that exploits people for profit and, as such, within the constraints of the law it has no moral compass that serves to prevent its activities harming others.[88]

69

Today, we are only too aware that the environmental consequences are becoming ever more acute, with no signs of abatement, and the social exploitation – both through the production methods employed and through market development to sustain growth – has been massive. Nair contends that it becomes necessary to move beyond the growth-based system that aims to sell electronic gadgets and automobiles to every person on the planet – a system that offloads the environmental and social costs of doing business onto the taxpayer, that concentrates wealth among companies and shareholders and is based essentially on self-interest and greed.[89, 90] As such, it is a system that is entirely antithetical to all the great spiritual and wisdom teachings down the ages.

Towards a wisdom economy

The design and production of consumer products has been on a steeply rising trajectory of innovation and growth for decades. The impacts have been enormous and while, undoubtedly, many of these have been positive, the products themselves, the methods employed and the side effects of their production, use and disposal are, in a multitude of ways, severely damaging in terms of *practical meaning* and the natural environment; *social meaning* and ideas of equity and justice; and *personal meaning* and the creation of conditions supportive of the spiritual self.

Today's most widely distributed, often least enduring, technological products are designed, produced, distributed and marketed by global-scale corporations whose priorities are largely incompatible with traditional understandings and values that seek to harmonize the inner person with outer activities and the world in general through ways that, crucially, include service, and concern for others. Scientific and technological advancements have provided us with unprecedented power over Nature, yet, in pursuit of profits, use of that power has tended to work against the common good.[91] This disparity with personal meaning is fundamentally linked to social equity and justice, and to respect for the natural environment. For these reasons, it would seem that any attempts to invoke substantive, meaningful change through design – or any other discipline for that matter – within the current corporate milieu would be a hiding to nothing. Attempting to internalize, within the company's economic accounting, problematic aspects of design and production for reasons of right action and ethical responsibility – aspects that are today consciously externalized – would have financial implications and therefore would conflict with the *raison d'être* of the organization.[92]

Approaches are needed that internalize costs, develop knowledge and skills, and nurture community, that provide good work, that yield products people can be proud of making and which can be appreciated and cared for. As we saw in Chapter 4, this would mean fewer, more expensive, more lasting products, which is entirely commensurate with reducing levels of consumption – an inescapable implication of sustainability. We can attempt to reduce consumption by proposing programmes such as fly less, eat local, switch off, etc.[93] But if considered in isolation, such well-meaning, self-imposed schemes, often perceived as a form of austerity, are likely to yield only failure, guilt and disillusionment because the whole trajectory of Western societies and economies is going in the other direction – a direction that depends on, and constantly encourages, consumption. Redressing the imbalance in our contemporary worldview to give greater recognition to age-old understandings that foster wisdom and inner development could yield more fundamental, lasting change. This would mean developing ways of living and ways of creating wealth that value *being* rather than *having*. Such a direction would recognize the importance of substantive values – ethics and social responsibility – and of spirituality and questions of ultimate meaning and purpose. Both are critical elements of an examined life and essential ingredients of a personally meaningful interpretation of sustainability. These factors, if given higher priority, would naturally lead to a disposition less preoccupied with external pursuits that require consumption.[94]

Hence, a *quadruple bottom line* that recognizes deeper notions of human meaning begins to move us from a *knowledge* economy based on what we *can* do, towards a *wisdom* economy based on what we *should* do. Such a direction would recognize the importance of knowledge acquisition but would place greater emphasis on priorities and practices that attain to wisdom via the examined life and development of inner values. A system that values wisdom, that combines knowledge with right judgement, would serve the common good through its attainment to virtue, and would reduce impacts on the natural environment because it would necessarily begin to moderate the place and significance of material goods in our ideas of the good life.

Greater appreciation of the contribution to human understanding of the core teachings contained within the traditional worldview, variously expressed by all the great philosophies and religions, can provide a sense of orientation and direction to life.[95, 96] Inherently, they steer us away from many of those contemporary preoccupations that are so closely associated with unsustainable practices – particularly our seemingly obsessive relationship with technological progress, growth and consumerism. The inclusion of spirituality within understandings of sustainability can begin to reverse the direction of motivation – from an external imposition of rules, regulations and sanctions to an internally driven, volitional repositioning of priorities. This would yield a more comprehensive approach to our design endeavours because it would include:

- a moderated, more environmentally responsible direction in the provision of material benefits – the major contribution of modernity;
- increased attention to social responsibility and justice – a characteristic of postmodernity;
- orientation and direction through inner growth and a sense of personal meaning – the major contribution of the traditional worldview.

This more balanced approach would have major implications for design because, in the milieu in which design operates, practices related to materials extraction, manufacturing, labour conditions, product disposal and economics, among others, would necessarily have to change. Such change, however, is to be welcomed because it would redirect our efforts away from the current, self-destructive, inherently unsustainable path, and lead us in a more positive and more hopeful direction.

6

The Narrow Door to Sustainability

from practically
useful to spiritually
useful artefacts

the thing to me is of greater importance than the words

Hermann Hesse

The Light of the World by the nineteenth-century artist William Holman Hunt portrays Christ knocking on a closed, long unused, weed-strewn door.[1] Hunt completed this painting in 1853, just two years after The Great Exhibition – that flamboyant celebration of Britain's dominance over international affairs, which it had achieved through trade, empire and industrial supremacy.[2, 3] Like Dickens' 'one thing needful', discussed in the previous chapter, Hunt's painting also suggests that in the pursuit of innovation, production and wealth, profound aspects of human concern had become neglected.

Some 60 years later another London-based artist became known for a very different painting but one that is not unrelated to the theme of Hunt's. Walter Sickert's *Ennui*, c.1914, depicts a middle-aged couple in a graceless parlour. The man sits smoking in the foreground while in the background the woman leans on a chest of drawers staring blankly at the wall.[4] It is a powerful portrait of boredom, apathy and vapidity, of lives without purpose. Here there is no door, no apparent way out.

Hunt's painting, with its weed-strewn door, can be interpreted as a representation of the neglect and decline of the traditional worldview, along with its conception of a hierarchical order to the universe; an order that for centuries was mirrored in human society.[5] While this ordering restricted social movement and individual freedom because one's place in society was more or less fixed, it also gave a sense of meaning to individual lives, to social endeavours and to the world itself. Indeed, within the traditional view, the constituents of Nature, because they occupied a place in the great chain of being, were regarded not merely as 'resources' but as inherently meaningful and significant.[6] Modern and subsequently early postmodern perspectives eroded and albeit eradicated this perspective. The modern worldview allowed more freedom but in the process there arose a disenchantment[7] – a state vividly captured by Sickert. Modernity's privileging of materialism and instrumental approaches to meaning-seeking through physical investigations may have raised our material standards of living but it also created a sense of meaninglessness and ennui that is intimately connected to the destruction of the natural environment.[8, 9]

Here, some of the options currently being pursued to foster a change in direction are described and the case is strengthened for a more substantive shift – one that reaches beyond mundane concerns. This is accompanied by an outline of the challenges this would pose, particularly a transformation in perspective to include inner values and spiritual sensibilities in our day-to-day activities. Furthermore, as was briefly mentioned in Chapter 3, historically, a spiritually significant artefact would have been expressed in the symbolism of a particular tradition. However, in a globalized world where international communications and travel and cultural intermingling have become commonplace this can create difficulties. Such objects can be divisive because of their association with distinct, exclusive claims to spiritual truth. They can also prevent discussion and inclusion of these important considerations in the secularized, neutral arena of public life. Therefore, following on from the propositional objects *Babel*, *Cana*, and *Whereof one cannot speak* (Figs. 3.1–3.3), which were based on the Judaeo-Christian tradition, this chapter considers the design of a spiritually useful object that brings to the fore the *personal meaning* facet of the *quadruple bottom line of sustainability* while also being trans-religious; it is also consistent with the social, environmental and economic facets through its localized sourcing of materials and its making. Unlike the earlier objects, the propositional design presented here draws on symbolism found in many traditions. By doing so, it offers a basis for reflecting on design's role in contributing to the development of a material culture for a post-materialist, post-consumerist and trans- and/or supra-religious time.

73

Extending design's ambit

For a century or more design's emphasis has been entirely in tune with the ideology of materialism. Under its auspices, instrumental reason, systematic investigation of the natural world and data acquisition to advance factual information and empirical knowledge have been put to human purpose through the continual advancement of science and technology. This contemporary understanding of progress, which is physically based, directed towards material benefits and in a constant state of evolution, has had a future-facing trajectory. Consequently, the next 'big thing' has been a major focus for design; it has driven consumption and fuelled economic growth.

A fundamentally different direction is advocated by some economists, as well as philosophers such as Gorz, who has called for a different kind of lifestyle to avoid environmental collapse. He suggests that our current capitalist system will have to end one way or another, either in a measured, civilized fashion or in a barbarous fashion.[10] Here, Gorz's arguments echo the warnings of Plato, from the third century BCE, that striving for a way of life based on immoderate consumption leads to conflict.[11]

It would seem to be true that 'there is nothing new under the sun'; at least there is nothing profoundly new, which is what this passage from the book of Ecclesiastes[12] signifies. Of course, there are an infinite number of ways of creating material novelties and in growth-based economies they tend to be granted disproportionate attention. This is because it is in the interests of business agendas to promote and encourage such attention in order to continually boost consumption. It is also important to recognize that the value ascribed to such novelties is subjective and has little to do with the costs of the labour and physical materials required to create them.[13, 14] Moreover, this kind of newness only attains significance when seen through the reductionist frame of materialism. This restricted ideology, which privileges scientific positivism and where meaning is sought via outer, worldly endeavours, has had a powerful effect on design's development,[15] and even though more human-centred design approaches have arisen in recent years, its overarching authority remains predominant. Today, however, the true costs of so many fleeting products and amusements have become far too high because we are paying for them with the ecological systems on which we all depend.

Emissions, consumption and options: Scientific studies suggest that to avoid dangerous increases in global temperatures, CO_2e (equivalent carbon dioxide) emissions will need to be very significantly reduced in coming decades.[16, 17] To achieve this overall reduction, at the same time as developing nations are raising their standards of living, per capita emissions and hence consumption levels[18] in affluent countries such as the United States,[19] the United Kingdom[20] and Australia[21] will have to be drastically lowered – by 90 per cent or greater compared to 1990 levels. Similarly, Sulston et al., in their People and the Planet report for the Royal Society, recognize the need for major reductions in consumption,[22] especially in the wealthy and emerging nations, and argue convincingly for alternatives to growth-based economic models.

Despite this, the ways being advocated to achieve such reductions are generally incommensurate with the magnitude of change required. The sheer scale of the reductions being proposed requires a fundamental shift in outlook, in behaviours and in our ways of living. Yet there appears to be little will, politically or otherwise, to get to grips with the issues and as we prevaricate, emissions continue to rise. It seems that short-term expediencies inexorably trump longer-term obligations, with potentially disastrous consequences. Most approaches to consumption reduction tend to promote green technologies and a transition to service solutions. Sulston et al. assert that techno-efficiencies will be of 'the greatest importance' in reducing waste, pollution and exploitation of Nature.[23] However, while such technologies may be a beneficial development compared to current modes, seeing them as a major contribution to change simply reinforces an eco-modernist approach to sustainability[24] and is regarded by some as naive.[25] A transformation to greener, more efficient technologies might reduce certain of the negative effects, but it does not confront the heart of the consumption issue. Capra calls this a crisis of perception, arguing that most people in Western society and its large social institutions adhere to ideas that are integral to an outdated worldview.[26]

Others advocate a transformation from a product-based economy to a service-based economy and the selling of performance instead of tangible goods.[27, 28] Again, these directions can offer benefits, but we must be circumspect about simply transferring our consumption habits from one form to another. First, services are not necessarily any more sustainable than conventional products.[29] Online services such as banking, education, social networking and entertainment often rely on a host of constantly changing, energy-hungry consumer electronics that are highly demanding in terms of energy. Power consumption by data storage centres is rising at an alarming rate and accounts for an increasing proportion of all power used worldwide.[30] Consequently, CO_2e emissions from IT use are rising much faster than those from other sectors and are predicted to double in the coming decade.[31] Second, use of online services can be time-consuming, intrusive and distracting, and can encourage behaviours that isolate individuals and atomize society.[32] Third, there can be rebound effects that offset the anticipated benefits.[33] Fourth, and most significantly because it underpins the other three, the key issue of consumption-based values and behaviours is not being addressed. Indeed, appealing to values associated with consumption and self-interest, such as prestige, status and image, can be counterproductive. This is because it serves to suppress those intrinsic and self-transcendent values that correlate with systemic concerns about bigger-than-self problems, which include social equity and environmental care.[34]

Instead of constantly looking for the next 'big thing', which could be a product including an eco-product, a service or an experience, we must ask ourselves how our priorities and values might develop if we were to set aside our preoccupation with externally acquired things. Capra argues that a more profound shift is required based in spiritual awareness which, he says, is deeply connected to ecological awareness.[35] His position is supported by many others from various fields, including psychology,[36] philosophy,[37, 38] education[39, 40] and design.[41] It is appropriate and, given the evident consequences, vitally important to consider what a different direction, with far less consumption and much greater emphasis on inner values, spiritual wellbeing and environmental care, might mean for the nature of our material culture and our ways of living. Such questions, and the assumptions they challenge, are not merely hypothetical. To substantially reduce consumption, along with a shift away from the tenets of materialism, an entirely different notion of material culture and material goods will be needed – one that is not only far more stable, enduring and environmentally benign, but also more conducive to human flourishing.

A less consumptive path: Clearly, compared to today, far less emphasis will have to be placed on the putative merits of technological products, especially those that are in a state of rapid development and change. Ways of life that are significantly less consumptive would mean far fewer material expectations and a turning away from the destructive interpretations of progress and growth that have characterized recent times. Instead of regarding such a direction as detrimental, potentially, it could be seen as a positive development, heralding a higher quality of life in terms of social and personal meaning. Rather than looking towards outer accoutrements, amusements and consumerism, it would promote an improved sense of community, civic society, cooperation and the common good, a cleaner, healthier environment, and a turning towards inner fulfilment and more profound notions of wellbeing.

Beyond the prosaic

76

To acknowledge deeper aspects of human meaning, which extend beyond the practical and the prosaic, people have always created artefacts that have had higher or spiritual purpose. These are artefacts that point, however nominally or inadequately, to the ultimate, impenetrable 'why' that lies beyond the scope of evidence-based justifications and logical arguments, and beyond what the poet Shelley called 'the painted veil' of everyday life.[42] Scruton refers to this as the *why of understanding*, which seeks meanings, in contrast to the *why of science* that seeks causes and explanations, and the *why of reason* that seeks arguments.[43] In recent times, design has concentrated its efforts virtually exclusively on the latter two but has assiduously avoided the why of understanding,[44] which is encountered through philosophy, art, religion and the inner path that leads to clarity of awareness. These are the things that distinguish us from other living creatures and help ensure that we give due consideration to other people and the planet itself.[45] They can generate within us a sense of right judgement and right action; that is, a basis for how we volitionally act towards others and the world – not merely in relation to externally imparted societal norms or moral codes, but in ways that are in accord with a deeper awareness of reality that is inherently meaningful.[46] If we are to raise our concerns above progress, narrowly interpreted in terms of prosaic practicalities, and above short-term financial gains, political expediencies, competitiveness and self-interest, we must look to these more profound areas of endeavour. They represent aspects of being human that acknowledge individuals as meaning-seeking subjects, not objects that can be explained in terms of scientific phenomena and rational argument or exploited as units of production and consumption.

In moving towards post-materialist, post-consumerist ways of living, artefacts that are spiritually symbolic rather than practically useful would serve as tangible reminders of, and a focus for, the inner path, long understood as the path of transformation, liberation and virtue.[47, 48, 49] Hence, they would be conducive to those very aspects of our humanness that have been given short shrift by materialism. We might think of these as spiritually useful objects. Their presence would contribute to the creation of physical conditions, as well as to modes of expression, that facilitate single-pointed attention, reflection and an awareness of the present. Such conditions are increasingly rare in our contemporary world, where technologies, particularly mobile communication technologies, intrude into every aspect of our lives, providing conduits for distraction, persuasion and consumption.

Extending design's ambit to include the development of a material culture that is commensurate with the inner path and deeper values and antithetical to consumerism may seem idealistic and impractical. Nevertheless, it is vital that the discipline of design contributes to the current debate by exploring and visualizing more sustainable, creative propositions based on systemically different tenets.

The inner path and sustainability

We have already referred to Ecclesiastes, which Wolfe regarded as the wisest and most lasting and powerful expression of humankind's life on Earth.[50] Perspectives from the world's great wisdom literature generally agree that concern for outer things and novelty hinders the path to fulfilment and true happiness.[51] Yet such concerns preoccupy consumer societies. There is a stark difference here between the directions advocated by contemporary corporations and governments and implicit in many research agendas, and what might be termed humanity's wisdom heritage. This divergence is not only an obstacle to human flourishing but it also obstructs effective responses to sustainability.[52]

Knowledge via praxis: The kinds of knowledge that can be acquired through observation, systematic inquiry, intellectual activity and reasoned argument are generally explicit and additive in nature and so can be passed on from one generation to the next; by such means scientific knowledge is able to accumulate and advance over time. However, there are other facets of human knowing that have to be learned anew by each individual. As we saw in the previous chapter, this kind of knowledge, which includes tacit knowledge and holistic understandings, is acquired through the direct experience afforded by praxis. As Cottingham explains, such knowledge must be attained through adherence to habituated, self-disciplined practices that progressively foster a capacity for discernment and right judgement, *prior to* theoretical or intellectual understanding.[53] Hence, it is our engagement in practice that leads to understanding, not the other way round. This form of knowledge is critical to design and other creative disciplines. It is also the form of knowledge that pertains to each individual's spiritual and ethical development, which is cultivated through contemplative practices, correlates with virtue and compassion and is inherently related to notions of social justice and ecological awareness.[54]

Traditional and emerging paths in the globalized public square: It is important to mention three factors that are impeding change towards post-materialism and post-consumerism.

1. **Marginalization of the spiritual:** Those aspects of human apprehension traditionally associated with religious practice have become diminished and marginalized in the modern/early postmodern era. Martin Palmer, Secretary General of the Alliance of Religions and Conservation, suggests that the UK – the first country to embrace industrialization – has become cut-off from its spiritual past. He contends that it has become a utilitarian and consumerist culture.[55] The UK is not alone in this – similar traits are present in many of the economically developed countries of the West; advanced capitalism within liberal democracies is inherently atheistic.[56] Anglican and Catholic church attendances plummeted in the UK during the second half of the twentieth century, and belief in a personal God dropped from 57 per cent of the population in 1961 to 26 per cent by 2000. However, in the same period, belief in a spiritual aspect of life rose from 22 per cent to 44 per cent.[57] Furthermore, and as might be expected in the interconnected yet increasingly atomized world fashioned by technology and consumption, distinctions between the major world religions have broken down and spiritual paths have become more complex and more individual.[58] So while adherence to traditional religious forms has waned, along with their public presence and significance, the spiritual side of our humanity has not disappeared; rather, it has been transferred to the private domain and its forms of expression have evolved. However, if, as many have argued, spirituality is an essential ingredient in tackling sustainability,[59, 60] it has to become a recognized and valued part of public debate and cognizance. If it is to do so it has to get beyond those traditional religious configurations that can be so controversial and divisive within Western democracies. Forms of expression are needed that not only rise above such contentions but also respond to contemporary and emerging trans-religious, supra-religious and non-religious modes of spiritual development.

2. **Ineffability of the spiritual:** These inner ways of knowing, attained through practice, are ultimately ineffable and have to be expressed and referred to indirectly. Conventionally, this has been through the use of symbolism, both in texts and objects. This means that their inclusion in

public discourse may not be straightforward; especially as such matters have long been excluded.

3   **Division over the spiritual:** Related to the foregoing, from a modern/ postmodern perspective permeated by philosophical materialism and largely unacquainted with longstanding approaches to sacred literature, the complex, anagogical meanings of traditional sacred texts are often interpreted literally, as if they were conveying explanatory knowledge. Consequently, they often tend to be dismissed as fallacious and their presence in the public realm, along with their associated symbolism, seen as inappropriate and unwelcome. Examples include controversies surrounding the display of religious symbols in the United Kingdom and France,[61, 62] and the display of religious texts in the United States.[63] In a globalized culture, such controversies can cause factionalism and division.

It becomes evident that the development of a fundamentally different direction – one that de-emphasizes materialism and consumerism and embraces a broader and deeper vista – will not only require significant changes in priorities and values, but also non-divisive forms of expression. For this reason, some prominent thinkers, including religious leaders, are suggesting new ways of recognizing profound aspects of human knowing – by reaching past the boundaries of traditional religion. In his book *Beyond Religion*, the Dalai Lama acknowledges that science has undermined certain aspects of religion, but he sees no conflict between scientific advancement and the development of inner or spiritual values.[64] Theological philosopher John Hick says that neither traditional religious beliefs nor materialistic accounts are, in themselves, sufficient. He argues for a new path that recognizes the truth of modern science along with the non-literal truths contained within the great traditions – especially those associated with allegory, symbolism and spirituality.[65] This recognition of the unifying themes of spiritual paths, which transcend religious differences, is reinforced by Frithoff Schuon's studies in comparative religion.[66]

79

Lynch sees signs that such a shift is already underway, with emerging trans-religious developments that draw together human rights and social justice, environmentalism and post-materialist values with issues of meaning, identity and progressive forms of spirituality.[67] The inherent relationship of these directions to social justice and environmental care makes them especially important for sustainability, and their trans-religious or supra-religious nature would seem entirely appropriate in a networked world – where self-transcendent values and cooperation, rather than self-interest values and competition, will be needed to tackle global-scale issues such as poverty and climate change.

Design shift

In advancing this shift, design can make an important contribution by creating alternative possibilities and by manifesting these possibilities in tangible, visual formats. It behoves us to consider what these directions imply for design and the creation of objects that acknowledge the sanctity of personhood and of the Earth itself, and a world not of consumption but of consequence.

Developing contemporary design approaches that pay greater heed to deeper meaning and inner values can help cultivate a renewed appreciation for wisdom and spiritual wellbeing. Such understandings would enable us to acknowledge the limitations of conventional perspectives and in so doing impart a greater humility. With such humility would come the realization that we cannot add anything significantly new to humanity's traditional knowledge about substantive values and discernment. However, this kind of design *can* provide new forms of expression that give this knowledge contemporary relevance and acceptability. While this is a never-ending project, today it is critically important for advancing our ideas and actions in response to the challenges posed by sustainability.

Design endeavours directed towards these inner facets of human knowing would not be concerned with the kinds of outer, worldly utility with which we normally associate the discipline. Moreover, because the inner path correlates strongly with ethics, social justice and environmental awareness, this direction for design can be a force for the good – not because the products of design would offer utilitarian benefits but because their presence as objects would be tangible reminders of ideas and understandings associated with deeper purpose, virtue and compassion.

80
From theory to practice

Based on the foregoing, an appropriate direction for design today would be to develop ideas and forms for inclusive, trans-religious artefacts that are suited to our spiritually pluralistic times. Designers have the opportunity to creatively explore what such a direction might mean for the nature of material culture. The designer's task would be to probe areas that could help redress the imbalances associated with materialism and consumerism. Consequently, any emerging design propositions would pertain to and acknowledge inner values rather than outer utility and, through such recognition, facilitate the inclusion of these deeper concerns in our workaday endeavours, public discourses and individual sensibilities. Naturally, such design expressions would have to reach beyond familiar, primarily religious, associations, which are often regarded as inappropriate today in anything but the private sphere.

The role of symbol: The symbolic modes of expression that are employed, along with practice, to address these inner ways of knowing have typically included such means as allegory, metaphor, poetry and parable. In the twelfth-century *Conference of the Birds* from the Sufi tradition, the spiritual path of the individual is told via an allegory of birds going on a journey to seek their king. Bunyan's *Pilgrim's Progress* from the Christian tradition and Bashō's *Narrow Road to the Interior* from the Japanese Buddhist tradition, both written in the seventeenth century, are also allegories that take the form of a physical journey.

These symbolic modes allude to that which cannot be expressed in the precise language of logical statement. Instead, the symbol is anagogical, i.e. it 'leads up' to metaphysical meaning.[68] Hence, the purpose of a designed artefact would be to provide a physical expression that helps direct one's thoughts away from outer, worldly preoccupations towards inner or higher notions of meaning and understanding. We see these forms of symbolism in traditional religious contexts. The physical and spiritual are represented respectively in the upward- and downward-pointing triangles that intersect in the hexagram or Jewish Star of David and, as we saw in Chapter 3, the same idea is conveyed in the Christian cross. These complementary, inseparable opposites are also represented in the interflowing forms of the Yin and Yang of Eastern tradition. Such symbols denote a comprehensive understanding of human apprehension, a union of temporal and timeless, physical and spiritual, ego and non-ego. Achieving this unity is the ultimate aim of spiritual development and of all religions.[69]

The basis for a spiritually useful object: The notion of spiritually useful design can be seen as an important ingredient in reconceiving the discipline to better align it with understandings of sustainability. It provides a creative path for bringing to the fore ways of knowing associated with inner values, ethics, virtue and compassion, which many now recognize as critical to any comprehensive interpretation of sustainability. Spiritually useful design can generate artefacts that draw upon tradition, that are more stable and whose appeal is not dependent on originality, newness or technological progress. As such, they represent a radical departure from much of today's consumer-driven product design – a departure that is urgently needed if current, highly damaging and potentially ruinous priorities are to be challenged and redirected. They are also consistent with wisdom teachings and unchanging notions of meaning, unity and deeper human purpose.

The following considerations are relevant to the development of the spiritually useful object:

- A designed artefact that aims to be spiritually useful will not be consequential or profound as a physical thing. It can only ever be an indicator or pointer – a symbol of significance, but not significant in itself.
- Being indicative rather than substantive, the physical artefact can and arguably should be inconsequential and somewhat cursory in its physical manifestation – requiring just enough to convey its meaning. Greater attention to detail or preciousness could be seen as misplaced because it would inappropriately focus effort and attention on physical, worldly concerns. However, given the history of lavishness that is often accorded such artefacts, opinions clearly differ on matters of appropriateness in this domain.
- Any claim to newness or originality will be in interpreting and presenting these longstanding ideas in forms that are relevant to our own time.

81

There is nothing new to be added in terms of that to which the artefact points.

- For wider recognition of inner values in our workaday endeavours, designs that are expressive of inclusiveness and pluralism would seem appropriate in the globalized culture in which we participate, i.e. expressions that embrace diversity, respect difference and foster conciliation and harmony.

With these aspirations in mind, the creative design process can be employed to explore how such encompassing ideas might be transmuted into tangible form. This would allow the discipline of design to develop routes and concepts for material artefacts that address notions of the profound and the spiritual in ways that are pertinent to today's sensibilities, as a step towards discovering new directions for design.

An appropriate symbolic form: Religious symbols such as those mentioned above are specific to, and identified with, one particular tradition. However, returning for a moment to William Holman Hunt's painting, a recurrent motif that is present in very many traditions is that of the door, gateway or threshold – the opening to the path of inner development and realization. Symbolically, it represents the connection between external reality and inner self, between physical and spiritual, lower and higher. Hence it represents the possibility of at-one-ment[70] or unity.[71] It is commonly found among the spiritual traditions of Europe, North America, the Middle East, Asia and Australia.[72]

The Hebrew Bible contains many references to gates, gateways and thresholds that give access to the spiritual or higher realm.[73] The New Testament refers variously to the strait gate or narrow door, making it clear that entering this path requires individual effort; one must strive to pass through.[74] In Islam the *mihrab*, or niche, located on the *qibla* wall of a mosque to indicate the direction of prayer, often takes the form of an entranceway and for this reason it is said to symbolize a door through which grace descends to Earth.[75] The Sufi tradition teaches that 'When the door has been opened throw away the key', making the point that the outward symbol is not a necessity but merely a support.[76] The Hindu *Upanishads* refer to the door of Truth (i.e. the true nature of reality) and the door to the World of Brahman,[77] and, similarly, Buddhism refers to the Path of Perfection.[78] In Shintoism, the *torii* or gate marks the entrance to a sacred place, representing the transition between the physical, temporal and finite and the spiritual, eternal and infinite.[79] And there are a wide variety of references to doorways in the world's shamanic traditions where the spiritual path is conveyed as an entrance that is difficult to negotiate. Commonly, the narrow gate or door is depicted as opening only momentarily and then only for those who are worthy.[80] Crossing the threshold traditionally requires purgation and purity of mind – as symbolized by the removal of shoes before entering a mosque.[81]

Hence, we see that the narrow door or gate has long been used as a metaphor for the connection between the physical/external and spiritual/internal sides of our humanness. In turn, these two facets of human apprehension are associated with different modes of thinking. Analytic, rational, linear and numeric modes, which have been associated with the left brain,[82] tend to characterize the scientific method and physical investigation of the natural world, whereas synthetic, intuitive, holistic and spatial modes, associated with the right brain, are closely related to spiritual understandings.[83] The narrow physical connection between the brain's hemispheres, the *corpus callosum*, has itself been referred to as a neural gatekeeper.[84] Edwards explicitly relates these left–right modes to the Yin–Yang of Taoism; left-mode equating broadly to Yang, which is rational, active and convergent, and right-mode to Yin, which is emotional, passive and divergent.[85] In Taoism, these two are said to spring from the same source, and again the analogy of a gate is evoked as the link between them, and thus between the physical and the spiritual.[86] It is, therefore, perfectly fitting that, according to legend, the writing of the *Tao Te Ching* was prompted by a request from a gatekeeper as its putative author, Lao Tsu, was about to leave the realm of worldly society.[87]

The universal presence of the door, gate or threshold as a symbol of the link between outer, worldly concerns and inner values, priorities and understandings makes it an appropriate motif for use in a trans-religious and supra-religious artefact whose purpose is to acknowledge and bring to the fore those concerns that have been largely excluded from public discourse in the modern/early postmodern era.

A spiritually useful, post-materialist, trans-religious object

An important part of this present study is the translation of the above ideas into physical form. The creation of an object provides a basis for synthesis and creative expression. In the process, it serves to demonstrate how conceptions of material culture, innovation and design for sustainability can be significantly different when the ethos by which we design is informed by broader apprehensions of human meaning. In addition, while intention is conveyed through the object, as with other kinds of artefacts its 'use' can benefit from supplementary information, which helps ensure that the intention is understood. This can take the form of instruction booklets or manuals; here this discussion serves a similar role.

Reflections on the making process: As would be expected, the approach taken in creating the object prioritizes considerations that are quite different from those found in industrial-scale, mass-production processes, i.e. those processes that have been so strongly linked to unsustainability.[88] Here, all the materials were acquired locally, and most of them had been discarded. The process of object-making was slow and considered. Time and care took priority over any concern for economic efficiency. The artefact was not precisely defined prior to making, but rather a way forward was found through the creative practice; a process that enables the maker to respond to the nature of the materials, their particular character and idiosyncrasies, and to reflect on the emerging form, to make adjustments, and to respond to chance occurrences in finishes and detail. The emphasis here was on making it 'right' in terms of intentions and aesthetics, rather than making it quickly or efficiently. A further consideration was for the artefact to have a certain robustness to it, so that it could be handled and accumulate the marks and grime of use – as all transient things do – but without fear of its newness quickly fading, thereby creating a sense of dissatisfaction. These factors would allow the artefact to age gracefully or, from time to time, to be easily freshened up through cleaning or re-finishing. In this way, the thinking and manner steering the process of making become aligned with principles of design for sustainability and related ideas such as Slow Design.[89] Moreover, re-using and re-dignifying rejected, seemingly value-less materials by incorporating them into new objects not only prevents those materials from becoming an eyesore on the landscape or the shoreline but infers an approach that challenges the idea and acceptability of waste.

The spiritually useful object: The object entitled *Oriel Triptych* shown in Figure 6.1 is rudimentary in its construction, being created from plywood jetsam, a piece of off-cut leather, glass and flour-based paste. Its overall form is akin to the wooden panel paintings, icons, altar triptychs, and small domestic shrines found in many spiritual traditions around the world.

84   The use of discarded, aged materials and an irregular patina enable the outer surfaces to absorb wear and tear without detracting from the overall appearance. Hinged side panels allow it to stand independently when open and, when closed, all the inner surfaces are protected. The interior finish was created by pouring a solution of flour and water into the recessed panels, carved out to a depth of c.4 mm. On drying, the mixture forms a hard, irregularly fissured texture unique to that particular piece. A coating of water-based whitener creates a sense of pristine purity and inviolability that contrasts markedly with the worn outer surfaces. Moreover, because the inner surfaces will inevitably become marred with the passage of time, pure white can be easily matched when periodic renewal is required. The hinges are created from cotton thread, as shown in Figure 6.2; a simple configuration that can be readily repaired or renewed. The motif that provides the central focus is a characteristic arched form – a minimal allusion to door, gate or threshold (Figure 6.3). When placed at a window, light passes through from behind via golden-coloured translucent glass; a modest reference to the Golden Disc said to cover the door of Truth in Hinduism.[90] The glass is kept in place with a piece of off-cut leather that has been fashioned into a frame and attached to the back of the panel with re-used screws (Figure 6.4).

Thus, the only strong colour in the piece occurs at its bright centre, which helps focus the viewer's gaze on the most significant part – the 'narrow door'. This crudely fashioned, asymmetric aperture, the shape of which was developed through gestural expression (Figure 6.5) is resonant with what has been called the art of artlessness whereby the image emerges without sensibility or style, where

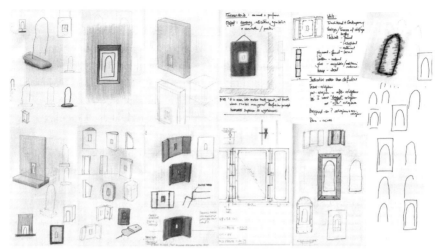

Figure 6.5
Development sketches
including gestural marks exploring potential aperture shapes

directness of emotion is expressed without ornament, and the image is 'as much felt as perceived'.[91]

As mentioned earlier, the symbol's purpose is anagogical and so what is required is just enough to provide a presence and reminder of that door which we can all individually strive to pass through, whether of a particular faith or of none. **85** Its intentionally rudimentary nature allows it to reference a variety of arched forms found in the world's great spiritual traditions without being distinctly attributable to any. These include, for example:

- the Gothic arches and prayer niches of Christian architecture, based on sacred geometry and the *vesica piscis*[92] – similar arches are found in Buddhism;
- the rounded Roman arch often used in Jewish sacred architecture as well as in Buddhist and Hindu temples;
- the Moorish arch and the *mihrab* in the Islamic mosque.

Rather than creating a crisp geometric form for the door, the intentional ambiguities of this looser design allow the viewer to bring their own, subjective perspective to it and to layer onto it that which is relevant to their own worldview and beliefs. This is in keeping with the conciliatory, inclusive teachings of figures such as Gandhi[93] and the Dalai Lama.

Through interpretation of the physical appearance of an object we are able to use it, if it has practical purpose, or we can contemplate it as a thing. In this case, the object is intended to serve as a visual signifier and focus for giving time and thought to spiritual matters, through reflection and contemplation. This anagogical intention differentiates it from a work of art even though, today, objects from the past created with similar purpose are often placed in galleries and presented as art.[94] However, it is a mistake to treat such objects as artworks because this deeper metaphysical purpose can become lost.[95] Drawing on the work of Hegel, Scruton points out that the manner in which we approach this kind of object involves two moments – communion and gift.[96] In its intention this object addresses communion by acting as a reminder of the need for focused attention on spiritual concerns and inner development – those most profound aspects of a meaningful life. Moreover, in its material presence – the nature of its localized, hand-rendered making and its re-used and renewable materials – it can be regarded as a manifestation of gift. Through both these aspects there is a recognition of the subjecthood of 'the other'; other persons and, by extension, the natural environment.

Hence, this is an object that invites the viewer to pause and reflect, whatever their beliefs and however their beliefs differ from those of others. At the same time, it recognizes the essential commonalities of the spiritual path. It is one attempt to offer common ground within a globalized, diverse world, but one that values the important and necessary differences emerging from the particularities of culture and place.

Conclusions

The gross social inequities between and within nations and the vast environmental destruction occurring in the world today have to be tackled in new ways that reach beyond the utilitarian, eco-modernist approaches that still dominate discussions around sustainability. Design can contribute to this debate by challenging industry conventions and contextualizing material culture within a broader and deeper frame of consideration. This involves being far more sensitive to the nature of human work that the making of our material culture represents, as well as to the kinds of materials used, where and how those materials are acquired, and the processes employed to transform those materials into objects. It also includes the nature of the objects themselves – their purpose, the manner of their use, the implications of their use in terms of materials and energy, their longevity, their legacy and the consequences of their disposal. All these things can violate people and planet through objectification and exploitation or they can be enriching and meaning-making. As the Japanese poet Bashō demonstrated in his linked prose and poetry, the spiritual and the timeless can be found, or at least striven towards, through our encounters in the physical, transient world.[97]

This discussion and the accompanying object represent an attempt to probe a different path for design – one that not only localizes and contextualizes the making of the physical thing, but which also addresses aspects of material culture rarely discussed in design and design education. However, it is these very aspects that are critically related to ethics, virtue and compassion and which many today are regarding as vital ingredients of sustainability. As such, they must become significant elements of design discourse and of wider public debate.

7

A Form of Silence design for doing no-thing

Action is consolatory.
It is the enemy of thought
and the friend of flattering illusions.

Joseph Conrad

In the woods a mile or two south of the town of Woodstock, New York is a crudely built, barn-like structure. This is the Maverick Concert Hall, which has been a venue for summer recitals since 1916. Over the years many distinguished musicians have played here, but it is especially well known for hosting the 1952 premiere performance of John Cage's controversial composition 4'33", also called the 'silent' piece because no notes are actually played. Cage wrote of this work, 'Silence is not acoustic. It is a change of mind, a turning around.'[1] Today, we are certainly in need of a change of mind, a turning around, and design's part in this will be to create conceptions of material culture that express new attitudes and evince sensibilities quite different from those associated with consumption and consumer society.

In earlier chapters I have explored how the nature and aesthetics of material goods might be more closely aligned with an understanding of sustainability that recognizes the critical role of inner values and spirituality. Here, these explorations are taken a stage further by developing a foundation for a contemplative object that is non-utilitarian, non-symbolic, supra-religious and, importantly, non-made.[2]

The discussion begins with an overview of some of the main obstacles to change; various extrinsic and intrinsic avenues for effecting change are then considered. The former includes technical innovation, consumption reduction and localization, while the latter involves a changed outlook or a change of mind, which has major implications for design's purpose. This leads to an exemplar object that expresses something further about this new outlook.

Obstacles to change

Systemic conventions that characterize our current, evidently unsustainable ways of living include: high levels of consumption; activities that hinder reflection; and forms of knowledge that intensify ideas of technological progress and encourage consumption. These are, of course, intricately linked. Lansley has pointed out that, to a large degree, our dependence on consumption, with apparently no upper limits, stems from the role of consumer products as indicators of status, referred to as 'positional goods'.[3] This occurs within an economic system that works against social cohesion[4, 5] and promotes competitive individualism and acquisitiveness; a condition that was boosted during the Thatcher–Reagan years of the 1980s when individualism took precedence, and any aspirations towards an equitable society were abandoned along with any moral or cultural restraints to an individual's accumulation of wealth.[6, 7] Positional goods, by their very nature, must be relatively expensive so that their owners can differentiate themselves from the average. Such goods nurture dissatisfaction and envy and are inherently socially divisive. In addition, incomes need to rise in order to purchase them and work hours tend to increase accordingly, with a corresponding reduction in leisure time. This accounts, in large part, for many of the inequities in the Western-style capitalist system where economic growth is the primary policy objective and superfluous consumption is vigorously encouraged, reaching levels well above those required to fulfil basic needs and reasonable levels of comfort.[8] Hence, the systemic conventions of growth-based consumer capitalism not only foster discontent and socioeconomic inequities, which have negative effects on individual wellbeing and community cohesion,[9] but also rely on over-production, which is extraordinarily damaging to the natural environment. Ironically, and despite much rhetoric to the contrary, market globalization and free trade, advocated by governments and corporations alike, do little to increase the wealth of poorer countries. Indeed, richer countries such as the United States and the United Kingdom became wealthy through subsidies, market protection and the very same strategies that today's free trade policies disallow.[10]

The continual production and promotion of consumer products and positional goods reached new levels of intensity with digital technologies. The unprecedented opportunities for distraction offered by these products has fostered even greater levels of atomization by facilitating habitual absorption, information inundation and unreflective amusement while giving the impression of busyness.[11, 12, 13] They also serve as an all-in-one advertising hoarding, shop window and payment counter at one's fingertips, which tends to encourage spontaneous, impulsive consumption – the nature of the medium, in its immediacy, convenience and targeted marketing, effectively deterring deliberation.

These are the characteristics of consumer capitalism and a society that privileges certain forms of knowledge over others. Contemporary academic research, for example, favours rational argument and the scientific method. The former calls on the intellectual mind, and builds a case using logical analysis, evidence and reasoned argument. The latter focuses on the systematic investigation of phenomena, empirical proof and repeatability of results. However, as we have seen in earlier chapters, there are other, vitally important facets of human knowing that have tended to be less well regarded within academia and within society in general. These are the forms of knowledge acquired through disciplined practice and personal experience. They include the kinds of knowledge that, in art and design, are gained via the creative process; both of these are practice-based disciplines, and it is notable that neither was to be found in UK universities until relatively recently. These practice-based forms of knowledge, so fundamental to creative disciplines like design, and crucial, also, to a person's inner or spiritual development, cannot be acquired through observation or through literary, scientific or intellectual inquiry. Such rationalized, abstracted modes of analysis and description can only point to, but can never entirely explain or embrace the fullness of, reality as it is experienced. Consequently, if we are to develop ways of living that are more meaningful and far less destructive, greater attention will have to be given to these other, practice-based, spiritually enriching ways of knowing.[14, 15, 16]

Significantly, experiential ways of knowing involve the subjecthood of the individual. As such, they transcend the notion of an objective, disinterested view based purely on intellectual understandings. Tacit, practice-based and experiential knowledge help to contextualize our more focused intellectual activities and enable us to acknowledge the wider implications of our endeavours. According to various spiritual traditions, we gain a more holistic outlook when these experiential ways of knowing are integrated with rational argument and intellectual knowledge. With this more inclusive outlook, rule-based moralities and limiting classifications imposed from without become superseded by ethical values and notions of virtue that emerge naturally from within.[17, 18] Clearly, these core ethical concerns, which guide our activities in the world, are linked to the social and environmental aspects of contemporary sustainability. Hence, the continuing lack of recognition of tacit modes of knowing and their relationship to inner values, especially within academia,[19] represent a considerable obstacle to more fundamental change.

Avenues for change

From the foregoing we see that the many extrinsic avenues for change that have been proposed over the years – such as recycling programmes, eco-technologies and CO_2e reduction agreements – are unlikely to be effective unless accompanied

89

by substantive changes in attitudes, values and priorities. More profound, intrinsic avenues for change, rooted in practices that cultivate inner values and new priorities, have the potential to take us significantly further. This section examines some of the more prominent extrinsic avenues before exploring in more detail the less discussed intrinsic avenues for change.

Extrinsic avenues for change

One of the main directions being promoted by governments and corporations is technological innovation and improved efficiencies. In contrast, others advocate consumption reduction, especially in the affluent countries, and see localization as an important feature of sustainable ways of living.

Technological innovation and efficiency: Many scientists and economists argue that solutions offered by science and technology will be crucial in attaining ways of living that correlate with the principles of sustainability.[20, 21] Some also argue for those technologies that provide access to the Internet to be more widely adopted in today's poorer countries because they offer greater benefits when more people are using them.[22] This, however, would seem to be an over-optimistic, rather partial view of advanced technologies and their implications. Indeed, it is the affluent countries' dependence on short-lived, energy-hungry technological products that is so closely associated with environmentally destructive and climate-changing emissions. Again, some argue that these shortcomings can be addressed through dramatic increases in efficiency and through urbanization,[23] and many schemes, regulations and legislations have been developed to improve the environmental performance of products and to address the implications of product disposal.[24, 25, 26] But without a more fundamental change in values and priorities, these directions are likely to only exacerbate social and environmental problems. Within an economic system of consumer capitalism, efficiency maximization in resource and energy use is a way of boosting financial return, but it is a system that depends on inefficiency maximization in the meeting of people's needs; in other words, it drives overproduction and wastage.[27] This raises several interrelated points:

- **Externalities:** True costs to people and environment are not accounted for.[28]
- **Obsolescence and waste:** While the fast pace of technological innovation is a key driver of the competitive edge, it also spurs obsolescence, waste and environmental degradation.[29]
- **Encouragement of consumption:** Within this system of innovation products have to be widely adopted to be profitable and so advertising becomes a major force. Hence, there is an internal contradiction in arguments that advocate both technological innovation and consumption reduction.
- **Product pricing too low:** If externalities were taken into account, products would be more expensive.

- **Implications of more expensive products:** More expensive products would not be readily discarded; they would have to be durable and upgradable. If products are significantly more expensive this would undoubtedly hinder their wider adoption, especially in poorer countries.
- **From products to services:** Companies that design products to be lasting would gain a larger portion of their income from repair and upgrade services.
- **A slower pace of innovation:** The pace of technological change and new product development would inevitably be slowed, along with a decrease in materials throughput, shipping and energy use.[30] This is in accord with calls for lower consumption levels and economic analyses that give greater regard to ethical and social responsibilities.[31] Such a direction is supported by research indicating that greater equality in society improves quality of life for everyone, and that when basic needs and reasonable comforts have been achieved, further affluence and the increased ability to consume have little bearing on wellbeing or happiness.[32]

Consumption reduction: To develop more sustainable ways of living that are practically, socially and personally meaningful, while also being economically responsible, there is a strong case for reducing our preoccupation with consumption. As we have seen, consumer society tends to increase atomization and social disparity; through its pervasive use of advertising it stimulates desires and acquisitiveness by encouraging competitive relations and inflaming envious feelings towards others, which in turn work against a spirit of fellowship and conviviality. Moreover, it reduces the overall quality of 'the commons' through decreased investment in social goods and thus shrinks public and social capacities.[33] According to Skidelsky and Skidelsky, it is associated with anxiety and depression, and damages personality. They argue that the social benefits of reducing consumption, and the provision of basic 'goods' of health, security, respect, personality, harmony with Nature, friendship and leisure are critically related to spirituality and the inspiration and social teachings that religion provides.[34] However, it has long been recognized that the ascendency of individualism within the culture and consumption-based economy of the West has severely undermined the vigour and validity of its own spiritual and contemplative heritage.[35] Consumption is seen as problematic, also, from an Islamic ethical perspective and some Islamic scholars are looking to other kinds of global cosmopolitan futures than the profit-oriented, middle-class consumption patterns promoted by the Euro-American economic system.[36]

Thus, there would seem to be a clear case for reducing consumption in order to positively enhance quality of life, social relationships and personal wellbeing while, simultaneously, reducing the burden on the natural environment. This would mean developing measures to decrease consumption, limit advertising and reduce new product development. As is to be expected, such a direction would mean a

91

radical reversal of many of the societal and economic norms that have become sacrosanct in contemporary, consumption-based societies.

Localization: Key aspects for achieving more sustainable lifestyles include localization of trade and economic scales, with fewer imported goods and greater community control, and a move towards localism, understood as a devolution of political decision-making and governance, and an attendant decline in centralization.[37, 38] Such directions serve to enhance a sense of community, self-determination and self-reliance; encourage use of local materials, products and enterprises; and reduce transportation needs, energy requirements, waste and pollution. It implies a stepping away from the dogmas of free-trade and globalization, and a reversal in regulations that favour large producers and obstruct local enterprises. As Saul has put it, 'Production doesn't need to be global to be successful. There is no noble global destiny in moving inanimate objects vast distances.'[39] Localization also serves to internalize the true costs of production, because environmental and social consequences are more directly felt and dealt with, not least through social pressures and community initiatives.[40] Indeed, it is these local-scale socio-ethical and eco-ethical considerations that link extrinsic and intrinsic avenues for change.

Intrinsic avenues for change: a changed outlook

92 The major shift in direction that will be required if we are to develop more sustainable ways of living will inevitably challenge our current, unsustainable conventions and bring to the fore areas of human knowledge that have received relatively little attention in recent times. This is perhaps especially important in those regions that have given precedence to a vision of economic growth based on technological progress and consumption. To achieve this shift it will be necessary to cultivate a different outlook – one that reflects altered priorities and a broader set of values.

Knowledge gained from scientific investigation and reasoned argument when enriched by forms of knowing that are experiential, subjective and tacit allow for a more comprehensive understanding of ourselves and our world. When *all* these forms of knowledge are taken into account, they offer a broader perspective of reality – as illustrated in the reconfigured arrangement of the *quadruple bottom line* shown in Figures 7.1–7.2.

Complementing knowledge of physical phenomena and causes, explanatory knowledge and knowledge attained through rational argument, this more holistic perspective includes knowledge associated with:

- the aesthetic sense, which includes the experience of the subject and pertains to the particularities of context;
- inner values that concern personal ethics, conscience, compassion and empathy, which are not necessarily the same as the moral norms of a particular community or society;
- the deeper, meaning-seeking, spiritual aspects of being human.

Figure 7.1 *The quadruple bottom line of sustainability: expanding areas of concern*

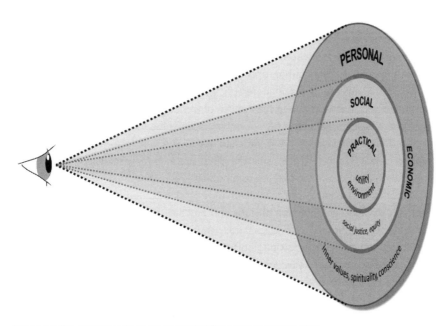

Figure 7.2 *The quadruple bottom line of sustainability: expanding perspectives*

These factors are critically related to issues of social justice and environmental care, and to creating more positive and more meaningful ways forward than those offered by ever more rabid consumerism.[41]

In taking greater account of these other forms of knowledge, especially in academia, Watts usefully explains that to acquire understanding involving non-intellectual, intuitive and tacit forms of knowledge, one has to engage in the field's disciplined practices. To be able to take into consideration and describe such knowledge, however, one must avoid becoming involved in its institutional obligations; otherwise there is a danger of becoming a partisan advocate.[42] It is imperative that a critical distance be maintained between the practitioner and the domain's institutional or organizational commitments and motives. With this in mind, greater recognition and development of these forms of subjective and tacit knowledge attained through practice and direct experience can contribute to the emergence of an altered outlook; one that is consistent with ways of living that adhere to principles of sustainability while also being capable of providing a deeper sense of meaning than that proffered by consumerism. Such an outlook would represent more than an intellectual grasp of a different worldview (Weltanschauung) as it would go further than a philosophical understanding of the physical world and one's place in it. The thirteenth-century Sufi mystic Mowlānā Jalāloddin said, 'The explaining mind sleeps like an ass in mud' and that some understandings are beyond concepts and beyond imagining.[43] Our deepest forms of knowing transcend concepts, rational formulae, theories and explanations. Through contemplative practices and a reorientation of one's priorities, we learn to place less emphasis on our rationalistic quest for explanations, and develop a disposition of humility, receptivity and attention to reality.[44] In a similar vein, Heidegger's view was that human existence can transcend both temporality and particular entities in the world, not towards some other-worldly entity, but by allowing a critical distance that, according to Inwood, gives 'free space in which to live'.[45] This represents a shift in perspective, from being that is essentially in the world to being that lies beyond the control of worldly particularities. This new perspective yields a kind of knowing that transcends the forms of knowledge acquired through everyday living, practical reasoning, intellectual inquiry and subject–object duality.[46] These understandings are intimately related to the nature and character of our responses to sustainability.

In both Eastern and Western contemplative traditions, true clarity of awareness is attained through a combination of study and practice. Study is required because concepts about inner values and spirituality can be grasped via intellectual knowledge; however, this knowledge alone is insufficient. One also has to engage in practice – such as self-reflection, meditation and contemplation – in order to transcend the ego and human will; the orientation of contemplative practice being that of emptiness, uselessness and purity.[47, 48] Teachings within Islamic contemplative traditions echo such thoughts.[49] Hence, clarity of awareness lies beyond intentional acts, strategies, measurements and evidence-based research, and it transcends dualistic notions of reality, so that the self is no longer regarded as separate from, but as inherent to or immanent in, the whole of reality.[50, 51] It is through practice that this clarity of awareness can be experienced and a changed outlook cultivated, evoking a world of transitions, processes and continuous flows.[52]

Implications of a changed outlook for design

This changed outlook has important implications for our actions in the world, as well as for our ability to see the broader repercussions of those actions. It enables us to more fully realize that the present state of a thing fully includes its past and future states, so that our notion of 'a product' becomes less certain. This realization deepens our understandings of design and its potential contribution in creating goods that not only offer material benefits as things but also, through their production and use, embrace approaches that are socially enriching and environmentally responsible. Furthermore, not only can it affect how we create material goods, but material goods themselves – our human-made world – can enhance and support the development of this changed outlook. It becomes clear that there is a symbiotic relationship between inner development and outer actions. Here, a positive relationship would be one in which external goods are created in ways that are supportive of inner development and spiritual wellbeing and are socially and environmentally sustainable in their production, use and after use. By contrast, a negative relationship would be one in which our material goods are created in ways that promote distractedness and divisiveness and are produced in ways that are socially and environmentally exploitative. Let us now consider in more detail some of the main implications of this changed outlook for design.

For design and design research, Watts' point, referred to above, is significant. That is, in order to acquire understanding involving intuitive and tacit knowledge one has to engage in a field's disciplined practices but avoid becoming involved in its institutional obligations. In the context of design, this means keeping a critical distance between the designer and the norms and priorities of commercial design practice and corporate and/or government agendas. All these tend to steer design in directions that prioritize continual economic growth and encourage consumption, both of which are proving incredibly harmful and increasingly dysfunctional. Ironically, given the lack of legitimacy academia has traditionally ascribed to practice-based endeavours, the most suitable place for maintaining this critical distance is academia. That said, there is constant pressure from governments to make academic research 'relevant', which usually means more business-focused, with less support for curiosity-based research and scholarship.[53] Nevertheless, study, learning and intellectual knowledge combined with academic design practice oriented to scholarly rather than commercial ends form a mode of engaged inquiry that is vital to the practice-based discipline of design. It is necessary for the advancement of the discipline and, ultimately, for commercial and political interests because it forms an important critical foundation – one that is capable of holding a mirror up to the discipline, of probing and challenging its conventions, exploring new, potentially significant directions and developing fresh ways of looking at and thinking about design and its changing role. This means that design must find suitable ways within academic research for appropriately recognizing the kinds of subjective decision-making, aesthetic judgements and personal 'feel' that are as crucial to design practice as rational analysis, empirical evidence and intellectual argument. If we confine design endeavours within the academy to modes of conventional academic scrutiny, which may be wholly unsuitable, we will constrain design researchers and scholars to act in ways that are contrary to their own discipline because such ways would lack adequate representation of design's creative core; a circumstance that Csikszentmihalyi refers to as alienation.[54] Unless we make efforts to understand, develop and value the discipline on its own terms, there is always the danger that its essential vitality will be nipped in the bud well before it has a chance to flower.

The discipline of design has traditionally created products as fixed entities for short timeframes, paying little attention to long-term implications. If our design endeavours are informed by deeper, more insightful notions of reality, which lie beyond definitive explanations,[55] they can lead to outcomes that are not conceived as fixed, autonomous units but, instead, as more mutable contributions that recognize a reality of continuous flux. Hence, there is an inseparable interdependence between: (1) a change in outlook based on development of inner values through spiritual practice, and (2) a change in the human-made environment through new priorities in design practice. Both are necessary if we are to make substantive contributions to *designing sustainability*.

Design and radical change: Combining inner values, spiritual development and design via study and practice leads to what we can term radical change, understood as change informed by a more comprehensive, more mindful attitude. It suggests a very different form of design from that which has characterized the discipline for many years — one that pays far greater attention to the continuous, interrelated effects of human actions and regards the outcomes of design as elements within a larger context of transition and flow. A variety of intimately related and entwined directions emerge from this notion of design and radical change.

Some suggest that the only way of achieving a more civil and more ethical way forward is to counter the capitalist ideology by withdrawing from the political sphere and developing a new monasticism.[56] Indeed there is a long history of such intentional communities and movements, from religious groups like the Shakers and the Hutterites, to environmental communes, and the voluntary simplicity and Slow movements. The impact of such counteractions, however, will tend to remain marginal unless the ideas they embrace find wider public and political support.

Less explicitly ideological, localization is regarded by many as essential to sustainability. Advocates see important connections between local actions, civility, and care for the environment and a spiritual or religious consciousness that focuses on that which is immediately present — the proximate, the here and the now; connections that are not recognized in purely scientific accounts.[57] Such connections are also a vital aspect of Zen Buddhism.[58]

Significant also is the Taoist concept of *wu-wei*, which means non-doing, no-action, non-busyness, non-duality, non-intention and not-making. It refers to an approach to life that does not try to grasp the world in terms of intellectual abstractions and fit it into human-made classifications and definitions. Instead of *enforcing one's will* and *constructing*, it is better described as *yielding* and *growing*, where confrontation and argument are avoided. Ways of doing are sought that are not impositional but are in harmony with the flow of Nature.[59, 60] Very similar ideas are present within the Christian tradition,[61] where the attitude arising from deeper ways of knowing, which lie beyond rational knowledge and categorization, is manifested as *agape*, charity or (non-sexual) love of one's fellow human beings and the whole of creation. This is a form of virtuous behaviour that originates from within a person; it is quite different from forms of behaviour imposed by externally constructed social norms, laws and moral codes.

For Heidegger, whose philosophy resonates strongly with Eastern thought and the teachings of Zen,[62] this changed outlook could be attained through the practice of art and poetry; that is through the process of 'bringing forth'.[63] Indeed, we see the reification of Heidegger's contentions in a wide spectrum of examples, which might include:

- the paintings and poetry of Blake, as well as the poetry of Wordsworth and other British Romantics;
- the monochrome ink paintings and Haiku poetry of Japanese Zen;
- the explorations of John Cage in the field of music in which he developed new kinds of composition that embraced chance, spontaneity and random events;
- the abstract *Suprematist* works of Malevich, who adopted a process of 'bringing forth' a black square though methodical pencil shading. Such works speak to the unconscious mind, beyond the rationalist view that seeks explanation. For Malevich they had spiritual significance[64] and have been interpreted as conveying ultimate emancipation or clarity of awareness;[65]
- the many repetitive practices found within spiritual traditions, which can be regarded as processes of 'bringing forth' a changed perspective on reality. These include the whirling dance found in the Sufi tradition, chant found in Tibetan Buddhism, chant and psalmody found in Christian monasticism and, perhaps especially, practices of contemplation and silence.

97

Significantly, too, all the contemplative traditions advocate behaviours that include, among other things, self-control of the passions and voluntary abstinence from worldly distractions,[66] such diversions being regarded as hindrances to clarity of vision. Skidelsky and Skidelsky link the social teachings emerging from spiritual traditions to ideas of sufficiency, distributivism and the duties rather than the rewards of ownership, and to the provision of public goods.[67] It is notable that contemporary consumer capitalism and the media it has spawned vigorously encourage behaviours that contravene such directions. People's susceptibilities are continuously exploited and feverish attention is given to discrete products and events, but their broader implications – within a more comprehensive view that recognizes reality as a continuously unfolding series of interrelated transitions and flows – are assiduously avoided.

An integrated view: We have seen that the inner path that leads to clarity of awareness does not result in an outlook that pits spirituality against physicality or romantic against industrial, but yields an integrated, non-dualistic view that recognizes inter-dependent relationships. Eastern thought, which perhaps most clearly expresses this integrated perspective of flow and continually unfolding processes, has, Williams contends in his discussion of what he calls *technê-zen*, become the ethos of late capitalism and the ideological framework for informatics networks.[68] While there may be parallels here in the flow enabled by networked technologies, such a view takes insufficient account of the technological optimism that is fundamental to the Euro-American economic system, including its wholly inadequate, technology-centred approaches to sustainability.[69] The rationalistic technocracy that Williams discusses cannot be separated from the commercial considerations and consumerism that drives it, which enables its continuously evolving presence. This has led to a burgeoning of outer, worldly distraction and preoccupation. It is this preoccupation with technology, powerful aspects of which tend to maintain the subject–object perspective, that Heidegger saw as an obstacle to attaining a new awareness of existence.[70] An example here would be the regular and influential launches of iconic but transient products by desirable brands, which encourage a preoccupation with object-ness, acquisition and status. In addition, so much of the output of this techno-economic system, in the form of transient, screen-based consumer products, offers only virtual, vicarious and often quite passive and manipulative encounters in place of the direct experiences of reality that are so critical to spiritual traditions such as Zen. The sheer variety and pace of information inundation, entertainment and marketing enabled by these contemporary technologies tend to impede more questioning, reflective modes. And as already mentioned, the widespread and affordable consumption of such products, their use and regular replacement is dependent on exploitation and environmental devastation on an unprecedented scale. Taken together, these things are anything but commensurable with 'the way of Nature' and 'the way of Zen' but are, it seems, more indicative of the persistence of modernity's narrow, over-rationalistic notion of reality.

The illusion of permanence: For design, this changed outlook can profoundly affect how we conceive of and create our material world. It implies a way of seeing the outputs of design as conditional phenomena arising from a prior state and flowing into a subsequent state. When the permanence of products is recognized as illusory, to continue to produce and market them *as if they were* permanent would be neither credible nor creditable. To illustrate this, let us consider a disposable plastic cup. In its present state, the cup fully includes its origins via land clearing, oil-well drilling, pipelines, refineries, air pollution, oil spills, thermoforming, packaging and shipping. It fully includes the fleeting convenience of its use, as well as trash cans, garbage collection trucks, exhaust fumes and its protracted existence in landfill, hedgerow or ocean. By accepting the present state of a disposable plastic cup we cannot but accept these other present states. This applies not only to overtly disposable products, such as plastic cups and plastic bags, razor blades and batteries, but also to phones, computers and appliances; these may be a little less fleeting but they have a similar array of other present states.

Material goods and the realization of a changed outlook: Visual imagery, analogy and symbolism serve important roles as mediators or pointers to ways of knowing that are essentially ineffable. But to strive towards these ways of knowing we must go beyond symbolism and beyond notions of the autonomous ego-centric self by engaging in practice. Thus, imagery, symbols and material things have their place within reality and should not be regarded as in any way inferior to the metaphysical and the spiritual. They can serve as aids to contemplative practice and in doing so they become part of the holistic, integrated reflective path.[71] It follows that, if appropriately conceived, images, tangible things and aesthetic experiences can be important factors in the realization of this changed outlook. Thus, materiality is not something to be ignored or renounced.[72] On the other hand, if they are given disproportionate significance and are inappropriately conceived, worldly desires in the form of material things can serve to endlessly engage us, diverting our thoughts and our lives away from the inner path. Such distractedness has undoubtedly become more prevalent during the periods of modernity and early postmodernity due to their emphasis on materialism. This potent but dangerously blinkered view of material benefit and economic expediency was recently illustrated by two newspaper stories published within a few days of each other. The first story reported research indicating that the area of Greenland's ice sheet showing signs of surface melt had increased from about 40 per cent to 97 per cent over a four-day period, which it described as 'the most frightening picture you will ever see'.[73] Only days later the same newspaper published an article that began 'Melting of icy surface opens up possibility of extracting rare earth metals and gemstones'.[74] A fundamental change in values, priorities and direction is called for when an indicator of serious environmental degradation is seen only in terms of the economic opportunities it offers, involving even further environmental exploitation.

99

Design advancement: The more comprehensive, inclusive view of legitimate knowledge that emerges from a changed outlook is vital to the discipline of design and to its advancement in ways that:

- acknowledge, develop and deepen design's particular contribution – a contribution that combines intellectual and intuitive thinking, objectivity and subjectivity, and the particular in the context of the whole;

- are congruent with a more holistic understanding of ourselves and with priorities that respond to increasingly acute social disparities and environmental breakdown.

Here, it is also important to recognize that attempts to adjust our behaviours from within conventional notions of legitimate knowledge and academic rigour are proving woefully inadequate.

From quantity to quality: A changed outlook yielding routes to human fulfilment that prioritize development of inner values, nurture community and cooperation, and care for the environment would also discourage consumerism. In turn, reduced levels of consumption would mean a slowing in new product development, production, marketing and distribution. This is the inevitable conclusion if we are to address both extrinsic and intrinsic avenues of change; a similar conclusion is reached from economic analyses.[75] Consequently, with fewer things and less frequent change, those products that remain would need to be of higher quality and repairable. This is commensurate with an understanding of objects as provisional rather than permanent. It is also commensurate with community and local services and with enhancing community relationships, inter-dependencies and employment opportunities. Direct, face-to-face encounters entail consideration of others, trust and integrity, and these things are allied with inner values and spiritual wellbeing. Hence, the making and caring of things can be considered in terms of how they help generate values – sociocultural, spiritual and political.[76] Increased product costs, as unit sales decline, would occur alongside a shift in priorities – from seeing product production as simply a means to wealth generation, to seeing it in broader terms. This would begin to emphasize the intrinsic value of producing high-quality goods well, by adopting approaches that are cooperative, environmentally responsible and personally meaningful, while also being sufficient in economic terms – in line with altered attitudes and principles.

Design process: A design process that corresponds with this changed outlook will be receptive but unpredictable. It will be less controlling and more open to improvisation and the kinds of non-linear sudden insight in which synthesis occurs abruptly, often in unexpected circumstances, but usually following long study and deep absorption in a particular theme. It becomes more flexible and yielding and more aligned with spiritual understandings such as *wu-wei*, described above. An outlook that pays greater heed to inner values, compassion and environmental care requires a process that is mindful of and immersed in the real world of people, place, and Nature, where one is able to be sensitive to the context of production, use and after-use. Such a design process is able to respond to context, chance encounters and serendipity by drawing on situated experiences, local skills, and tacit knowledge. Similarly, it is a process that engages directly with materials, textures and colours, is cognizant of their provenance and aesthetic qualities, and nurtures an organic emergence of ideas. In other words, a design process that is able to appreciate the tangible, physical world that our design decisions affect.

Such a process allows for extemporization and variation around a basic idea, e.g. for a chair, lamp or other product, so that each artefact is seen as a temporary coming together of materials in a unique configuration. In this way, physical things can be regarded as part of a process of growing, transition, evolution and change. Here, design becomes less about planning ahead and developing proposals made up of lines, letters and symbols, which are all abstractions, and less about defining, systematizing and categorizing. Instead it becomes a process of thinking-and-doing that seamlessly combines intellectual and intuitive knowledge, facts and feel, study and practice in ways that are intimately embedded in the real world of people and place.

This is far removed from design processes that are locked down by extrinsic determinants, fixed objectives and rigid, rationalized forms of accountability. It is also far removed from processes that limit themselves to the creation of seductive but sterile 'idealities' – made possible within computer-generated environments. These rationalized but vicarious design processes are detached from individual personality, cultural idiosyncrasy and the particularities of place, all of which can endow human-made environments and artefacts with meaning, richness and distinction. Such generalized, one-size-fits-all approaches, which have characterized globally distributed, but thereby fragmented and unsituated mass-manufacturing for decades, are part of a system that is proving insatiable in terms of materials and energy. By contrast, the more holistic outlook described here is fundamentally embedded in the specificities of context and locale.

101

StoneWork: an exemplar object

In moving from generalized theory (study) to a specific propositional artefact, a basis for engagement (practice) is required. In developing such a basis, two important factors should to be borne in mind. First, such propositions – in all their diversity – are bound together by their question-asking role.[77] This is the nature of creative exploration and disciplinary advancement. In the field of music, for example, Cage said, 'What can be analysed in my work, or criticized, are the questions that I ask.'[78] Understood as a manifest question rather than a solution, the propositional artefact is a specific but non-definitive constituent of a continually unfolding process. Second, any proposition must be fully compliant with the *quadruple bottom line of sustainability*.

Responding to both of these factors, the intention of the propositional artefact presented here is to support the transition to altered priorities and values, to draw the user's attention to the importance of this changed outlook and to its unending development. It follows, therefore, that its purpose is contemplative rather than utilitarian. In addition, and as noted previously, because the kind of knowing that this changed outlook reveals is ineffable, material goods that refer to it serve as mediators or pointers. Furthermore, an object that is intended to serve a contemplative purpose has to be not only a tangible reminder of, but also consistent with, these most profound, inner aspects of human knowing.

Here, *StoneWork*, shown in Figure 7.3, is proposed as just such a 'sensible' mediator. It is a simple pebble that has not been modified in any way. Significantly, against the backdrop of the earlier discussion, *StoneWork* is not a symbolic object but rather one that directly embodies the natural environment and, *ipso facto*, larger ideas of meaningfulness, particularly that of the self no longer being regarded as separate from but immanent in the whole of reality. Intentionally, it does not draw on the symbolic language of this or that tradition, as explored in Chapters 3 and 6. Being completely natural, it lies beyond the realm of such human-made concepts.

As an object, its contribution can be considered from a variety of interrelated perspectives:

Non-made: *StoneWork* is a non-made, unprocessed object that is readily and freely available to all. Through direct experience of an entirely natural element it offers a point of focus. It is stone, earth, water – a manifestation of process, flow, continuity and change. As such, it can be regarded as time contained in a moment – an instance of being, a particular state in a continuum of states. Its unmodified, natural condition means that it is not pinned to anything, it is not founded on any formula, concept, image or intention, it simply is. There is nothing done, aimed for or aspired to; and, as we learn from Taoism, 'If nothing is done, then all will be well.'[79] This absence of artifice is entirely in keeping with its function as a reminder of and focus for contemplative practice (see below).

As an element of the natural environment, it offers an appropriate presence that transcends religio-cultural divisions. Being entirely natural, it offers a direct experience of reality and, as such, it serves as an apposite reminder that busy-ness, ulterior purpose, mundane aspirations and routinely invoked methods and formulae can all serve to divert us from more profound notions of human meaning. Unquestioned busy-ness can encourage a superficial, unreflective view of the world and humanity's place in it. In recent times, busy-ness has undoubtedly been stimulated by technological progress and pervasive ideas that encourage a life absorbed by prosaic benefits. In turn, this has fostered a view of the world that is lacking in deeper meanings; but as Eagleton has pointed out, the postmodern hostility to traditional spiritual foundations – and their replacement with 'culture' – ultimately proves inadequate in meshing universal truths with ordinary, everyday lives.[80]

Silent: *StoneWork*, in its stillness and silence, conveys an important feature of spiritual and religious practices. In philosophy, silence can be regarded as the antithesis to logic and in aesthetics it frees us from the limitations imposed by interpretation, which places critical judgement between us and the work.[81]

Non-utilitarian: While it has a functional purpose, the object is freed from the shackles of mundane pragmatism. This allows it to be regarded not in instrumental terms but as a natural object with its own inherent characteristics and intrinsic value. Its functional purpose, which is concerned with inner work rather than outer utility, does not involve using the object in any active sense. Hence, *StoneWork* is the antithesis of the many contemporary devices that distract, entertain and encourage compulsive use. It is commensurate with an outlook that will be essential to the emergence of a sustainable frame of mind. In contrast to our prevailing direction, *StoneWork* serves as a simple visual reference, a tacit object for doing no-thing; an object that has been temporarily singled out to draw one's attention away from notions of consumption and status and to guide one's thoughts elsewhere. The modest act of singling out affirms its role as an object of contemplation, inviting one to pause, reflect and focus one's attention on a deeper, more integrated view of reality and one's place in it, and where the transient baubles and diversions of consumerism are seen within a broader sphere.

Non-positional: Being natural, freely available and of no monetary value, it stands outside the positional realm of consumer goods, novelty and competitive individualism.

Sustainable: As a propositional object, it is fully congruent with the principles of sustainability. In its acquisition, re-contextualization, use and eventual return it requires nothing in terms of additional energy use or processes and has no harmful social or environmental repercussions.

103

Beyond categorization: In its realization as an object of design there are similarities with certain art works. For example, the creative act is limited to one of selection, which has parallels with the *Readymades* of Duchamp whereby ordinary manufactured products, such as a snow shovel, a bottle rack and a urinal, were selected and exhibited but with no utilitarian or aesthetic intention.[82] However, unlike these objects, *StoneWork* is non-made and as such it does not bear the marks of human concepts, aesthetic expression or judgements of value. Rather, in it we see immanent reality in its unadulterated state – unaffected by utilitarian goals, logical methods or worldly aspirations. Accordingly, it is free of the mundane benefits, short-term gains and ulterior motives that prevent us from emptying ourselves and bar us from that clarity of awareness of which the contemplative traditions speak. There is perhaps closer alignment with Cage's 4'33", which he described as an art without work,[83] which is also free of concepts, impositions and presuppositions. However, there are also considerations that allow us to regard *StoneWork* not only as a legitimate object of design, rather than of art, but also as an object that transcends such categorizations.

First, *StoneWork* is not intended to be, nor is it presented as, art. This propositional object has a functional purpose, which is to serve as a tangible reference for contemplative activity. Second, individual creativity is de-emphasized. Even the notionally creative act of selection perhaps gives too active an impression to a modest act of temporary relocation. One pebble would serve as well as another. It is not this pebble or that pebble but any pebble. Or it could be a handful of sand or a fallen leaf. In picking up an ordinary element of the natural environment, taking it out of its context, and placing it so that it can be seen anew, not as just one element among endless similar elements but as an object worthy of our attention and an object of contemplation, its original significance remains the same but is accentuated through the singularity of its presentation. It matters little which natural element is selected. Each has its own aesthetic qualities and its place in manifest reality, and each can draw one's attention to the contemplative path and serve as a tangible reminder of the ego-less sense of unity with all creation that, according to teachings from various contemplative traditions, we must realize for true clarity of awareness.[84]

Seen in this context, human-made abstractions, definitions and classifications such as 'art' and 'design' become restrictive and divisive. They foster a certain kind of perspective that separates and isolates elements of reality into discrete silos. Clarity of awareness reaches beyond such abstractions to recognize and accept reality as it simply is, complete and uncategorized. As Cage said of 4'33", 'it leads out of the world of art into the whole of life', Duchamp said much the same of his work.[85] According to Hindu teachings, this holistic, interconnected outlook is the basis of true happiness.[86] It is also the polar opposite of the individualistic, atomized directions encouraged by consumer capitalism.

Physical-spiritual: With respect to the materiality and tacit presence of *StoneWork* in relation to spirituality and inner values, the non-dualistic, interrelationship of the physical and the spiritual is a continual theme among contemplative traditions. In Sufi writings we read, 'If spiritual explanation were enough, creation of the world were all in vain';[87] and the path to fully comprehending and experiencing this, we are told, is through contemplative practice: 'Be silent for a while and understand.'[88] In Christianity, the inseparable relationship between the physical and the spiritual is denoted in its symbols[89] and referred to in its canonical and non-canonical writings.[90, 91] In Buddhist teachings, contemplation of the object is linked to a subject's self-transcendence[92] and the Zen tradition teaches that pebbles, grass, trees and earth endlessly expound the profound truth taught by the Buddha, which is inexpressible and beyond concepts but key to self-awakening, where self is inseparable and indistinguishable from ever-unfolding external reality.[93] Ruskin voiced somewhat similar sentiments in *The Two Paths*,[94] as did Blake in his poem *Auguries of Innocence* when he wrote of seeing 'a world in a grain of sand/And a heaven in a wild flower'.[95] Thus, we see that various spiritual traditions convey non-dualistic notions of reality. It is not a case of spiritual or physical, Yin or Yang or in the modern era, as Williams has pointed out, romantic or rationalistic thinking. He argues that the problem is not fundamentally one of industry and technology, but a disproportionate emphasis on rationalistic patterns of thought.[96] In this view, modernity's dualistic notions of science vs. religion and physical vs. spiritual yield to a broader vision that recognizes a more comprehensive notion of reality; one that includes rationalistic thinking, science and the physical universe, *and* intuitive apprehension, spirituality and religion, and 'the whole of things'.[97] It includes ethical responsibilities to one's fellow human beings and society and extends to environmental ethics and responsible stewardship of the Earth.

Conclusions

We all seek meaning in our lives and in this endeavour we can learn much from the insights of those who have taken the contemplative path. These traditions from diverse cultures and religions have, down the ages, taught ways of living that lead to a sense of personal meaning in one's life, and are socially just and environmentally responsible. Inner pursuits of study and contemplative practice are combined with outer pursuits of simplicity of living and service towards others and the world in general.

Our present course, characterized by a consumption-oriented economic system that sees no value in the idea of sufficiency, is not only socially and environmentally harmful but also largely deficient in qualities that give a deeper sense of fulfilment and meaning to one's life. One cannot purchase meaningfulness and spiritual wellbeing; each of us has to find them for ourselves. Furthermore, a large-scale systemic shift in direction – by decree or imposition – is neither feasible nor desirable. Systemic transformation and a change in course will occur, if at all, through changes in the attitudes of many individuals volitionally placing greater emphasis on the study, practice and living of reflective, examined lives; and in such an endeavour, we are all beginners.[98]

In fostering such a course, the designer can make a valuable contribution by developing new understandings of material culture and new understandings of the place and role of design. The designer must also offer new kinds of post-materialist, post-consumerist propositional objects, which are not only aligned with and supportive of such a life, but also fitting for increasingly globalized, multicultural times.

8

A New Game
function, design
and post-materialist
form

A song of Enchantment I sang me there,
In a green-green wood, by waters fair

Walter de la Mare

To this point, we have looked at the *quadruple bottom line* and the implications of
including personal meaning in our understandings of sustainability. Also, we have
explored in some depth the notion of a personally meaningful 'spiritually useful'
object. These ideas about inner values and meaningfulness can now be brought
to bear in the design of a practically useful object.

We will look first at the context, or lack of it, in which we encounter our
material culture today, and how this relates to object meaning. Through the use of
examples, we will consider how the form of an object is a function of values and
priorities and is, therefore, a physical expression of meanings. Specifically, the
Bauhaus chess set of 1923/24, designed by Josef Hartwig, is discussed in relation
to a new propositional design, the *Balanis* chess set. Where the Bauhaus design is
a physical expression of the ideas and principles of modernity, the *Balanis* design
represents an attempt to embody the ideas and principles of the *quadruple bottom
line of sustainability*. Its physical form is a function of a variety of interconnected
factors such as localization, empathy with Nature and relationship to the spiritual

self. Each of these chess set designs can be seen as attempts to encompass and express issues relevant to their time.

Context, story and the value of objects

Many of the ways in which we encounter our world today lack context and clarity, in large part due to vested interests. Media headlines proclaim half-truths and revelations to stimulate curiosity and their prevailing negativity builds an atmosphere of controversy, anxiety and discontent. The accompanying news stories are presented without background or follow-up. Similarly, new products appear on the store shelves seemingly out of nowhere, attended by advertising messages that hail their benefits and disregard their deficiencies – the intention being to generate dissatisfaction, stoke desire and stimulate consumption.[1] And when evidence or ethical concerns are raised that might interfere with their agendas, corporations will often quite intentionally work to confuse the debate, thereby sowing doubt in the minds of the public and dissipating any threats to consumerism. In the past this was done to confound public perceptions about the dangers of smoking. Today, millions of dollars are being spent to undermine public discourse about the scientific evidence for human-caused climate change and its links to fossil fuels, production, pollution and consumption.[2, 3] Throughout broadcast, online and print media, context and clarity are lacking, and anxieties and dissatisfactions are nurtured. This phenomenon, however, is not new, even if the preponderance of wireless devices has made access to information far easier. In the mid-nineteenth century the American philosopher Henry David Thoreau dismissed much so-called news as mere gossip, saying,

107

> If we read of one man robbed, or murdered, or killed by accident, or one house burned, or one vessel wrecked, or one steamboat blown up, or one cow run over on the Western Railroad, or one mad dog killed, or one lot of grasshoppers in the winter, – we never need read of another. One is enough. If you are acquainted with the principle, what do you care for a myriad instances and applications?[4]

The phenomenon may not be new but the scale and pace of information inundation has reached new heights today, making reflection and discernment increasingly difficult.[5] Consequently, we become ever more susceptible to the disquieting influences that feed consumerism.

Designers are part of this milieu, both through their contribution to a product's creation and because, in a digital age, many of these products are conduits for media and marketing. Obviously, the mass-produced, globally distributed products that designers help create are aimed squarely at the 'consumer' – itself a mean, contrived concept that reduces personhood to purchaser. Furthermore, because of their lack of connection to place, when these products are launched onto the market, people have little basis for understanding the environmental and social implications of their production: where the materials came from, how they were produced, the working conditions of the employees and so on. Likewise, their design makes no reference to the context of their use – they have no relationship to the culture, the climate, the traditions or any of the other factors that contribute to a rich and meaningful life. There is certainly no relationship to community, cooperation and interdependencies. On the contrary, consumer capitalism thrives on atomization and the purported choices made available to the individualized consumer; the primary objective is the sale, after which attention immediately moves on to the next product and the next potential 'consumer'.

It becomes apparent that only an impoverished kind of product value is afforded by the design profession's continuing compliance with modernity's emphasis on function, efficiency and progress-interpreted-as-technological-innovation. In this context it is inevitable that as a product's functionality becomes faulty or technologically superseded it will cease to be of value. Critically connected to this, in a consumption-based economic system, technological displacement is a carefully planned corporate act – a considered stratagem to kindle dissatisfaction and drive sales. Going hand in hand with this and strenuously encouraged by advertising is the inferred social cachet of owning the most technologically up-to-date version of a product.

Designing sustainability must challenge such inadequate notions of value and develop ways of talking about and engaging in design that reflect and support deeper understandings. When a functional object is considered within a larger landscape of human needs, which includes concern for others, for place and for consequence, its value can be understood in quite different terms. These extend beyond mere utility and have little to do with either the morally questionable exclusivity ascribed to many mass-market products, an attribution that is self-evidently incongruous, or the purported social standing that advertising campaigns would have us associate with product ownership. Instead, the value of a product can be appreciated in terms of its broader meaning as a thing. These aspects of product meaning can be found, for example, in its provenance and conveyed through its story. Only by knowing something of the origin and contextual significance of our material culture, and its relationship to people and to the natural environment, can we begin to more fully appreciate the meaning of our objects and thereby find them of value in ways that surpass both function and self-regarding notions of status. Objects will then possess both instrumental and intrinsic value and will warrant more considered care. Such contextual understandings may also make us think twice about purchasing certain kinds of objects; for example, if they are associated with exploitative production practices or if their use is known to foster compulsive or unreflective behaviour patterns. They may even encourage us to reduce our overall consumption levels. Indeed, this is one of the most important ways of contributing to sustainability and it may also allow us to live more wisely and more contentedly; to again quote Thoreau, 'With respect to luxuries and comforts, the wisest have ever lived a more simple and meagre life than the poor.'[6]

108

Spirituality, virtue and sustainability in human activities

A variety of institutional failings became apparent in the early years of the twenty-first century, including: unethical and illegal banking practices and corruption; an increasing divide between rich and poor; economic recession; and increasing evidence of acute environmental problems coupled with an inability of national governments to come together, agree and act decisively in ways that go beyond narrow, chiefly economic, self-interests. These failings have spurred a growing recognition that substantive change is needed to effectively address contemporary social and environmental concerns. Michaels argues that the economic story, which has become the central premise of our time, has changed our outlook by encouraging us to see everything in the terms of the market.[7] This has altered our attitudes to all aspects of life – how we think about relationships, community, health care, education, creativity, spirituality and the natural environment. All these things tend to lose their richness and become reduced to the language of commodification and saleable products. As this language and this kind of thinking become pervasive, they erode ideas about intrinsic value and the common good. For example, in a discussion about introducing a new degree programme and its various courses, a senior university professor recently wrote, 'you don't develop good products for the market by just reconfiguring old components'; while it may be sound advice not to simply re-shuffle existing materials, the phrasing itself clearly demonstrates how the education of our young people tends to be considered within the dominant economic monoculture. Similarly, universities and university departments talk about their brand, a term that has become ubiquitous but which reveals an educational culture of products, competitive markets, service providers and customers; in other words, higher education, along with many other areas of life, is increasingly being viewed through the lens of the dominant economic narrative. To counter this, we have to enlarge our vision and embrace a broader spectrum of values, which reach beyond utility and self-interest and embrace social, environmental and personal meanings, as shown in Figure 7.2.

109

The mid-twentieth-century academic C. S. Lewis, a specialist in medieval and Renaissance literature, argued that throughout the course of human history the wisdom of sages and the reasonings of philosophers not only guided ordinary people, but helped steer society and the whole pattern of life. Their teachings made their way into the social order of things via authority and tradition, and this remained the case until modern times when such teachings became neglected or were actively rejected.[8] This abnegation was especially evident in the twentieth century's cultural responses and outputs, particularly in the period known as Modernism. The overarching aim of artists, designers and writers during the early part of the century was 'out with the old and in with the new', a sentiment forcefully characterized in Marinetti's Futurist manifesto of 1909.[9] It is notable that these were the cultural responses of a society that had, over several centuries, embraced materialism, instrumental rationality, industrialization, progress and capitalism, i.e. modernity. However, even though to some extent the priorities of modernity have become superseded in recent decades, late-modern or postmodern sensibilities have done little to restore any extensive or cogent recognition of traditional wisdom teachings. In fact, continual advances in science, technology, information distribution and consumer-capitalism serve to keep the focus of contemporary society firmly on rapid progress, apparently for its own sake as a self-evident good, as well as for the sake of economic growth. These urgent strivings, which are typically characterized as a race in which we must not fall behind, leave little time or inclination for reflection.

As a consequence, it seems that in contemporary society we must either dedicate our own lives to the pursuit of wisdom, an astringent course that few may be inclined to follow, or we must do without it. On this point Lewis cautioned that a society that neither heeds the wisdom of humanity that has come down to us through the ages nor seeks wisdom for itself is fated to become superficial, base and ugly, and such a course will ultimately prove fatal.[10]

It is perhaps not surprising, then, that today ideas about values are finding renewed tenure and many contemporary thinkers and commentators are suggesting that there is a need for an alternative path to that which continues to be so zealously promoted by Western-style capitalism. Even the Director-General of the World Trade Organization, an organization that has been the target of huge anti-globalization protests, has acknowledged that globalized capitalism has to change in order to improve social justice.[11] From various quarters there are calls for a renewed emphasis on moral principles, ethics and trust, especially in the business environment, a recognition of the importance of inner values and spirituality and their relationship to personal wellbeing, and a turning away from consumerism. All these are inter-linked and are related to the development of ways of living that are personally meaningful and sustainable, in that they encourage a sense of responsibility towards others and society as a whole and towards the care and prudent use of the natural environment. Longley points to the virtue ethics of Aristotle, which are associated with an individual's spiritual development and wellbeing and are included in Catholic social teaching[12] (see also Chapter 7). In contrast to the pervasive culture of our times, virtue ethics teach that that which is good for the individual is not associated with money, possessions, honour or pleasure, but with 'being' well and 'doing' well, achieved by living according to the virtues.[13] The virtues include self-restraint, courage, fortitude, magnanimity and truthfulness,[14] and social teachings based on virtue ethics include the dignity of the human person, the needs and rights of the poor, economic justice, charity, promotion of the common good and stewardship of the Earth.[15] Virtue ethics, also known as *aretaic* ethics, differ from utilitarian ethics, which aim to maximize the good for the greatest number of people, but which can result in the ends justifying the means. Virtue ethics also differ from duty ethics, or *deontic* ethics, which are founded on universal principles and rules. Instead, virtue ethics are based in the idea of each individual developing moral character and striving to do the right thing. This is quite different from codes of ethics found in organizations and rules that outline minimal ethical standards, and is a long way from approaches that encourage a culture of box-ticking compliance. Learning to act virtuously is not dependent on principle or systemized methods; rather, it is to act and to feel in particular ways and to be inclined to do so because one has cultivated the virtues through moral education.[16] It follows that virtue ethics require and contribute to the building of a culture of trust, which in turn supports the common good.

The growing recognition of the need for substantive change is not restricted to those living in the economically developed nations. As Western-style growth-based economic policies spread eastward and those nations develop along the route of consumer-capitalism, a number of writers from countries in Asia are also raising concerns. Pankaj Mishra paints a rather bleak picture, seeing no convincing alternative to Western political and economic ideas arising in Asia today. He suggests that the teachings of Gandhi, which were so firmly grounded in an ethics of virtue, are practically forgotten in today's India, and Confucian ideas of harmony are making no difference in China, despite lip service from the ruling elites. Consequently, the adoption by these countries of Western-style economic growth is having the effect of dramatically widening social divisions and, while the privileged minority aspires to nothing more than modern conveniences and technological gadgets, the majority are in despair. This, he concludes, together with massive environmental destruction and dwindling resources, may well lead to conflict and bloodshed in coming years.[17] The President of the World Bank has also warned of the likelihood of conflict, over water and food supplies, if current trends in climate change continue.[18]

More promisingly, there are some signs of changing sensibilities within private sector organizations and within academia. Spiritual considerations and inner experience are entering discussions about sustainability in major international companies such as Puma and Unilever, and in academia there is an increasing recognition of the relationship between inner values and our responses to environmental degradation. Research at the London Business School has found a strong connection between a company's sustainability programmes and the inner experiences and inner values of its leaders or other employees. And the director of the Grantham Institute for Climate Change recognizes that scientific knowledge alone will not be enough to spur change, that inner experience is a crucial factor.[19] There are also dedicated scholarly journals and academic conferences that focus on the connections between religion, spirituality, business management, industry and economics.[20]

Nature and the spiritual self

The term 'spiritual' can simply refer to that which is not the bodily or material person – all that is immaterial, including emotions, passions and memories, whether or not these are judged to be good.[21] However, all cultures have developed traditions aimed at ensuring that the spiritual life of the individual is channelled towards the good. And as we have seen, through the language of symbolism and metaphor, they all point to that which lies beyond words but which, nevertheless, is knowable through practice and experience. Hence, there is an inextricable relationship between one's individual conduct and actions in the world, and one's inner or spiritual development towards the good.

Today, it is probably not too far off the mark to suggest that we live in dispirited times. We have not only disenchanted the world,[22] we have cast doubt on its future. For too long and to all intents and purposes we have regarded it in terms of scientific facts, material resources and economic opportunity, and in doing so we have distanced ourselves from the intimacies of the world. For too long we have separated our work lives from Nature – from seeing it, feeling it, heeding it – from directly experiencing its fullness, its majesty and its, sometimes awful, beauty. Having replaced familiarity with desiccated abstractions and reduced Nature to data, tonnage and profits, we show little compunction in plundering it, polluting it, littering it and relentlessly abusing it with ever more developments and innovations. If we are not to completely eradicate the world's purity and goodness we have to learn once more to love it, to find it beautiful and enthralling. It is increasingly palpable that the natural world's splendour, its rhythms and its restorative potency will only be maintained if we can love it liberally and care for it copiously. As Chesterton said, 'Men did not love Rome because she was great. She was great because they had loved her.'[23] Only by learning to love the world will it be a place of beauty and enchantment for us.

Of course, in former times, too, the world was seen as a provider of resources for human benefit, but this instrumental view was accompanied by a more profound connection that was nurtured not by facts but by experience, through tacit knowledge and by human creativity and imagination. At one level, in the lore of ordinary people, a tree was not just a tree, it was the home of a nymph, and a cave behind a waterfall was the palace of the fairy queen. The world was filled with the human imagination – with sprites, sirens and genies, crocks of gold and enchanted wells. At another level, the world was sacred – a place of sanctity and sanctuary – a holy place where we found repose in mountains, woods and desert. Magical stories are, of course, still told and they still fire the human imagination. A schoolboy wizard who can fly on a broomstick and defeat dark forces is testament that reason has not eradicated our appetite for the fantastic. But unlike ancient lore, such stories, each from a particular imagination, are not deeply connected into a shared consciousness of the natural world, nor do they emerge from a collective imagination. And while many still find refuge and succour in natural places, the sentiments that may arise from such times do not transfer easily into our work lives; these experiences are compartmentalized and disconnected.

Part of the restorative process will be to give greater affirmation to other ways of knowing and other ways of encountering the world and to include these in our own thinking and our own lives – including, critically, our work lives. This may not be straightforward or unproblematic, given how far we have veered from an empathetic relationship with Nature. Nevertheless, it will be a necessary facet of change. Other ways of knowing, that bring to the fore values and priorities that extend beyond the rational mind, have been expressed and evoked down the ages through song, poetry, prose and art. William Wordsworth (1770–1850) wrote of how our preoccupations have distanced us from the natural world, fomenting dissonance and insensitivity,

> The world is too much with us; late and soon,
> Getting and spending, we lay waste our powers:
> Little we see in Nature that is ours;
> We have given our hearts away, a sordid boon!
> This Sea that bares her bosom to the moon;
> The Winds that will be howling at all hours,
> And are up-gathered now like sleeping flowers;
> For this, for everything, we are out of tune;
> It moves us not. [24]

Wordsworth urged 'being' in the natural environment and seeing and feeling from the heart, rather than doing and reasoning. In a poem to his sister, he wrote of setting aside reason and daily routines that are so busy and regulated – instead, he called upon us to experience the natural world directly, tacitly,

> Put on with speed your woodland dress,
> And bring no book, for this one day
> We'll give to idleness.
>
> No joyless forms shall regulate
> Our living Calendar:
> We from to-day, my Friend, will date
> The opening of the year.
>
> Love, now a universal birth,
> From heart to heart is stealing,
> From earth to man, from man to earth,
> – It is the hour of feeling.
>
> One moment now may give us more
> Than years of toiling reason;
> Our minds shall drink at every pore
> The spirit of the season. [25]

113

In another culture, in another time, Matsuo Bashō (1644–94) used the spare poetry form of *haiku* to express direct experiences of the natural world. A master of the form, he possessed a rare ability to poignantly distil and capture a moment and, in doing so, he makes the reader aware of the relationship of the particular to the transcendent: [26]

At the ancient pond
a frog plunges into
the sound of water

A hundred years!
All here in the garden in
these fallen leaves[27]

As a follower of Zen Buddhism, Bashō sought spiritual and artistic insight through unmediated experiences and he strove to express these through uninterpolated – or self-less – poetry and prose. However, while he taught that we should learn about Nature from direct experience and observation and through a forgetting of self, he recognized that 'the unconditioned was attainable only within the conditioned, nirvana within samsara – that the illumination sought was to be found in the here and now of daily life', an understanding that accords with the Zen teaching that 'noumenon and phenomena are identical'.[28] Hence, his poetry creates a vision of the eternal in and through that which is finite, a notion of the spiritual in and through that which is physical.[29]

A similar idea of the infinite being present in the finite is apparent in some of the early Christian writings, such as this excerpt from the late first or early second century Gospel of Thomas:[30]

114

Split a piece of wood;
I am there.
Lift up the stone, and
you will find me there.[31]

Needleman says of these early texts that they speak of a transformational knowing, which is of critical importance to our contemporary condition because of our ever-widening gap between intellectual knowledge and 'being' in the world. He contends that our lack of attention to inner growth and ethical knowing is leading us towards environmental disaster because 'knowledge without virtue can neither bring us good nor show us truth'. The kind of knowledge we have acquired is not transformational, 'it does not elevate our level of being and it does not nourish the development of moral power'.[32] Traditional sacred writings, from all cultures, present a different kind of knowledge. These texts are not analytical writings, they do not present facts or physical evidence, but are concerned with ways of knowing that cultivate the inner values and spiritual development of the individual.

Echoing the Gospel of Thomas, the presence of the sacred in mundane phenomena is also referred to by the second-century satirist Lucian of Samosata, who wrote 'god is not in heaven but pervades all things, like sticks and stones and even the humblest of creatures'.[33] The connection between spiritual development and our relationship to the natural world was a crucial aspect of Celtic Christianity, which flourished in the western regions of the British Isles between the fourth and seventh centuries. Celtic theology regarded Nature as a gift to humanity that was to be cherished and honoured. Worldly wealth, status and luxury were criticized and a life of simplicity and living in harmony with Nature were advocated. The natural world was regarded as a way of spiritual insight and 'knowing God', where 'Animals, birds, plants, and running water were all seen as tangible intimations of divine glory'.[34] Also in the Western tradition, St. Francis of Assisi developed a spirituality that extended beyond humanity to embrace a larger reality. He is said to have had an affinity with all of creation, which included living creatures, plant life and natural inanimate objects. He saw all of creation as coming from the same source and regarded it with concern and compassion.[35, 36]

The nineteenth-century American essayist Ralph Waldo Emerson wrote powerfully of the natural world and its relationship to spiritual growth and wellbeing: 'Nature is loved by what is best in us. It is loved as the city of God.' And when we are in natural places, we see our day-to-day affairs in a new perspective – Nature 'shames us out of our nonsense' and it detects 'the presence or absence of the divine sentiment in man'. He suggested that natural places are medicinal, that they heal us and minister both to the imagination and to the soul. Contrasting our experiences of Nature with modern society and modern nations, he argued that in the pursuit of technological benefits we have created foolish expectations and in our strivings for wealth we have become aimless. 'The world is mind precipitated', he said, and natural objects in their virtue and their pointedness have a beneficial influence because 'wisdom is infused in every form'.[37]

115

A few years ago wildlife biologist Karsten Heuer and his filmmaker wife Leanne Allison completed a 1500 km trek from the Yukon to Alaska, following the caribou herds across the Canadian wilderness to their calving grounds. The trails they walked had been followed by the caribou for some 27,000 years. The aim of their journey was to raise awareness of the risk to these herds of drilling oil wells in the calving grounds, as was being proposed. Heuer recalls that several weeks into the trek, when they had left the city far behind, both physically and mentally, and had become attuned to the rhythms and flow of the herd, he became aware one day of a hitherto unrecognized phenomenon,

> It was there, immersed in the history and energy of multiple migrations, that I clearly heard what had registered as only a subtle rumbling before.... The land was vibrating underneath me, as though the ground itself were alive.... A trained scientist, I was vexed by its formlessness: neither loud nor subtle, it was a strong beckoning I could hardly hear.... I lay back, wondering if I was imagining things, and if not, what the thrumming meant. Was the sound because of the convergence of all the animals, or was the convergence prompted by the sound? Did it come and go, or was it me who was changing, hearing something that has always existed, only noticing it for the first time?[38]

And recollecting Bashō's *haiku* above, in which he attempted to express unmediated awareness of the natural world, Heuer goes on to say,

> I felt that I was on the cusp of something, on the edge of uncovering an innate but forgotten wisdom. After years of only applying a rational and scientific approach, I was beginning to see and hear directly, rather than filter every feeling through my mind.[39]

Such ideas are very familiar in Native American spiritual traditions, which contend that the spiritual and the commonplace are one, and the essence of daily life: 'The spiritual world is everywhere! If you listen, you will hear.' As a consequence, the design and making of artefacts in Native American cultures reflect the belief that the source of materials is sacred.[40] Many contemporary forms of 'progressive spirituality' also see the spiritual embedded within the material world.[41] Thus, as King has pointed out, while it may be expressed in a variety of different ways, all societies and cultures have recognized a relationship between the natural environment and humanity's sense of the spiritual.[42]

By giving greater recognition to the critical, interwoven relationships between, on the one hand sustainability, spirituality and the natural world and, on the other, the creation of our material culture, we become aware that very different approaches are required from those that have dominated design and manufacturing for many decades. There is a need to develop design in directions that are far more sensitive to and respectful of the natural environment, not just for Nature's sake, but for our sake too. Aligning the provision of our practical needs with environmental care not only creates a healthier place in which to live, but is also conducive to the development of inner values and spiritual wellbeing.

116

Values and priorities expressed through form

We can now turn to design and consider the implications of these ideas for the definition and making of our material culture. To do this, we must refer to particular examples, because design is concerned not with generalities but with specifics. For purposes of illustration, a new design, the *Balanis* chess set, developed to address the principles and priorities discussed above, will be discussed in relation to the Bauhaus chess set created by Josef Hartwig in 1923/24, which in many respects epitomizes the 'modern' and still dominant approach to product design. Through such discussion we can more clearly discern the differences between what has come to be regarded as conventional product design and design for a *quadruple bottom line of sustainability*.

Modernist sensibilities still dominate design education and design practice – from the content of foundation courses to the design of furniture, appliances, housewares and electronic products; and the legacy of the Bauhaus still guides debate about design and the value of design.[43] The modernist approach has been the most significant influence on the discipline in recent times, and for this reason it is inseparably linked to contemporary concerns about unsustainable practices. Fundamentally, the Bauhaus school, at least in its latter years, was geared towards design for mass-production and, in creating designs for this type of manufacturing it sought a universal aesthetic by emphasizing rationalistic approaches, simplifying form, rejecting decoration and abandoning convention;[44] and we see all these traits expressed in the mass-produced products of today that are aimed at global markets. With these developments, aesthetic references to tradition, which can contribute to cultural continuity and are often deeply meaningful, were actively stripped away. Instead, the modernist approach was thought to be 'honest and democratic' and rooted not in tradition and culture but in 'the logic of mass manufacturing'.[45] However, these proved to be untenable assertions – modernism's *form follows function* maxim turned out to be nothing more than a style.[46] Despite this, and even with its integrity diminished by philosophical deficiencies and economic efficiencies, it remains obstinately prevalent.

Significantly, important shifts in purpose were occurring in the Bauhaus at the very time Hartwig was developing his chess set design. Idealism and artistic notions of self-expression were giving way to rationalism and semi-scientific approaches.[47] In 1923 Johannes Itten, a specialist in colour theory and a mystic who had been teaching at the school since 1919, was forced to leave by Walter Gropius. Gropius wished to distance the Bauhaus from Itten's influence and introduce a more 'realistic' approach. He brought in the Constructivist Lázló Moholy-Nagy and from that point the direction changed. It was at this time, according to Schlemmer, that 'design for industry was born'.[48] Subjective expression, an intimate and direct knowledge of traditional materials, craft-based approaches, unconscious associations with the creative process and links between creativity and spirituality were all de-emphasized. Priorities shifted to the needs of industry, focusing on design for mass-production, materials technology and design for efficiency.[49]

In retrospect, this decision by Gropius can be seen as a turning point in the history of design and production, one that reverberates down the years to today's concerns about sustainability. Intimate and important connections between our human-made material culture, the natural environment and our spiritual needs become stifled and obscured by rationalistic approaches that emphasize abstraction and efficiency and, when coupled with commercial priorities, promote fragmentation, self-interest and a placeless individualism. In the process, a perilous division is forged between, on the one hand, our decisions, actions and productions, and on the other, the natural world, locality and our communal, ethical and spiritual needs. Seen in today's context, in which the cumulatively devastating effects of mass-production, consumerism, pollution and waste are only too evident, the significance of this re-directed emphasis becomes clear. The influence of the Bauhaus approach proved to be overarching, setting the direction for design education and design practice throughout the twentieth century and into the twenty-first.

When we look at Hartwig's design (Figure 8.1), as we might expect we see an abandonment of references to cultural tradition and hierarchy; characteristics that are clearly present in the Staunton chess set designed by Nathaniel Cook some 75 years earlier (Figure 8.2).

Figure 8.1
Bauhaus chessmen
designed by Josef Hartwig, 1923/24
pear wood, natural and stained black, with cloth
bases
Photograph by Klaus G. Beyer, Weimar,
© Constantin Beyer, Weimar,
reproduced with permission

Figure 8.2
Staunton chessmen
designed by Nathaniel Cook, 1849
boxwood, natural and stained black

The Staunton set features a castellated rook, a horse's head for the knight and an ascending height across the range of pieces from pawn to king, thereby expressing through form historical precedents and distinctions rooted in custom, rank and heritage. Chess has long been known as 'the royal game', both because it holds a principal place among intellectual pastimes and because in feudal Europe it was played by kings and nobles.[50] Where Cook paid homage to this history, Hartwig, in the spirit of the age, effectively rejected it through a design approach that emphasized functionalism. Not only are hierarchical distinctions considerably diminished, the shape of each piece has lost any figurative expression and is, instead, indicative of its movement on the board – an uncompromising translation of the *form follows function* principle.

A design path that attempts to comprehensively adopt sustainable principles will differ significantly from this modernist approach. The differences will be found in the underlying motivators, the methods of making, the aesthetic expression and the overall meaning. An expansive understanding of *designing sustainability* brings to the fore considerations that extend beyond conventional rationalizations, quantifications and reductionist, quasi-scientific approaches. It calls upon sensibilities and connections that have long been dismissed as irrelevant and therefore have been absent from discussions of design. However, many of these will be important in bringing to prominence aspects of design that reach beyond both functionalism and narrow economic ends. By taking these into account within a simple artefact like a chess set, we can begin to more clearly recognize how *designing sustainability* can affect the definition and nature of our material culture.

As we saw in Chapter 4, the *quadruple bottom line of sustainability* encompasses:

- *practical meaning* – utilitarian needs and environmental considerations;
- *social meaning* – moral considerations, duty and matters of social justice;

- *personal meaning* – inner values, matters of conscience and spiritual wellbeing;
- *economic means* – consigned to a lower, more appropriate place.

It follows that, compared to conventional design approaches, this more expansive view will allow our design endeavours to be rooted more deeply, to contribute more abundantly, and to be appreciated more comprehensively. Moreover, these various facets of design have to be considered from a perspective that is integrative and which recognizes their interdependencies – design being primarily a discipline not of analysis but of synthesis. Clearly, also, many of these factors lie outside the scope of physical evidence and quantification, residing instead in realms of human meaning that are rooted in history, tradition, beliefs, ritual, myth, emotion, experience and imagination. They are expounded and understood not through theories, measurements and generalized abstractions, but through the qualities and characteristics of the particular – in narrative, story, poetry, practice, place and artefact. And they are appreciated holistically, through subjective responses and aesthetic experiences. Such inclusive, experiential understandings and realizations cannot be pointed to or measured; they are incompatible with reductionism and tangible evidence. Nevertheless, they constitute vital facets of being human. They also represent an important, and arguably the most critical, contribution of the designer who wishes to explore a more sustainable, more substantive and more desirable path for the discipline. It follows that in order to appreciate the meanings of a particular design proposition, we must know something of its provenance.

119

A propositional design for sustainability: the *Balanis* chess set

Most politicians and corporate leaders continue to advocate a progress- and growth-based economic system in which progress is narrowly interpreted as technological innovation and growth as a continuous rise in GDP. This kind of economic system is fundamentally locked into rising levels of consumption and, with it, rising levels of energy use, pollution and waste. For many years philosophers, environmentalists and academics from a variety of fields have been arguing for fundamental change. More recently, as noted, change has also been called for by such influential figures as the Director-General of the WTO and the President of the World Bank.

Even though these global-scale issues may seem far removed from the design of an individual object such as a chess set, they are, in fact, inseparable. The ways in which we think about our material culture, conceive it, produce it, use it and dispose of it are fundamentally connected to matters of environmental care and social equity, and it is through the act of designing – how we conceptualize and define an object – that we tie the particular to the global. The cumulative effects of millions of 'particulars' can have major social and environmental impacts.

Meanings, priorities and values are embedded into an object at the design stage.[51] It is here, in the individual design decisions – many of which may seem minor – that the designer can sow the seeds of change. It is here, in decisions about the conceptual nature of the artefact, and in the specification of materials and production processes, that the die is cast, as it were. The consequences of these decisions, when combined with those made by many other designers working on many other projects, can be far reaching.

The *Balanis* chess set (Figure 8.3) was developed as a vehicle for exploring the nature of a functional object that adheres as fully as possible to the priorities of the *quadruple bottom line of sustainability*. These priorities guided decisions about intention, materials, designing and making, use and after-use, and influenced the chess set's aesthetic expression and the nature of its physical presence. Let us now consider each of these factors.

Intention: We can consider the intention of the *Balanis* chess set design, first, in terms of the *intention of the object*, and the compatibility of this intention with sustainability, i.e. we can ask ourselves whether this object is even warranted; and second, in terms of the *intention of the design* of this specific chess set.

When we consider the *intention of the object*, and the compatibility of this with sustainability, irrespective of any specific design articulation, we have to reflect on the meaning of the object, what it represents and whether it is compatible with the ethos and principles of sustainability. In other words, we must ask ourselves if this kind of object's presence in the world can be justified. The answer to such a question may not always be clear-cut. We have to weigh the pros and cons and make a judgement based on our values. Now, many might object to this, arguing that it is not up to the designer to decide which products should or should not be produced, and they would have a perfectly valid point. However, it *is* up to the designer to make a value-based judgement about the things that he or she, personally, is willing to work on. Making such judgements is part of being an ethical human being. By way of example, a highly regarded product designer once told me that, over a long career, the only project he had turned away on ethical grounds was a commission to design an all-plastic handgun. No doubt many would regard this decision as rather straightforward, raising as it does significant ethical questions about firearms use, concealment and security but, as has become evident in the light of 3D printing, some designers have no such qualms.[52] Others might have similar ethical concerns about the design of cigarette packaging or landmines. Generally, however, these kinds of decisions are not so straightforward. A product may be justifiable in one situation but not in another, and different people will have different perspectives and come down on opposite sides of the fence. Or, again, a designer may have to weigh taking on a project that they have ethical concerns about and earning a salary to provide for their family. And it is all too easy to avoid the issue by convincing ourselves that if we don't take on a particular project, someone else will.

Ethical judgements may be fraught with difficulties, but that does not mean we should avoid them. With particular relevance to sustainability, some people object strongly to the design and production of disposable plastic water bottles, regarding them as unethical because of their environmental consequences (they require large amounts of energy to produce and transport and are a severe cause of litter) and because bottled water commodifies a basic human right.[53] Their sale has been banned in some towns and in New South Wales all state departments and agencies have been prohibited from purchasing bottled water.[54, 55] Others regard plastic water bottles as a convenient, reliable and hygienic way of distributing, acquiring and carrying clean drinking water. Bottled water may be seen as a preferable alternative to drinks with high sugar content and it may have considerable health benefits in areas where tap water is contaminated.[56] So we see that there are ethical obligations, and sometimes ethical dilemmas, related to the design and subsequent production of material things. Moreover, as issues related to sustainability become more critical, we will need to ask ethical questions that in the past may have been of little or no concern.

Turning now to the *Balanis* chess set. While this is not the place for a detailed discussion of the merits of chess as a game, we can consider its general characteristics and their relationship to sustainability, regardless of the design and production of the physical artefact. Clearly, if the activity itself were somehow in conflict with the ethos of sustainability, there would be little benefit in creating a 'sustainable' version of the game pieces.

Chess is a game for two people which has a long tradition; it can be traced back at least 1500 years. Consequently, it is steeped in cultural history and over the centuries it has developed rules, game theories and strategies. When playing the game one has to scan the board and think ahead about possibilities and options, the goal being to place the opponent's king in checkmate. Essentially it is a pleasurable pastime that is engaged in for its own sake, and its complexity allows for continual development and improvement. While some players compete in championships, often for prize money, and it may be used as a basis for gambling, which could raise ethical concerns, for the most part it is an amateur pursuit, played for the love of the game itself. Its rewards are associated with the challenges it offers, along with the human interaction. While it is possible to play via the Internet or against a computer, in its traditional form it requires two people to sit together and, as such, at least when played recreationally, it is inherently convivial in nature even though it is an abstracted battle. Unlike passive forms of entertainment, it is a leisure activity that demands the involvement and concentration of the participants. Unlike many electronic games that can foster addiction-like behaviours and absorb considerable amounts of time, chess has a fixed goal and a game can be completed in less than an hour.

None of these things conflict with sustainability. On the contrary, for the most part chess is played as a face-to-face, socially reifying, enjoyable activity. It requires a sense of fair play, and offers opportunities for continual improvement in one's ability. In its basic form it consists of simple wooden pieces and a wooden or cardboard playing board; it requires no batteries or other power supply and creates no waste. Hence, in terms of its personal, social and environmental meanings, the basic game is perfectly in keeping with the ethos and principles of sustainability. These considerations apply to the game itself, and can be taken into account by the designer before embarking on any creative activity related to a specific chess set design. By doing so, the contribution of the designer can be more clearly differentiated and discerned.

The designer's contribution lies not in any change to the game itself, but rather in the creative development and specification of the chess pieces and the wider implications of those design decisions. Here, these wider implications relate to sustainability and, as such, the designer's task is to develop forms for our material culture that help move us away from a system – economic, political, technological – that is dependent on consumerism, escalating use of natural materials and energy and environmental harm. The design intentions that guided the development of the *Balanis* chess set can be summarized as follows:

- To design in a way that is sensitive to, and responsive to, the materials being used.
- To use materials and processes that are not harmful to the natural environment.
- To use materials that are natural and, wherever possible, locally sourced.
- To maintain a sense of closeness to the natural environment in regard to materials acquisition and use, materials transformation, aesthetics, product use and after-use.
- Through effective design, to achieve a desirable result while:
    - minimizing time, effort and energy spent on making;
    - employing simple, quiet forming processes that require little in the way of tools and specialized skills but which take into consideration the characteristics and quality of labour required, so as to ensure good work and equity via widespread, localized availability;
    - minimizing the impact of the artefact in its making, use and eventual return to the natural environment;
    - expressing a relatively low level of concern for material goods and eschewing qualities that provoke acquisitiveness.

Materials

The *Balanis* chess set is fashioned from the wind-fallen branches of a local tree, which happened to be a large holm oak (*Quercus ilex*). This particular holm oak grows in the grounds of an old hospital on the northwest coast of England. It is close to my current home, which means that the wood was collected as locally as possible. Its many and varied associations can add to our appreciation of both the material and the chess set. Obviously, other locally available woods could be used to create similar chess sets elsewhere and they would be accompanied by equally meaningful associations.

The holm oak is not native to Britain but was introduced from the Mediterranean in the 1500s. It grows particularly well in coastal areas that are less susceptible to frost,[57] which helps explain its presence in the grounds of the old hospital. It probably dates from the early part of the nineteenth century; the hospital was completed in 1816 and the gardens would have been planted around the same time. It stands close to the entrance and therefore, when it was a very young tree, the holm oak from which these chess pieces are made would once have fallen under the gaze of Charles Dickens, who visited the hospital in 1857.[58, 59]

In its native lands, the holm oak has both utilitarian and symbolic meanings. The ancient Romans valued it for its functional qualities, especially its strength and durability, using it for agricultural tools and cartwheels.[60] For the ancient Greeks it had symbolic and ritualistic meanings – its acorns were a sign of fertility and its evergreen leaves were used to tell the future.[61] In Chaucer's *Knight's Tale*, as Emily prepares to pray at the temple of Diana, 'Her shining hair was combed and loose, and a crown of evergreen oak leaves set neatly and becomingly on her head.'[62] In Greek mythology, *hamadryads* or wood-nymphs inhabited the trees, and lived and died with them; the nymph of the holm oak being *Balanis*. The nineteenth-century folklorist Folkard tells us that in ancient Greece the holm oak was regarded as both a funereal tree and a symbol of immortality, and that the Fates wore wreaths fashioned from its leaves. He also recounts a legend about the crucifixion of Jesus in which all the trees held a council and together agreed not to allow their wood to be used for the cross. As attempts were made to fell a tree, the axe would split the trunk into a thousand fragments. The holm oak alone did not shatter, and so it became the instrument of the crucifixion. Even up to his day, Folkard tells us, woodcutters in Greece had an aversion to the tree, fearing to cut it down or bring it into their homes. However, another interpretation suggests that the holm oak generously gave up its life to die with Jesus. A legend from Russia tells of it being a martyr-tree; here it was thought to be capable of curing sick children by taking on their illnesses.[63] These various associations with natural environments, functional benefit and cultural and sacred meanings can foster a deeper appreciation of materials and, in doing so, can potentially lead to more moderate, more respectful attitudes to their acquisition and use.

123

The other material in the *Balanis* design is flax, which is present in two forms. Flaxseed oil, also known as linseed oil, thickens and hardens when exposed to air. It has been applied to all outer surfaces to seal and protect the wood. Flax cord, in contrasting colours, is used to differentiate the two opposing sides. The cord is wound tightly round the base of each piece and finished with a simple knot at the back, as shown in Figure 8.4. Here, the use of an exposed knot, rather than a concealed method of joining, such as a whipping-knot or adhesive, is in keeping with making the object explicit, comprehensible and visually accessible. This contributes to a sense of being in control of and at ease with the artefacts of our material culture.

Designing and making: The chess pieces were made without accurate measurement, but through approximation; lengths and angles being determined by eye. The tree bark was left in place and the cut faces were given a light sanding

Figure 8.4 *Sketch book with Balanis chess pieces*

to remove rough edges and bring out the end grain. This lack of refinement not only minimizes the intervention, it also retains the qualities and attributes of the natural material. Inexactitude, rather than machined precision, becomes a quality of the design, and the chess set maintains a recognizable aesthetic connection with Nature; when the pieces are being used, the player is directly handling elements and textures of the natural world. This contrasts starkly with conventional manufacturing processes that force organic materials into our predetermined notions of what they *should* be as forms. Such processes remove the innate contours and eliminate the raw textures and, in so doing, they physically and cognitively distance us from Nature's presence. In the *Balanis* design, each piece is simply a short length cut from the branch. This minimization of processing is a formal expression of an attitude of sufficiency, which aligns with the priorities and values of sustainability. Just enough has been done to create a usable, aesthetically pleasing chess set.

The only tools required were a fine-toothed cross-cut saw and sandpaper. Waste and pollution are minimal because the naturally occurring forms are essentially retained. Unused materials are entirely natural. The impact of this kind of approach relates not only to the making of a particular artefact, but extends to the 'non-use of' and 'non-need for' machine tools and *their* materials, manufacture, shipping, operation, draw on energy supplies, creation of emissions and eventual disposal. So we see that the ripple effects of our design decisions, even for an object as simple as this, can be wide-ranging and, potentially, could make a substantial contribution to sustainability.

A comparison of the Hartwig and *Balanis* designs, summarized in Table 8.1, demonstrates the relationship between the design of physical artefacts and the

Table 8.1 A comparison of the design factors in the Hartwig and the _Balanis_ chess sets

Design factors	'Hartwig' chess set design for industrial production	'Balanis' chess set design for sustainability
Materials	Selected on suitability for purpose. Materials are based on their ability to achieve the specifications of a predefined design. Prototyped in pear wood and stained pear wood.	Selected on availability for purpose. The design emerges by considering the particular qualities of an environmentally responsible, local material. Created from discarded, wind-fall, locally grown holm oak, with flax cord binding.
Form	Purely functional: expressive of its movement on the board.	Retains the character of the branch from which it came. Pieces are differentiated through height, girth and angle of the upper face.
	Formal differences in stature have been reduced, in line with modernity's emphasis on egalitarianism.	Formal differences in stature are indicative of identity and rank, in acknowledgement of the game's traditional form and aspect.
	Indications of rank via figurative forms have been eliminated. Differences here are indicative of the role and contribution of the piece in the game, and are in accord with meritocratic values.	Indications of rank via figurative forms are absent in recognition of modern sensibilities. Rank is indicated through stature, combined with upright aspect and cut angle, in recognition of the game's rich history.
	Standardized for mass-production and large markets – resulting in forms that are not specific to or reflective of any particular place.	Particularized through local production for local use – resulting in forms that are specific to and reflective of place, i.e. via local wood and 'raw' aesthetic.
	Machined, exact, geometric, uniform, repeatable.	Natural, irregular, organic, varied, unique.
	Anonymous, universal, instrumental, mass produced, narrow, form-follows-function.	Appreciative, located, intrinsic, one-off, holistic, form-follows-meaning.
Tools and making	In design for industrial production, which the Bauhaus was exploring, the pieces are accurately machined into predetermined shapes. Precision machine tools are required, necessitating their manufacture, shipping, use, draw on energy supplies, emissions and eventual disposal.	The shape of each piece is determined partly by Nature and partly through selection of the natural branch. Variations in height and angle of cut, both determined by eye, create formal differences between pieces. Tools required are minimal – a cross-cut hand saw and sandpaper.
	Controlling, energy-intensive, polluting, noisy, wasteful.	Yielding, low-energy, clean, quiet, prudent.
Finishing	Natural forms and textures have been completely eliminated.	Natural forms and textures have been largely retained.
Design ethos	The shape of each piece fits within a rationalized system that governs the relationship of form to function.	The shape of each piece is partly natural, partly imposed, and is a function of a particularized response to natural elements.

125

stories and moralities a society tells itself to justify its actions in the world. Modernity's ideas of morality are clearly expressed in Hartwig's chess set, whereas the *Balanis* design represents an attempt to express a broader, more inclusive set of values that combine (1) contemporary concerns for the natural environment and social equality with (2) the importance of tradition and history, and priorities that challenge the still dominant place of rationalization, efficiency and functionalism.

Design outcome

An important property of this chess set design is its rudimentary form, which speaks not of meticulousness, accuracy and control but of connectedness, not of artifice and prescribed allure, but of Nature's inherent beauty and non-fabricated is-ness. The design intervention is intended to be *just enough* to convey the character of each piece. This minimal, non-aggressive intervention is achieved through an approach that combines intuitive responses with gentle, adaptive ways of working. By combining direct, personal awareness of the material at hand with the spontaneously 'felt', the features and innate properties of the material are retained. Through its visual and tactile qualities, the design is a tangible, lightly modified memento of Nature, reminding us of our closeness to the earth and our dependence on its provision. This is a different kind of connectedness from that afforded by digital devices and offers a counterpoint to their synthetic materials and globalized mass-production methods.

126   Rather than attempting to control Nature and force-fit it to match our precise desires, this design is in keeping with ways of being and doing that flow with and yield to the warp and weave of Nature – an ethos that is perhaps most clearly expressed in the Taoist tradition.[64] The forming of materials is with Nature, not against it, and this is apparent in the design outcome. In minimizing the intervention, the form of each chess piece becomes a function of Nature's forms – produced as much by sun, wind and rain as by human hand and will. As a consequence, artefacts for human use become tangible expressions of a less invasive attitude and more closely aligned with a culture of environmental care.

The overall form of the chess set – in its upright aspect and its hierarchical character, with the king being the tallest, stoutest piece and the pawn the shortest, narrowest piece – is true to the traditional societal hierarchy in which chess is rooted. This traditional hierarchy is quite different from that found in modern, secular meritocracies in which moralities emphasize fairness, autonomy and egalitarian relationships but place less emphasis on loyalty, authority, sanctity, duty and tradition.[65] However, notions of tradition and obligation, as well as spirituality and sanctity, tend to be more prominent aspects of contemporary discussions around environmental care, social justice and spiritual wellbeing, which attempt to counter the perceived narrowing and shallowing effects of 'consumer' society. In addition, in this chess set design, figurative elements that would result in a more literal expression of rank and identity have not been included, partly in recognition of contemporary sensibilities, and partly to minimize both the extent of the intervention and any unnecessary detail.

Hence, the design is the result of a conscious attempt to arrive at a suitable outcome through modest means. By doing less, we retain Nature's forms and textures. Rather than strictly defining every detail, we allow natural characteristics to remain and their presence bestows unique details and aesthetic qualities. Thus, the design can be seen as an attempt to reach a fitting conciliation between human imposition and the existing, natural condition. The design outcome is neither wholly natural nor wholly prescribed.

Conclusions

This discussion is not about chess *per se* but, because design is located in the details of the particular, we are bound to explore *designing sustainability* and the issues it raises within the domain of the specific. Here, the chess set – a traditional, simple, non-technological object – is used as a vehicle for exploring these specifics of design. The details of the design considerations and decisions, the story of its provenance, and its comparison with a modernist chess set from the Bauhaus, collectively reveal how *designing sustainability* differs from the modernist approaches that continue to dominate contemporary design. It illustrates how meanings related to history, myth and location can add to one's understanding and appreciation of an object. It shows how, through design decisions, minimal intervention combined with a sensitivity to the qualitative characteristics of materials can lead to an outcome that is functionally useful and aesthetically – visually and tactilely – both distinctive and close to Nature; and as discussed, this closeness to Nature has long been associated with notions of spiritual wellbeing. The minimal form of the design – where the identity of each piece is attained essentially through one saw-cut – makes a local, handmade product readily achievable, obviating the need for machine tools, energy use and pollution, packaging and transportation. Locally made artefacts, using simple techniques, can help create good work and contribute to a local economy. And the fact that the object is made entirely of natural materials means that its eventual disposal will not be environmentally harmful.

127

The simplicity of this object brings key design issues to the fore. It illustrates how the *quadruple bottom line* can allow design to contribute to the practical, social and personal meanings of our material culture while, potentially, also offering economic opportunities at the local level. The challenge lies in how such approaches might be effectively extended to inform the design of more technologically sophisticated products – products that often tend to distance us further from a direct relationship with the natural environment.[66]

We can start to address this challenge by reflecting on the approaches explored here, which centre on the contemplative and the cognizant. They involve being aware of materials, their origins and their historical and cultural associations. They involve being more fully aware of the materials themselves and their particular characteristics and features, which can be built on rather than eradicated during the creative process. And they involve being aware of the forming processes – the making – and their effects on ourselves, our locality and our planet. Energy use, pollution and waste are part of this, but we can also consider the violence and violation of many of the processes we have come to take for granted, the noise pollution and the manner in which we have come to industrialize Nature's bounty, and the potential benefits of imprecision and sufficiency. Being cognizant of and contemplating these things can enable us to better appreciate the correlation between our ways of thinking and doing, and their effects – not just on the natural environment, but also on ourselves. If there is a relationship between spiritual wellbeing and our experiences of the natural environment, as so many traditions down the ages have suggested, then in damaging Nature and distancing ourselves from it, we are also eroding our own routes to peace of mind and happiness.

9
Epilogue

In this strange school the inward eye detects
A hundred thousand yearning intellects,
But failure dogs the analytic mind

Farid Ud-Din Attar

According to Tolstoy, our contrived, blinkered world of abstracted rationality should be seen as a strange psychological condition, one that pronounces sounds independently of concepts, that generates fear, strains memory and attention and crushes imagination and creativeness.[1] To glimpse beyond this impoverished view of reality, we have to learn to see anew, with a widened perspective and a deeper level of attention. And we have to learn to approach such seeing with a different attitude – one that quietens our tendencies towards inquisitiveness and acquisitiveness and instead seeks repose, openness and acceptance; an attitude that seeks not to *do* or to *have* but to *be*. It is here, in *being*, that we find composure, a respect for what is and a more modest idea of needs.

Following Merton's description of contemplation,[2] the design approach discussed in this book, with its emphasis on inner values and spiritual development, is one rooted in the natural processes of life and suffused by an attitude of humility, attention to reality, receptivity and flexibility. One that attempts to set aside cynicism, hardness of heart, coarseness of mind and an ignorance of reality through narrowness, technological distancing and abstraction. Cultivating such design draws us towards an outlook that is more accepting, more yielding and less grasping. One that enables us to see our current endeavours from a new perspective, that challenges assumptions and allows us to move forward in ways that are creative, constructive and, importantly, that are taking a different path from that which has characterized so many design decades of busy-ness, dis-harmony and environmental destruction.

The discussions and the artefacts I have presented here represent one attempt to reach beyond entrenched attitudes and conventions to show, through creative practice, some possible routes for reconceiving our notions of material culture and its relationship both to the natural environment and to our perennial search for meaning and fulfilment. Through a series of inquiries that explored values and attitudes, design and spirituality, knowledge and wisdom and non-utilitarian contemplative objects in various guises – the religious, the subordinate, the trans-religious and the non-made – we returned, finally, to the functional object, in the form of a simple chess set. The route taken permitted the inclusion of new insights and the adoption of what might be understood as a more pliant approach in which the natural and the human-made are combined – neither seeking dominance but both, hopefully, residing in balanced accord. Comparing this design outcome with the chess set from the Bauhaus school allowed us to distinguish how our values and attitudes affect and become articulated through the designed object.

130

From such explorations and discussions it becomes clear that, in changing our values and attitudes, the nature of material culture is also changed. As a result our understandings of and responses to material culture are altered and this, in turn, reinforces a shift in values and attitudes. In this way we see that design can make an important and potentially powerful contribution to a dynamic, virtuous circle of positive development that helps take us towards more meaningful, more fulfilling and, critically, more sustainable ways of living. In advancing this course, design can be seen as a continual inquiry and propositional objects as a series of questions. Moreover, propositional objects, such as those presented here, are not created with multiple repetitions in mind. The discipline of design, as it emerged over the twentieth century and as it is still largely conceived, aims to define an object that can be accurately reproduced; the precise design definition being meticulously followed. Propositional objects are not for reproduction. Their reliance on local and found materials and serendipitous features – such as the knots in wood bark or the markings and shape of a rock, make exact reproduction impossible. Instead, these objects serve as pointers to a way of creating our material culture that 'allows in' the unpredictable and uncontrolled contributions of nature and, in doing so, diminishes the designer's impositions on the natural world. But the purpose is not simply damage control. By minimizing our will over Nature and doing less, we become more cognizant of the natural world. Unadulterated materials, textures, colours and unmanufactured complexities provide a positive and affirming backdrop to our daily lives. By reducing our control over Nature and allowing Nature's objects to be purposeful while also being themselves, we begin to reach a conception of material culture that is both sustainable and meaningful.

Putting these contributions in perspective, it is important to recognize that today's problems of economic disparity, social injustice, conflict and environmental degradation are not new. These things have characterized human societies for millennia. The human project has always been one of seeking justice, wisdom and virtue in a world that continually seems to thwart such hopes. Throughout history certain individuals have spoken out against such iniquities, advocating self-restraint and sobriety and spurning worldly wealth, extravagance and superfluity. In Plato's Republic, Socrates describes life in an imagined city. His first suggestion for a just city, which provides the basis for subsequent dialogues, is one in which people's needs are met through ways of living that are moderate and limited. Material goods are made from natural constituents and are basic and unpretentious. Meals are simple and mainly vegetarian, and some modest luxuries are afforded. This city of sufficiency allows for social justice to prevail and poverty and injustice to be avoided. People live healthily, happily and in peace. However, as the discussion continues, it becomes clear that the pursuit of luxurious ways of life and unlimited material possessions is a formula for injustice and conflict and is the origin of war.[3] The Republic was written over two millennia ago but despite all our advances in scientific knowledge and technological capability, the same questions about how we should live confront each new generation.

Inequality, immorality and injustice in today's world are only too prevalent and plain to see. Enormous wealth exists alongside debilitating poverty and, invidiously, the poor and the least able are often blamed and vilified by the wealthy for their neediness.[4] Going hand in hand with these gross disparities is rampant environmental destruction which, in the stripping of the earth's substance, often makes the wealthy wealthier while simultaneously intensifying the deprivations of the most disadvantaged. The engine for this, which has made contemporary societies so voracious in their procurement of natural materials, is consumerism – this is the prime mover for the creation and concentration of wealth. The immoderate production and consumption of non-essential goods is the critical driver of our economic system and therefore can be seen as the critical driver of resource use, energy use, waste production, pollution of air, water and land, the creation of individual dissatisfaction, social disparity, inequity and injustice. It is this system, therefore, that has to change.

To do this, we will need something to put in the place of consumerism. Hence, we will need to develop an outlook that finds fulfilment in things other than the accoutrements of convenience and status. Fortunately, there are precedents from which we might learn – a philosophical precedent has already been mentioned. Another, more prevalent in times prior to modernity, was that of the spiritual path, which was manifested via religion. This was a path that generally shunned material wealth and luxury because they were seen as obstacles to inner development. It

131

was also a path that defied simplistic literalness and reached beyond the compass of philosophical materialism, which so characterized modernity. Today, in a period of postmodernity, we must find a similar inner path, but one more suited to our globalized, multicultural times – a path informed by one's own culturally rooted tradition but generous and cooperative enough to recognize the spiritual truths, inner values and ethical teachings of all the great traditions, including atheist and humanist forms of inner development.

Furthermore, in acknowledging and learning from other ways of encountering the world – ways that are potentially more benign, just and meaningful – we must apprehend the entrenched and often debilitating characteristics of our own conventions and cultural norms. Today, in our insatiable pursuit of knowledge, we tend to view the world through a specialized and therefore confined frame. Within this frame, our individualized rationalizations gain an atomized logic but such knowledge, derived from a restricted perspective, binds us to mundane minutiae and in doing so prevents us from gaining a more holistic view and from appreciating the wider ramifications of our decision-making. Hence, these narrow, discipline-specific viewpoints tend to inhibit a more meaningful joined-up understanding of our world and ourselves. This seeking after and continual advancement of mundane knowledge, which has become the primary preoccupation of our universities, is a function of the modern mind. Prior to modernity the acquisition of knowledge and engagement in argument were seen as lesser occupations to the pursuit of spiritual advancement, charitable love and wisdom. 'Knowledge without love does not edify', recalls the fourteenth-century English mystic Richard Rolle.[5, 6] Such teachings offer a quite different way of looking at the world from our own. As such, they provide a useful counterpoint to contemporary preoccupations and show us that a powerful alternative to consumption is at least possible. It is an alternative that has, over generations, offered a path to individual fulfilment and meaning while concurrently advocating charitable love and compassion towards others, particularly society's neediest. So it would seem not unreasonable to pause in our endeavours and consider these other ways of looking at the world and what we might learn from them in developing more healthy, more sustainable and more meaningful ways forward, particularly as it is the modern rather than the pre-modern perspective that is associated with unprecedented scales of environmental devastation, social disparity, overpopulation and disenchantment.

These earlier teachings advised of the dangers of yielding to base pleasures and desires, and that love of worldly things distanced us from spiritual advancement. In stark contrast, worldly luxury is, today, constantly promoted as the ultimate goal because 'we deserve it' and unbridled curiosity is seen as a good thing, not least because it can spur innovation, technological advancement and profit. But traditionally the acquisition of knowledge was seen as a potential source of individual pride and puffery and such worldly things were regarded as obstacles to the spiritual path and the pursuit of wisdom, which were considered the source of goodness, virtue and individual happiness.[7]

It would seem, therefore, that to come to grips with the project of sustainability we have to move towards a way of looking at and understanding the world that is more holistic, where perspectives and conventional specialties become more interconnected, interdependent and transcategorical.[8] Such an outlook is antithetical to the main principles of modernity, which tended to separate, disconnect and invariably narrow our field of vision. Yet the influence of modernity still dominates the economically developed countries, despite inroads associated with postmodernity, and it offers a powerful precedent to the economically emerging nations.

Consequently, the pursuit of sustainability behoves us to consider:

- notions of meaning-seeking beyond our own, including the world's great philosophical and religious traditions;
- practical needs and wants within a larger notion of personhood;
- notions of social justice beyond an ethics of compliance but contextualized within a panorama that includes universal, spiritually reifying understandings of empathy, compassion and neighbourly love;
- the effects of damage and destruction on the natural world;
- the effects of human-made environmental abuse and degradation on others and on our own individual sense of spiritual wellbeing and inner peace.

However, perhaps the biggest shift we have to make is from an attitude of *doing* and *having* to one of *being*. Therefore, we should measure our contribution to sustainability not by how much we can do, but by how much we can do without.

Notes

1 Introduction

[1] The UK Prime Minister, David Cameron, asserts that, 'Britain is in a global race to succeed today'. Speech to the CBI, 19 November 2012, available at www.number10.gov.uk/news/speech-to-cbi, accessed 5 February 2013.

[2] Cain, S. (2013) *Quiet: The Power of Introverts in a World that Can't Stop Talking*, Penguin Books, London, p74.

[3] Papanek, V. (1971 [1984]) *Design for the Real World: Human Ecology and Social Change*, 2nd edition, Thames & Hudson, London.

[4] John Keats (1795–1821) wrote, 'A thing of beauty is a joy forever', in the poem 'Endymion', *Selected Poems*, Penguin Books, London, p38.

[5] O'Neill, S. J., Boykoff, M., Niemeyer, S. and Day, S. A. (2013) 'On the use of imagery for climate change engagement', *Global Environmental Change*, Elsevier, pp1–9, available at SciVerse ScienceDirect, http://sciencepolicy.colorado.edu/admin/publication_files/2013.02.pdf, accessed 30 January 2013, p8.

2 The Object of Nightingales: design values for a meaningful material culture

An earlier version of this chapter appeared in the *Design and Culture Journal*, vol 4, no 2, pp149–170 (copyright 2012). With kind permission of Berg Publishers, an imprint of A&C Black Publishers Ltd.

[1] Mason, D. (1998) *Bomber Command: Recordings from the Second World War*, CD Liner Notes, Pavilion Records Ltd, Wadhurst, UK.

[2] RAF History (2005) *Bomber Command: Campaign Diary May 1942*, available at www.raf.mod.uk/bombercommand/may42.html, accessed 18 March 2011.

[3] Stevenson, R. L. (1888) 'The lantern bearers', in Treglown, J. (ed.), *The Lantern Bearers and Other Essays*, Cooper Square Press, New York, 1988, p231.

[4] Tucker, S. (1998) 'ChristStory nightingale page', *ChristStory Christian Bestiary*, available at ww2.netnitco.net/users/legend01/nighting.htm, accessed 19 March 2011.

[5] The term 'the great wisdom traditions' refers to those philosophical, religious and/or spiritual traditions that emerged from the so-called Axial Age. These include the Abrahamic religions, Buddhism, Hinduism, Taoism, Confucianism and the classical European philosophies of Plato, Socrates and Aristotle.[6] Even though there is clearly much diversity among these traditions, all respond to humanity's deepest questions about the nature of reality, its values, its meaning and its purpose.[7] While acknowledging that their cosmologies and social conventions have been superseded, Smith maintains that their teachings about how we should live and about the nature of reality represent the essential wisdom of humanity. In addition, he indicates where these traditions speak with a more or less common voice:

- Ethical principles – how we ought to act; i.e. do not murder, steal, etc.
- Virtue – how we ought to be if we are to live authentic lives; i.e. not putting oneself above others (humility), giving due regard to the needs of others (charity) and truthfulness to the way things really are (veracity).
- A recognition that humanity's limited perspective allows only a partial, fragmented view of reality – one that leaves us unaware of its integrated nature. The great wisdom traditions represent humanity's most enduring and profound inferences and teachings about the meaning of, and our relationship to, this whole, which is considered *better* than any concept of it we may infer, indeed, it is regarded as perfection itself (*Tao, Nirvana, Brahman, Allah*, etc.). Moreover, this unity, this highest value, is beyond human capacity to fully grasp; at most, we perceive only fleeting glimpses.[8]

Lewis, among others, expresses similar sentiments, arguing that these understandings of meaning and human values have never been surpassed and are as relevant today as ever.[9]

[6] Armstrong, K. (2002) *Islam: A Short History*, Phoenix Press, London, p6.

[7] Smith, H. (1991) *The World's Religions* (revised edition), HarperSanFrancisco, New York, pp386–389.

[8] Smith, H. (1991) *The World's Religions* (revised edition), HarperSanFrancisco, New York, pp386–389.

[9] Lewis, C. S. (1947) *The Abolition of Man.* HarperCollins Publishers, New York, p43.

[10] Nietzsche, F. (1889 [2003]) *Twilight of the Idols and the Anti-Christ*, Penguin Group, London, pp61–81.

[11] Thoreau, H. D. (1854 [1983]) 'Walden in Thoreau', H. D., *Walden and Civil Disobedience*, Penguin Group, New York, 1983, pp45–382.

[12] Horkheimer, M. and Adorno, T. W. (1947 [2010]) 'The culture industry: enlightenment as mass-deception', in Leitch, V. B. (ed.), *The Norton Anthology of Theory and Criticism*, 2nd edition, W. W. Norton, London, pp1110–1127.

[13] Schumacher, E. F. (1973) *Small is Beautiful*, Sphere Books Ltd, London.

[14] Hick, J. (2002) *Science/Religion*. A talk given at King Edward VI Camp Hill School, Birmingham, March 2002, available at www.johnhick.org.uk/jsite/index.php?option=com_content&view=article&id=52:sr&catid=37:articles&Itemid=58, accessed 19 February 2011, p1.

[15] Taylor, C. (2007) *A Secular Age*, The Belknap Press of Harvard University Press, Cambridge, MA, p28.

[16] Taylor, C. (2007) *A Secular Age*, The Belknap Press of Harvard University Press, Cambridge, MA, p246.

[17] Taylor, C. (2007) *A Secular Age*, The Belknap Press of Harvard University Press, Cambridge, MA, pp716–717.

[18] Tillich, P. (1952 [2000]) *The Courage to Be*, 2nd edition, Yale University Press, New Haven, CT, pp105–111.

[19] Mathews, F. (2006) 'Beyond modernity and tradition: a third way for development', *Ethics & the Environment*, vol. 11, no. 2, p90.

[20] Beattie, T. (2007) *The New Atheists: The Twilight of Reason & The War on Religion*, Darton, Longman & Todd Ltd, London, p134.

[21] Holloway, R. (2000) *Godless Morality*, Canongate, Edinburgh, pp16, 151–157.

[22] Jessop, T. E. (1967) 'Nietzsche, Friedrich', in MacQuarrie, J. (ed.), *A Dictionary of Christian Ethics*, SCM Press Ltd, London, p233.

[23] Smith, H. (2005) 'Foreword' in Johnston, W. (ed.) *The Cloud of Unknowing and the Book of Privy Counseling*, Image Books, Doubleday, New York, p1.

[24] Cottingham, J. (2005) *The Spiritual Dimension: Religion, Philosophy and Human Value,* Cambridge University Press, Cambridge, pp109–110.

[25] Smith, H. (1996 [2005]) 'Foreword' in Johnston, W. (ed.) *The Cloud of Unknowing & the Book of Privy Counseling*, Image Books, Doubleday, New York, pp1–2.

[26] Cottingham, J. (2005) *The Spiritual Dimension: Religion, Philosophy and Human Value,* Cambridge University Press, Cambridge, p110.

[27] Walker, S. (2011) *The Spirit of Design: Objects, Environment and Meaning*, Earthscan, Abingdon, pp185–210.

[28] Hick, J. (1989) *An Interpretation of Religion: Human Responses to the Transcendent,*Yale University Press, New Haven, CT, pp129–171.

[29] Comte-Sponville, A. (2007) *The Book of Atheist Spirituality: An Elegant Argument for Spirituality without God*, trans. Huston, N. Bantam Books, London, pp168–169.

[30] Hick, J. (2004) 'The real and it's personae and impersonae', a revised version of an article in Tessier, L. (ed.) (1989) *Concepts of the Ultimate*, Macmillan, London, available at www.johnhick.org.uk/jsite/index.php?option=com_

content&view=article&id=57:thereal&catid=37:articles&Itemid=58, accessed 19 February 2011.

[31] King, U. (2009) *The Search for Spirituality: Our Global Quest for Meaning and Fulfilment*, Canterbury Press, Norwich, p14.

[32] Needleman, J. (1989) 'Introduction' in *Tao Te Ching*, trans. Feng, G. F. and English, J., Vintage Books, New York 1989, pvi.

[33] Cottingham, J. (2005) *The Spiritual Dimension: Religion, Philosophy and Human Value*, Cambridge University Press, Cambridge, p140.

[34] Papanek, V. (1971 [1984]) *Design for the Real World: Human Ecology and Social Change*, 2nd edition, Thames & Hudson, London.

[35] Jackson, T. (2009) *Prosperity without Growth: Economics for a Finite Planet*, Earthscan, London, p32.

[36] Eagleton, T. (2009) *Reason, Faith and Revolution: Reflections on the God Debate*, Yale University Press, New Haven, CT, p39.

[37] Lindsey, E. (2010) *Curating Humanity's Heritage*. TEDWomen, December, available at www.ted.com/talks/elizabeth_lindsey_curating_humanity_s_heritage. htm, posted February 2011, accessed 21 March 2011.

[38] Lewis, C. S. (1947) *The Abolition of Man*, HarperCollins Publishers, New York, p13.

[39] Lewis, C. S. (1947) *The Abolition of Man*, HarperCollins Publishers, New York, pp39–40.

[40] Yamakage, M. (2006) *The Essence of Shinto: Japan's Spiritual Heart*, Kodansha International, Tokyo, p12.

[41] Hick, J. (1989) *An Interpretation of Religion: Human Responses to the Transcendent*, Yale University Press, New Haven, CT, p11.

[42] Tillich, P. (1952 [2000]) *The Courage to Be*, 2nd edition, Yale University Press, New Haven, CT, pp180–181.

[43] Comte-Sponville, A. (2007) *The Book of Atheist Spirituality: An Elegant Argument for Spirituality without God*, trans. Huston, N. Bantam Books, London, p168.

[44] Aristotle's *Ethics*, 1106a.

[45] *Analects of Confucius*, 6.29.

[46] Lewis, C. S. (1947) *The Abolition of Man*, HarperCollins Publishers, New York, p18.

[47] Cottingham, J. (2005) *The Spiritual Dimension: Religion, Philosophy and Human Value*, Cambridge University Press, Cambridge, p168.

[48] Aristotle's *Ethics*, 1103b, 1104b, 1144b.

[49] Lewis, C. S. (1947) *The Abolition of Man*, HarperCollins Publishers, New York, p18.

[50] Lewis, C. S. (1947) *The Abolition of Man*, HarperCollins Publishers, New York, p19.

[51] *Analects of Confucius*, 15.23.

[52] Plato's *Crito*, 49c–d.

[53] *Tao Te Ching*, 49.

54 *Bhagavad Gita*, 12.

55 *Dhammapada*, 10.130.

56 *Leviticus*, 19:18.

57 *Matthew*, 7:12.

58 *Hadith of an-Nawawi*, 13.

59 Bakan, J. (2004) *The Corporation: The Pathological Pursuit of Profit and Power*, Constable & Robinson Ltd, London, p134.

60 *Tao Te Ching*, 3.

61 *Dhammapada*, 16.

62 Camus, A. (1942 [2005]) *The Myth of Sisyphus*, Penguin Books, London, pp115–116.

63 Tillich, P. (1952 [2000]) *The Courage to Be*, 2nd edition, Yale University Press, New Haven, CT, pp171–190.

64 Stevens, D. (2007) *Rural*, Mermaid Turbulence, Leitrim, Ireland, pp97–175.

65 Manzini, E. and Jégou, F. (2003) *Sustainable Everyday: Scenarios for Urban Life*, Edizioni Ambiente, Milan, pp172–177.

66 Power, T. M. (2000) 'Trapped in consumption: modern social structure and the entrenchment of the device', in Higgs, E., Light, A. and Strong, D. (eds), *Technology and the Good Life*, University of Chicago Press, Chicago, IL, p271.

67 Carr, N. (2010) *The Shallows: How the Internet is Changing the Way we Think, Read and Remember*, Atlantic Books, London, p119.

68 Chan, J., de Haan, E., Nordbrand, S. and Torstensson, A. (2008) *Silenced to Deliver: Mobile phone Manufacturing in China and the Philippines*, SOMO and SwedWatch, Stockholm, Sweden, available at www.germanwatch.org/corp/it-chph08.pdf, accessed 30 March 2011, pp24–26.

69 Jackson, T. (2009) *Prosperity without Growth: Economics for a Finite Planet*, Earthscan, London, pp32–33.

70 Day, C. (1998) *Art and Spirit: Spirit and Place – Consensus Design*, available at www.fantastic-machine.com/artandspirit/spirit-and-place/consensus.html, accessed 28 March 2011.

71 Armstrong, K. (1994) *Visions of God: Four Medieval Mystics and their Writings*, Bantam Books, New York, pp x–xi.

138

3 Design on a Darkling Plain: transcending utility through questions in form

An earlier version of this chapter appeared in *The Design Journal*, vol. 15, no. 3, pp347–372 (copyright 2012). With kind permission of Berg Publishers, an imprint of A&C Black Publishers Ltd.

1 Carlson, D. and Richards, B. (2010) *David Report: Time to ReThink Design*, Falsterbo, Sweden, issue 12, March, available at http://static.davidreport.com/pdf/371.pdf, accessed 20 May 2011.

[2] EIA (2011) *System Failure: The UK's Harmful Trade in Electronic Waste*, Environmental Investigation Agency, London, available at www.eia-international. org/files/news640-1.pdf, accessed 20 May 2011.

[3] SACOM (2011) 'Foxconn and Apple fail to fulfill promises: predicaments of workers after the suicides', Report of Students and Scholars against Corporate Misbehaviour, Hong Kong, 6 May 2011, available at http://sacom.hk/wp-content/uploads/2011/05/2011-05-06_foxconn-and-apple-fail-to-fulfill-promises1.pdf, accessed 20 May 2011.

[4] Turkle, S. (2011) *Alone Together: Why We Expect More from Technology and Less from Each Other*, Basic Books, New York, pp278, 293–296.

[5] Lanier, J. (2010) *You Are Not a Gadget: A Manifesto*, Penguin Books, London, p75.

[6] Branzi, A. (2009) *Grandi Legni* [exhibition catalogue essay], Design Gallery Milano and Nilufar, Milan.

[7] Bhamra, T. and Lofthouse, V. (2007) *Design for Sustainability: A Practical Approach*, Gower, Aldershot, pp27, 66.

[8] Davison, A. (2001) *Technology and the Contested Meanings of Sustainability*, State University of New York Press, Albany, NY, pp22, 39.

[9] Senge, P., Smith, B., Kruschwitz, N., Laur, J. and Schley, S. (2008) *The Necessary Revolution: How Individuals and Organizations are Working Together to Create a Sustainable World*, Nicholas Brealey Publishing, London, pp6–8.

[10] Princen, T. (2006) 'Consumption and its externalities: where economy meets ecology', in Jackson, T. (ed.), *Sustainable Consumption*, Earthscan, London, pp50–66.

[11] Scharmer, C. O. (2009) *Theory U: Leading from the Future as it Emerges*, Berrett-Koehler Publishers, San Francisco, CA, p5.

[12] Senge, P., Smith, B., Kruschwitz, N., Laur, J. and Schley, S. (2008) *The Necessary Revolution: How Individuals and Organizations are Working Together to Create a Sustainable World*, Nicholas Brealey Publishing, London, p11.

[13] Burns, B. (2010) 'Re-evaluating obsolescence and planning for it', in Cooper, T. (ed.), *Longer Lasting Products: Alternatives to the Throwaway Society*, Gower, Farnham, pp39–60.

[14] Park, M. (2010) 'Defying obsolescence', in Cooper, T. (ed.), *Longer Lasting Products: Alternatives to the Throwaway Society*, Gower, Farnham, pp77–105.

[15] Nair, C. (2011) *Consumptionomics: Asia's Role in Reshaping Capitalism and Saving the Planet*, Infinite Ideas, Oxford, p35.

[16] Daly, H. E. (2007) *Ecological Economics and Sustainable Development: Selected Essays of Herman Daly*, Edward Elgar Publishing, Cheltenham, pp117–123.

[17] Jackson, T. (2009) *Prosperity without Growth: Economics for a Finite Planet*, Earthscan, London, p123.

[18] Borgmann, A. (2003) *Power Failure: Christianity in the Culture of Technology*, Brazos Press, Grand Rapids, MI, p81.

[19] Herzfeld, N. (2009) *Technology and Religion: Remaining Human in a Co-Created World*, Templeton Press, West Conshohocken, PA, p87.

139

[20] Steele, T. J. (1984) *Santos and Saints: The Religious Folk Art of Hispanic New Mexico*, Ancient City Press, Santa Fe, NM, p1.

[21] Ware, K. (1987) 'The theology and spirituality of the icon', in *From Byzantium to El Greco: Greek Frescoes and Icons*, Royal Academy of Arts, London, pp37–39.

[22] Carr, N. (2010) *The Shallows: How the Internet is Changing the Way we Think, Read and Remember*, Atlantic Books, London, pp168, 220.

[23] Herzfeld, N. (2009) *Technology and Religion: Remaining Human in a Co-Created World*, Templeton Press, West Conshohocken, PA, p89.

[24] Scharmer, C. O. (2009) *Theory U: Leading from the Future as it Emerges*, Berrett-Koehler Publishers, San Francisco, CA, pp90–92.

[25] Orr, D. W. (2003) *Four Challenges of Sustainability*, School of Natural Resources – The University of Vermont, Spring Seminar Series 2003 – Ecological Economics, available at www.ratical.org/co-globalize/4CofS.html, accessed 17 May 2011.

[26] Porritt, J. (2007) *Capitalism as if the World Matters*, Earthscan, London, p322.

[27] Lanier, J. (2010) *You Are Not a Gadget: A Manifesto*, Penguin Books, London, p75.

[28] Eagleton, T. (2007) *The Meaning of Life*, Oxford University Press, Oxford, p20.

[29] Smith, H. (2001) *Why Religion Matters: The Fate of the Human Spirit in an Age of Disbelief*, HarperCollins, New York, p200.

[30] Buchanan, R. (1995) 'Rhetoric, humanism and design', in Buchanan, R. and Margolin, V. (eds), *Discovering Design: Explorations in Design Studies*, University of Chicago Press, Chicago, IL, pp23–66.

[31] Borgmann, A. (2000) 'Society in the postmodern era', *The Washington Quarterly*, Winter, available at www.twq.com/winter00/231Borgmann.pdf, accessed 26 April 2011, pp196–197.

[32] Bakan, J. (2004) *The Corporation: The Pathological Pursuit of Profit and Power*, Constable & Robinson, London, p34.

[33] Kelly, M. (2001) *The Divine Right of Capital*, Berret-Koehler, San Francisco, CA quoted in Porritt, J. (2007) *Capitalism as if the World Matters*, Earthscan, London, p199.

[34] Gandhi (1925) *The Collected Works of Mahatma Gandhi*, vol. 33, no. 25, September 1925–10 February 1926 (excerpt from *Young India*, 22 October 1925), available at www.gandhiserve.org/cwmg/VOL033.PDF, accessed 12 May 2011, p135.

[35] Borgmann, A. (2001) 'Opaque and articulate design', *International Journal of Technology and Design Education*, vol. 11, pp5–11.

[36] Leonard, A. (2010) *The Story of Stuff*, Constable, London, pp78, 281–291.

[37] Arnold, M. (2006 [1869]) *Culture and Anarchy*, Oxford University Press, Oxford, pp34, 55, 153.

[38] Horkheimer, M. and Adorno, T. W. (1947 [2010]) 'Dialectic of enlightenment', in Leitch, V. B. (ed.), *The Norton Anthology of Theory and Criticism*, 2nd edition, W. W. Norton, New York, pp1110–1127.

[39] Papanek, V. (1971 [1984]) *Design for the Real World*, Human Ecology and Social Change 2nd edition, Thames & Hudson, London, pp ix, 248–284.

[40] Papanek, V. (1995) *The Green Imperative: Ecology and Ethics in Design and Architecture*, Thames & Hudson, London, p54.

[41] Daly, H. E. (2007) *Ecological Economics and Sustainable Development: Selected Essays of Herman Daly*, Edward Elgar Publishing, Cheltenham, p89.

[42] Daly, H. E. (2007) *Ecological Economics and Sustainable Development: Selected Essays of Herman Daly*, Edward Elgar Publishing, Cheltenham, pp19–23.

[43] Meroni, A. (ed.) (2007) *Creative Communities: People Inventing Sustainable Ways of Living*, Edizioni Poli.design, Milan.

[44] Peters, G. P., Minx, J. C., Weber, C. L. and Edenhoffer, O. (2011) 'Growth in emission transfers via international trade from 1990 to 2008', *Proceedings of the National Academy of Sciences of the United States of America (PNAS)*, open access article published online 25 April, available at www.pnas.org/content/early/2011/04/19/1006388108, accessed 26 April 2011.

[45] Jackson, T. (2009) *Prosperity without Growth: Economics for a Finite Planet*, Earthscan, London, pp171–185.

[46] Buchanan, R. (1995) 'Rhetoric, humanism and design', in Buchanan, R. and Margolin, V. (eds), *Discovering Design: Explorations in Design Studies*, University of Chicago Press, Chicago, IL, pp23–66.

[47] Lewis, C. S. (1947) *The Abolition of Man*, HarperCollins Publishers, New York, p18.

[48] Grayling, A. C. (2011) 'Epistle to the reader', foreword of *The Good Book: A Secular Bible*, Bloomsbury Publishing, London.

[49] Schumacher, E. F. (1973) *Small is Beautiful: A Study of Economics as if People Mattered*, Abacus, Reading.

[50] Schumacher, E. F. (1977) *A Guide for the Perplexed*, Vintage Publishing, London, p58.

[51] Schumacher, E. F. (1977) *A Guide for the Perplexed*, Vintage Publishing, London, p143.

[52] Schumacher, E. F. (1977) *A Guide for the Perplexed*, Vintage Publishing, London, p148.

[53] Buchanan, R. (1995) 'Rhetoric, humanism and design', in Buchanan, R. and Margolin, V. (eds), *Discovering Design: Explorations in Design Studies*, University of Chicago Press, Chicago, IL, p26.

[54] Orr, D. W. (2003) *Four Challenges of Sustainability*, School of Natural Resources – The University of Vermont, Spring Seminar Series 2003 – Ecological Economics, available at www.ratical.org/co-globalize/4CofS.html, accessed 17 May 2011.

[55] Hawken, P. (2007) *Blessed Unrest: How the Largest Movement in the World Came into Being and Why No One Saw It Coming*, Viking, New York, pp184–188.

[56] Ehrenfeld, J. R. (2008) *Sustainability by Design: A Subversive Strategy for Transforming Our Consumer Culture*, Yale University Press, New Haven, CT, p23.

[57] Easwaran, E. (trans) (1985) *The Bhagavad Gita*, Vintage Books, New York, p xix.

141

[58] Needleman, J. (1991) *Money and the Meaning of Life*, Doubleday, New York, pp69, 95.

[59] Nicoll, M. (1954) *The Mark*, Vincent Stuart Publishers, London, pp3–4, 201.

[60] Nicoll, M. (1950 [1972]) *The New Man*, Penguin Books Inc., Baltimore, MD, pp1–2.

[61] Walker, S. (2009) 'The spirit of design: notes from the shakuhachi flute', *International Journal of Sustainable Design*, vol. 1, no. 2, pp130–144.

[62] Nicoll, M. (1954) *The Mark*, Vincent Stuart Publishers, London, pp3–4.

[63] Scruton, R. (2009) *Beauty*, Oxford University Press, Oxford, pp52–53.

[64] Jackson, T. (2006) 'Consuming paradise? Towards a social and cultural psychology of sustainable consumption', in Jackson, T. (ed.), *Sustainable Consumption*, Earthscan, London, pp367–395.

[65] Taylor, C. (2007) *A Secular Age*, The Belknap Press of Harvard University Press, Cambridge, MA, p717.

[66] Hick, J. (1989) *An Interpretation of Religion: Human Responses to the Transcendent*, Yale University Press, New Haven, CT, pp10–11.

[67] Wittgenstein, L. (1921b) *Tractatus Logico-Philosophicus*, Proposition 7, trans. C. K. Ogden, available at www.kfs.org/~jonathan/witt/tlph.html, accessed 17 May 2011.

[68] See the story of the Tower of Babel in Genesis 11:3 and its interpretation by Maurice Nicoll in Nicoll, M. (1950) *The New Man*, Penguin Books, Baltimore, MD, pp11–15.

[69] See the story of the Marriage of Cana in the Gospel of John 2:6–9 in the New Testament and its interpretation by Maurice Nicoll in Nicoll, M. (1950) *The New Man*, Penguin Books, Baltimore, MD, pp32–36.

[70] Scruton, R. (2009) *Beauty*, Oxford University Press, Oxford, p188.

[71] Dormer, P. (1990) *The Meanings of Modern Design*, Thames & Hudson, London, p43.

[72] Sparke, P. (2004) *An Introduction to Design and Culture: 1900 to the Present*, 2nd edition, Routledge, London, p65.

[73] Heskett, J. (1987) *Industrial Design*, Thames & Hudson, London, pp20–21.

4 Contemplative Objects: artefacts for challenging convention and stimulating change

An earlier version of this chapter appeared in *Behaviour Change, Consumption and Sustainable Design*, Crocker, R. and Lehmann, S. (eds), Earthscan Series on Sustainable Design, Routledge, Abingdon, Oxford, 2013, pp198–214. With kind permission of Routledge.

[1] Senge, P., Smith, B., Kruschwitz, N., Laur, J. and Schley, S. (2008) *The Necessary Revolution: How Individuals and Organizations are Working Together to Create a Sustainable World*, Nicholas Brealey, London, p5.

[2] Nair, C. (2011a) *Consumptionomics: Asia's Role in Reshaping Capitalism and Saving the Planet*, Infinite Ideas Ltd, Oxford, p76.

[3] Scruton, R. (2012a) *Green Philosophy: How to Think Seriously about the Planet*, Atlantic Books, London, pp2, 399.

[4] Jackson, T. (2009) *Prosperity without Growth: Economics for a Finite Planet*, Earthscan, London, pp130, 196.

[5] Walker, S. (2011) *The Spirit of Design: Objects, Environment and Meaning*, Earthscan, Abingdon, pp187–190; Figure 4.1 is a development of the version on p190 in this earlier work.

[6] Buchanan, R. (1989) 'Declaration by design: rhetoric, argument, and demonstration in design practice', in Margolin, V. (ed.), *Design Discourse: History, Theory, Criticism*, University of Chicago Press, Chicago, IL, pp91–109.

[7] Fry, T., Tonkinwise, C., Bremner, C., Fitzpatrick, L., Norton, L. and Lopera, D. (2011) *Future Tense: Design, Sustainability and the Urmadic University*, ABC National Radio, Australia, broadcast 4 August 2011, transcript available at www.abc.net.au/radionational/programs/futuretense/design-sustainability-and-the-urmadic-university/2928402, accessed 12 January 2012.

[8] Smith, H. (2001) *Why Religions Matters*, HarperCollins, New York, pp12, 59, 81.

[9] Davison, A. (2001) *Technology and the Contested Meanings of Sustainability*, State University of New York Press, Albany, NY, pp36–42.

[10] Northcott, M. S. (2007) *A Moral Climate: The Ethics of Global Warming*, Darton, Longman and Todd Ltd, London, pp175–177.

[11] Eagleton, T. (2011) *Why Marx Was Right*, Yale University Press, New Haven, CT, p8.

[12] Smith, H. (2001) *Why Religion Matter*, HarperCollins, San Francisco, CA, pp150–152.

[13] Eagleton, T. (2011) *Why Marx Was Right*, Yale University Press, New Haven, CT, pp9, 15.

[14] Duhigg, C. and Bradsher, K. (2012) 'How U.S. lost out in iPhone work', *New York Times*, 21 January 2012, available at www.nytimes.com/2012/01/22/business/apple-america-and-a-squeezed-middle-class.html, accessed 22 January 2012.

[15] Duhigg, C. and Bradsher, K. (2012) 'How U.S. lost out in iPhone work', *New York Times*, 21 January 2012, available at www.nytimes.com/2012/01/22/business/apple-america-and-a-squeezed-middle-class.html, accessed 22 January 2012.

[16] Borgmann, A. (2010) 'I miss the hungry years', *The Montana Professor* vol. 21, no. 1, pp4–7.

[17] Curtis, M. (2005a) 'Distraction technologies', in *Distraction: Being Human in the Digital Age*, Futuretext Ltd, London, pp53–69.

[18] Examples include: from Hinduism – the Katha Upanishad, (Mascaró, J. (trans.) (1965) *The Upanishads*, Penguin Group, London, pp.55–66, especially Part 2, p58); from Christianity – The Epistle of St. Paul to the Corinthians Ch. 7, vs. 30–32 in the New Testament of the Bible; and from Islam – the Spiritual Verses of Molānā Jalāloddin Balkhi, known in the West as Rumi (Williams, A. (trans) (2006)

Rumi: Spiritual Verses – The First Book of the Masnavi-ye Ma'navi, Penguin Books, London, vs. 2360–2364, p221).

[19] This summary description is a development of the *Quadruple Bottom Line of Design for Sustainability*, first presented in: Walker, S. (2011) *The Spirit of Design: Objects, Environment and Meaning*, Earthscan, Abingdon, pp187–190.

[20] Marx, K. and Engels, F. (1848 [2004]) *The Communist Manifesto*, Penguin Group, London, 2004.

[21] Thoreau, H. D. (1854 [1983]) 'Walden', in Thoreau, H. D. *Walden and Civil Disobedience*, Penguin Group, New York, 1983.

[22] Briggs, A. S. A. (ed.) (1962) 'Socialism', various writings in *William Morris: News From Nowhere and Selected Writings and Designs*, Penguin Group, London, pp158–180.

[23] Ruskin, J. (1862–63 [1907]) 'Essays on the political economy, part 1: maintenance of life – wealth, money and riches', in Rhys, E. (ed.), *Unto This Last and Other Essays on Art and Political Economy*, Everyman's Library J. M. Dent & Sons Ltd, London, p198.

[24] Ruskin, J. (1857) 'The political economy of art: addenda 5 – invention of new wants' in Rhys, E. (ed.), *Unto This Last and Other Essays on Art and Political Economy*, Everyman's Library J. M. Dent & Sons Ltd, London, 1907, p96.

[25] Ruskin, J. (1884) *The Storm-Cloud of the Nineteenth Century*, two lectures delivered at the London Institution 4 and 11 February, available at www.archive.org/stream/thestormcloudoft20204gut/20204-8.txt, accessed 21 January 2012.

[26] Habermas, J. (1980 [2010]) 'Modernity', in Leitch, V. B (ed.), *The Norton Anthology of Theory and Criticism*, 2nd edition, W. W. Norton & Co., London, pp1577–1587.

[27] Carey, G. and Carey, A. (2012) *We Don't Do God: The Marginalization of Public Faith*, Monarch Books, Oxford.

[28] Eagleton, T. (2009) *Reason, Faith, and Revolution: Reflections on the God Debate*, Yale University Press, New Haven, CT, pp153–154.

[29] Woodhead, L. (2012a) 'Restoring religion to the public square', *The Tablet*, 28 January, pp6–7.

[30] Sparke, P. (1986) *An Introduction to Design and Culture in the 20th Century*, Allen & Unwin, London, pp179–181.

[31] Smith-Spark, L. (2007) 'Apple iPhone draws diverse queue', BBC News, 29 June, available at http://news.bbc.co.uk/1/hi/technology/6254986.stm, accessed 17 January 2012.

[32] Gladwell, M. (2000) *The Tipping Point*, Abacus, London, pp4–5.

[33] Nair, C. (2011a) *Consumptionomics: Asia's Role in Reshaping Capitalism and Saving the Planet*, Infinite Ideas Ltd, Oxford, p76.

[34] Eagleton, T. (2011a [1961]) *Why Marx Was Right*, Yale University Press, New Haven, CT, p15.

[35] Wittgenstein, L. (1921) *Tractatus Logico-Philosophicus*, trans. Pears, D. F. and McGuinness, B. F., Routledge, London, 1961, pp2, 3, 11, 31, 32.

[36] IEA (2011) *Prospect of Limiting the Global Increase in Temperature to 2°C is Getting Bleaker,* International Energy Agency, 30 May, available at www.iea.org/index_info.asp?id=1959, accessed 11 January 2012.

[37] Perry, G. (2011) *The Tomb of the Unknown Craftsman*, The British Museum Press, London, p73.

[38] Leonard, A. (2010) *The Story of Stuff*, Constable, London, pp261–268.

[39] Taylor, C. (2007) *A Secular Age*, The Belknap Press of Harvard University Press, Cambridge, MA, pp716–717.

[40] Eagleton, T. (2009) *Reason, Faith and Revolution: Reflections on the God Debate*, Yale University Press, New Haven, CT, pp153–154.

[41] Scruton, R. (2009) *Beauty*, Oxford University Press, Oxford, pp75–78, 172–175.

[42] Krueger, D. A. (2008) 'The ethics global supply chains in China: convergences of East and West', *Journal of Business Ethics*, Springer, Berlin, vol. 79, pp113–120.

[43] Manzini, E. and Jégou, F. (2003) *Sustainable Everyday: Scenarios for Urban Life*, Edizioni Ambiente, Milan.

[44] Porritt, J. (2007) *Capitalism: as if the World Matters*, Earthscan, London, p306.

[45] Walker, S. (2011) *The Spirit of Design: Objects, Environment and Meaning*, Earthscan, Abingdon, pp187–190.

[46] Scruton, R. (2009) *Beauty*, Oxford University Press, Oxford, pp62, 90–92.

[47] IDSA (2012) *Industrial Design: Defined,* Industrial Designers Society of America, available at www.idsa.org/content/content1/industrial-design-defined, accessed 10 February 2012.

145

5 Design and Spirituality: creating material culture for a wisdom economy

An earlier version of this chapter appeared in *Design Issues*, vol. 29, no. 3, pp89–107 (copyright 2013). With kind permission of The MIT Press, USA.

[1] The Gospel of Luke, Ch.10, vs.42, in the New Testament of the Bible.

[2] See, e.g. Johnston, W. (ed.) (2005) *The Cloud of Unknowing and the Book of Privy Counseling,* Doubleday, New York, p67.

[3] Dickens, C. (1854 [2003]) *Hard Times: For These Times*, Penguin Group, London, p28.

[4] Dickens, C. (1854 [2003]) *Hard Times: For These Times*, Penguin Group, London, p14.

[5] Chandran Nair is founder of the Asian think tank Global Institute for Tomorrow – the point referred to here was made in an interview on *Business Daily*, BBC World Service Radio, 21 September 2011.

[6] Taylor, C. (2007) *A Secular Age*, The Belknap Press of Harvard University Press, Cambridge, MA, p264.

[7] Tarnas, T. (1991) *The Passion of the Western Mind*, Harmony Books, New York, pp314–315.

[8] Smith, H. (2001) *Why Religion Matters: The Fate of the Human Spirit in an Age of Disbelief* , HarperCollins, New York, pp59, 60, 84.

[9] Sheldrake, R. (2013) 'The science delusion', *Resurgence & Ecologist,* May/June, no. 278, pp40–41.

[10] Taylor, C. (2007) *A Secular Age*, The Belknap Press of Harvard University, Cambridge, MA, p266.

[11] Schumacher, E. F. (1977 [1995]) *A Guide for the Perplexed,* Vintage Publishing, London.

[12] Papanek, V. (1995) *The Green Imperative: Ecology and Ethics in Design and Architecture*, Thames & Hudson, London, pp49–74.

[13] Hick, J. (1999) *The Fifth Dimension: An Exploration of the Spiritual Realm,* Oneworld Publications, Oxford, pp1–2.

[14] Needleman, J. (1989) 'Introduction', in *Tao Te Ching*, trans. Feng, G. F. and English, J., Vintage Books, New York, p xii.

[15] Needleman, J. (1989) 'Introduction', in *Tao Te Ching*, trans. Feng, G. F. and English, J., Vintage Books, New York, pp xii–xiii.

[16] Davison, A. (2008) 'Ruling the future? Heretical reflections on technology and other secular religions of sustainability', *Worldviews*, vol. 12 pp146–162, available at http://ade.se/skola/ht10/infn14/articles/seminar4/Davison%20-%20 Ruling%20the%20Future.pdf, accessed 30 August 2011.

[17] Orr, D. W. (2002) 'Four challenges of sustainability', *Conservation Biology*, vol. 16, no. 6, pp1457–1460, available at www.cereo.wsu.edu/docs/Orr2003_ SustainabilityChallenges.pdf, accessed 30 August 2011.

[18] Inayatullah, S. (2011) 'Spirituality as the fourth bottom line', available at www. metafuture.org/Articles/spirituality_bottom_line.htm, accessed 30 August 2011.

[19] Mathews, F. (2006) 'Beyond modernity and tradition: a third way for development', *Ethics & the Environment*, vol. 11, no. 2, pp85–113.

[20] Berry, T. (2009) *The Sacred Universe*, edited by Mary Evelyn Tucker, Columbia University Press, New York, p133.

[21] Van Wieren, G. (2008) 'Ecological restoration as public spiritual practice', *Worldviews*, vol. 12, pp237–254, available at www.uvm.edu/rsenr/greenforestry/ LIBRARYFILES/restoration.pdf, accessed 30 August 2011.

[22] Porritt, J. (2002) 'Sustainability without spirituality: a contradiction in terms?', *Conservation Biology*, vol. 16, no. 6, p1465.

[23] See Smith, H. (2001) *Why Religion Matters: The Fate of the Human Spirit in an Age of Disbelief* , HarperCollins, New York, p26.

[24] Eagleton, T. (2007) *The Meaning of Life*, Oxford University Press, Oxford, p89.

[25] Smith, H. (2001) *Why Religion Matters: The Fate of the Human Spirit in an Age of Disbelief,* HarperCollins, New York, pp11–12.

[26] Armstrong, K. (2002) *Islam: A Short History*, Phoenix Press, London, p6.

[27] Lewis, C. S. (1947) *The Abolition of Man*, HarperCollins Publishers, New York, p43.

[28] Eagleton, T. (2007) *The Meaning of Life*, Oxford University Press, Oxford, p20.

[29] Armstrong, K. (2002) *Islam: A Short History*, Phoenix Press, London, p122.

30 Smith, H. (2001) *Why Religion Matters: The Fate of the Human Spirit in an Age of Disbelief*, HarperCollins, New York, p150.

31 Smith, H. (2001) *Why Religion Matters: The Fate of the Human Spirit in an Age of Disbelief*, HarperCollins, New York, p20.

32 Smith, H. (2001) *Why Religion Matters: The Fate of the Human Spirit in an Age of Disbelief*, HarperCollins, New York, p12.

33 Erlhoff, M. and Marshall, T. (eds) (2008) *Design Dictionary: Perspectives on Design Terminology*, Birkhäuser Verlag AG, Basel, pp354–357.

34 Wilson, A. N. (2011) *Dante in Love*, Atlantic Books, London, p342.

35 Herzfeld, N. (2009) *Technology and Religion: Remaining Human in a Co-Created World*, Templeton Press, West Conshohocken, PA, p134.

36 Hick, J. (1999) *The Fifth Dimension: An Exploration of the Spiritual Realm*, Oneworld Publications, Oxford, p2.

37 Huitt, W. (2007) 'Maslow's hierarchy of needs', *Educational Psychology Interactive*, Valdosta State University, Valdosta, GA, available at www.edpsycinteractive.org/topics/regsys/maslow.html, accessed 30 August 2011.

38 Hick, J. (1989) *An Interpretation of Religion: Human Responses to the Transcendent*, Yale University Press, New Haven, CT, pp148–158.

39 Eagleton, T. (2007) *The Meaning of Life*, Oxford University Press, Oxford, p71.

40 Eagleton, T. (2007) *The Meaning of Life*, Oxford University Press, Oxford, p89.

41 King, U. (2009) *The Search for Spirituality: Our Global Quest for Meaning and Fulfilment*, Canterbury Press, Norwich, pp3–4.

42 Hick, J. (1982) *God Has Many Names*, The Westminster Press, Philadelphia, PA, pp9, 18.

43 See Johnston, W. (ed.) (2005) *The Cloud of Unknowing and the Book of Privy Counseling*, Doubleday, New York, p68.

44 Schumacher, E. F. (1977) *A Guide for the Perplexed*, Vintage Publishing, London.

45 Johnston, W. (ed.) (2005) *The Cloud of Unknowing and the Book of Privy Counseling*, Doubleday, New York, pp66–70.

46 Mascaró, J. (trans.) (1962) *The Bhagavad Gita*, Penguin Group, London, pp56, 62.

47 Johnston, W. (ed.) (2005) *The Cloud of Unknowing and the Book of Privy Counseling*, Doubleday, New York, p67.

48 Johnston, W. (ed.) (2005) *The Cloud of Unknowing and the Book of Privy Counseling*, Doubleday, New York, p67.

49 See Plato's *Apology 38A*, (in, for example, (1997) *Plato: Symposium and the Death of Socrates*, Wordsworth Editions Ltd, Ware, p109.

50 See, e.g. Nicoll, M. (1950 [1972]) *The New Man*, Penguin Books Inc., Baltimore, MD, pp110–128.

51 Nasr, S. H. (1966 [1994]) *Ideals and Realities of Islam*, Aquarian/HarperCollins Publishers, London, p93.

52 Mascaró, J. (trans.) (1973) *The Dhammapada*, Penguin Group, London, pp29–32.

53 See Patton, L.L. (trans. and ed.) (2008) 'Introduction', in *The Bhagavad Gita*, Penguin Group, London, pp xiv–xv.

147

54 Easwaran, E. (trans.) (2000) *The Bhagavad Gita*, Vintage Books, New York, pp74–76.

55 See Johnston, W. (ed.) (2005) *The Cloud of Unknowing and the Book of Privy Counseling*, Doubleday, New York, pp80–81.

56 Merton, T. (1967) *Mystics and Zen Masters*, Farrar, Straus & Giroux, New York, p235.

57 See Johnston, W. (ed.) (2005) *The Cloud of Unknowing and the Book of Privy Counseling*, Doubleday, New York, p83.

58 Humphreys, C. (1949) *Zen Buddhism*, William Heinemann Ltd, London, p116.

59 Humphreys, C. (1949) *Zen Buddhism*, William Heinemann Ltd, London , p116.

60 Johnston, W. (ed.) (2005) *The Cloud of Unknowing and the Book of Privy Counseling*, Doubleday, New York, p84.

61 The relationship between rational, analytic, evidence-based modes and intuitive apprehension, spontaneous insight and spiritual understandings is discussed further in Chapter 6, The Narrow Door to Sustainability: from practically useful to spiritually useful artefacts, and also, in relation to the design process, in: Walker, S. (2013) 'Imagination's promise: practice-based design research for sustainability', in Walker, S. and Giard, J. (eds), *The Handbook of Design for Sustainability*, Bloomsbury Academic, London, pp446–465. The point here is that study, reasoned argument and use of techniques and systemized methods are all important in advancing understandings and cognitive knowledge. They can also help prepare the ground and facilitate – but cannot guarantee – the kinds of spontaneous insight, moments of synthesis and intuitive ways of knowing that are related both to inner development and to the creative process, all of which *may* arise from contemplative practice and 'non-doing'.

62 Rowell, M. (ed.) (1986) *Joan Miró: Selected Writings and Interviews*, Da Capo Press, Cambridge, MA, p275.

63 Schumacher, E. F. (1977) *A Guide for the Perplexed*, Vintage Publishing, London, 1995, p143.

64 Harries, R. (1993) *Art and the Beauty of God*, Mombray, London, p101.

65 Harries, R. (1993) *Art and the Beauty of God*, Mombray, London, p106.

66 Johnston, W. (ed.) (2005) *The Cloud of Unknowing and the Book of Privy Counseling*, Doubleday, New York, pp77, 83

67 Humphreys, C. (1949) *Zen Buddhism*, William Heinemann Ltd, London, p1.

68 Herrigel, E. (1953 [1999]) *Zen in the Art of Archery*, Vintage Books, New York, p6.

69 Johnston, W. (ed.) (2005) *The Cloud of Unknowing and the Book of Privy Counseling*, Doubleday, New York, pp80–83.

70 Mascaró, J. (trans.) (1965) *The Upanishads*, Penguin Group, London, pp58–60.

71 Alexander, C. (1979) *The Timeless Way of Building*, Oxford University Press, New York, p ix.

72 Alexander, C. (1979) *The Timeless Way of Building*, Oxford University Press, New York, pp xiv, 7, 26.

73 Van der Ryn, S. and Cowan, S. (1996) *Ecological Design*, Island Press, Washington, DC, p63.

74 Scruton, R. (2012a) *Green Philosophy: How to Think Seriously about the Planet*, Atlantic Books, London, pp71–79.

75 Scruton, R. (2012a) *Green Philosophy: How to Think Seriously about the Planet*, Atlantic Books, London, pp288–289.

76 Hawken, P. (2007) *Blessed Unrest: How the Largest Movement in the World Came into Being and Why No One Saw It Coming*, Viking Publishing, New York, p184.

77 Tucker, M. E. (2003) *Worldly Wonder: Religions Enter their Ecological Phase*, Open Court, Chicago, IL, pp7–8.

78 Berry, T. (2009) *The Sacred Universe*, edited by Mary Evelyn Tucker, Columbia University Press, New York, pp131–133.

79 For example, see Herman Daly's arguments for a steady state economic model in Daly, D. (2007) *Ecological Economics and Sustainable Development: Selected Essays of Herman Daly*, Edward Elgar Publishing, Cheltenham, pp228–236. Also see Jackson, T. (2009) *Prosperity Without Growth: Economics for a Finate Planet*, Earthscan, London, pp150–151; and Borgmann, A. (2006) *Real American Ethics*, University of Chicago Press, Chicago, IL, p194. An example from the business world includes the international office floor covering company Interface Inc.; see Anderson, R. (2009) *Confessions of a Radical Industrialist*, Random House, London, pp238–243.

80 Day, C. (2002) *Spirit and Place*, Elsevier, Oxford, pp234–235.

81 Papanek, V. (1995) *The Green Imperative: Ecology and Ethics in Design and Architecture*, Thames and Hudson, London, pp49–74.

82 Branzi, A. (2009) *Grandi Legni* (exhibition catalogue essay), Design Gallery Milano and Nilufar, Milan, p59.

83 Nicoll, M. (1950) *The New Man*, Penguin Books Inc., Baltimore, MD, pp118–119.

84 See, e.g. Patton, L.L. (trans. and ed.) (2008) 'Introduction', in *The Bhagavad Gita*, Penguin Group, London, p34.

85 Korten, D. C. (1999) *The Post-Corporate World: Life After Capitalism*, Berrett-Koehler Publishers, San Francisco, CA and Kumarian Press, West Hartford, CT, p187.

86 Friedman, M. (1962 [1982]) *Capitalism and Freedom*, University of Chicago Press, Chicago, IL, p112, available at www.4shared.com/document/GHk_gt9U/Friedman_Milton_Capitalism_and.html, accessed 10 September 2011.

87 'About certified B corps', available at www.bcorporation.net/about, accessed 10 September 2011.

88 Bakan, J. (2004) *The Corporation: The Pathological Pursuit of Profit and Power*, Constable & Robinson Ltd, London, pp53, 69.

89 See Nair, C. (2011) Interview, *Business Daily*, BBC World Service Radio, 21 September.

90 Nair, C. (2011a) *Consumptionomics: Asia's Role in Reshaping Capitalism and Saving the Planet*, Infinite Ideas Ltd, Oxford, p65.

149

91 Smith, H. (2001) *Why Religion Matters: The Fate of the Human Spirit in an Age of Disbelief*, HarperCollins, New York, p161.

92 Leonard, A. (2010) *The Story of Stuff*, Constable, London, p314.

93 For examples, see *Reduce Your Carbon Footprint* at the David Suzuki Foundation website, available at: www.davidsuzuki.org/what-you-can-do/reduce-your-carbon-footprint, accessed 30 April 2013.

94 Johnston, W. (ed.) (2005) *The Cloud of Unknowing and the Book of Privy Counseling*, Doubleday, New York, p90.

95 Smith, H. (2001) *Why Religion Matters: The Fate of the Human Spirit in an Age of Disbelief*, HarperCollins, New York, p26.

96 Nicoll, M. (1950 [1972]) *The New Man*, Penguin Books Inc., Baltimore, MD, p125.

6 The Narrow Door to Sustainability: from practically useful to spiritually useful artefacts

An earlier version of this chapter appeared in the *International Journal of Design for Sustainability*, vol. 2, no. 1, pp83–103 (copyright 2012). With kind permission of Inderscience, Switzerland, who retain copyright of the original paper.

1 Keble College (2012) *Keble Chapel Treasures: The Light of the World*, Oxford University, Oxford, available at www.keble.ox.ac.uk/about/chapel/chapel-history-and-treasures, accessed 24 May 2012.

2 Hobsbawm, E. (1962) *The Age of Revolution 1789–1848*, Abacus, London, p229.

3 Raymond, R. (1986) *Out of the Fiery Furnace: The Impact of Metals on the History of Mankind*, Pennsylvania State University Press, University Park, PA, pp187–188.

4 Tate Britain (2012) *Walter Richard Sickert, Ennui, c.1914*, available at www.tate.org.uk/art/artworks/sickert-ennui-n03846, accessed 24 May 2012.

5 Hobsbawm, E. (1962) *The Age of Revolution 1789–1848*, Abacus, London, p229.

6 Taylor, C. (1991) *The Malaise of Modernity*, Anansi, Concord, ON, p3.

7 Taylor, C. (1991) *The Malaise of Modernity*, Anansi, Concord, ON, p4.

8 Eagleton, T. (2007) *The Meaning of Life*, Oxford University Press, Oxford, pp20–22.

9 Porritt, J. (2002) 'Sustainability without spirituality: a contradiction in terms?', *Conservation Biology*, vol. 16, no. 6, p1465.

10 Gorz, A. (2010) *Ecologica*, trans. Turner, C., Seagull Books, London, pp26–27.

11 Plato (fourth century BCE [2000]), *The Republic*, edited by Ferrari, G. R. F., trans. Griffith, T., Cambridge University Press, Cambridge, 372e–373e, pp55–56.

12 Ecclesiastes 1:9.

13 Daly, H. E. (2007) *Ecological Economics and Sustainable Development: Selected Essays of Herman Daly*, Edward Elgar Publishing, Cheltenham, pp119.

[14] Gorz, A. (2010) *Ecologica*, trans. Turner, C., Seagull Books, London, p30.

[15] Swann, C. (2002) 'Action research and the practice of design', *Design Issues*, vol. 18, no. 2, *Design Issues*, pp49–61.

[16] Harrison, K. (2012) *End of Growth and Liberal Democracy*, lecture, Australian Centre for Sustainable Catchments, University of Southern Queensland, available at http://vimeo.com/41056934, accessed 17 May 2012.

[17] Roadmap 2050 (2010) *Roadmap 2050: A Practical Guide to a Prosperous, Low-Carbon Europe: Technical Analysis*, vol. 1 April, McKinsey & Company, KEMA, The Energy Futures Lab at Imperial College London, Oxford Economics and the ECF, available at www.roadmap2050.eu/attachments/files/Volume1_fullreport_PressPack.pdf, accessed 26 November 2012, pp9–17.

[18] Schmidt-Bleek, F. (2008) *FUTURE: Beyond Climatic Change*, position paper 08/01, Factor 10 Institute, available at www.factor10-institute.org/publications.html, accessed 5 September 2012.

[19] Bianco, N. M. and Litz, F. T. (2010) *Reducing Greenhouse Gas Emission in the United States Using Existing Federal Authorities and State Action*, World Resources Institute, Washington, DC.

[20] Hill, K. (2008) *Legal Briefing on the Climate Change Bill: The Scientific Case for an 80% Target and the Proposed Review of the 2050 Target: Legal Briefing*, ClientEarth, London, available at www.clientearth.org/publications-all-documents, accessed 5 September 2012.

[21] Harrison, K. (2012) *End of Growth and Liberal Democracy*, lecture, Australian Centre for Sustainable Catchments, University of Southern Queensland, available at http://vimeo.com/41056934, accessed 17 May 2012.

[22] Sulston, J., Bateson, P., Biggar, N., Fang, C., Cavenaghi, S., Cleland, J., Mauzé, J. C. A. R., Dasgupta, P., Eloundou-Enyegue, P. M., Fitter, A., Habte, D., Jackson, T., Mace, G., Owens, S., Porritt, J., Potts Bixby, M., Pretty, J., Ram, F., Short, R., Spencer, S., Xiaoying, Z. and Zulu, E. (2012) *People and the Planet*, The Royal Society, London, available at http://royalsociety.org/policy/projects/people-planet/report, accessed 26 April 2012.

[23] Sulston, J., Bateson, P., Biggar, N., Fang, C., Cavenaghi, S., Cleland, J., Mauzé, J. C. A. R., Dasgupta, P., Eloundou-Enyegue, P. M., Fitter, A., Habte, D., Jackson, T., Mace, G., Owens, S., Porritt, J., Potts Bixby, M., Pretty, J., Ram, F., Short, R., Spencer, S., Xiaoying, Z. and Zulu, E. (2012) *People and the Planet*, The Royal Society, London, available at http://royalsociety.org/policy/projects/people-planet/report, accessed 26 April 2012, p87.

[24] Davison, A. (2001) *Technology and the Contested Meanings of Sustainability*, State University of New York Press, Albany, NY, pp27–30.

[25] Senge, P., Smith, B., Kruschwitz, N., Laur, J. and Schley, S. (2008) *The Necessary Revolution: How Individuals and Organizations are Working Together to Create a Sustainable World*, Nicholas Brealey Publishing, London, p41.

[26] Capra, F. (2012) 'Ecological Literacy', in *Resurgence*, The Resurgence Trust, Bideford, UK, no. 272, pp42–43.

151

[27] Stahel, W. (2010) 'Durability, function and performance', in Cooper, T. (ed.), *Longer Lasting Products: Alternatives to the Throwaway Society*, Gower, Farnham, pp157–176.

[28] Peattie, K. (2010) 'Rethinking marketing', in Cooper, T. (ed.), *Longer Lasting Products: Alternatives to the Throwaway Society*, Gower, Farnham, pp243–272.

[29] Simon, M. (2010) 'Product life cycle management through IT', in Cooper, T. (ed.), *Longer Lasting Products: Alternatives to the Throwaway Society*, Gower, Farnham, pp351–366.

[30] Kumon, K. (2012) 'Overview of next-generation green data center', *Fujitsu Scientific & Technical Journal*, vol. 48, no. 2, pp177–178.

[31] Uddin, M. and Rahman, A. A. (2012) 'Energy efficiency and low carbon enabler green IT framework for data centers considering green metrics', *Renewable and Sustainable Energy Reviews*, vol. 16, no. 2, pp4078–4094.

[32] Turkle, S. (2011) *Alone Together: Why We Expect More from Technology and Less from Each Other*, Basic Books, New York, p157.

[33] Fuad-Luke, A. (2009) *Design Activism: Beautiful Strangeness for a Sustainable World*, Earthscan, London, p49.

[34] Crompton, T. (2010) *Common Cause: The Case for Working with our Cultural Values*, WWF-UK, available at http://assets.wwf.org.uk/downloads/common_cause_report.pdf, accessed 14 June 2012, pp33–34.

[35] Capra, F. (2012) 'Ecological Literacy', in *Resurgence*, The Resurgence Trust, Bideford, UK, no. 272, pp42–43.

[36] Crompton, T. (2010) *Common Cause: The Case for Working with our Cultural Values*, WWF-UK, available at http://assets.wwf.org.uk/downloads/common_cause_report.pdf, accessed 14 June 2012, pp82–85.

[37] Borgmann, A. (2003) *Power Failure: Christianity in the Culture of Technology*, Brazos Press, Grand Rapids, MI, pp81–94.

[38] Mathews, F. (2006) 'Beyond modernity and tradition: a third way for development', *Ethics & the Environment*, vol. 11, no. 2, pp85–113.

[39] Orr, D. W. (2003) *Four Challenges of Sustainability*, School of Natural Resources, University of Vermont, available at www.ratical.org/co-globalize/4CofS.html, accessed 11 June 2012.

[40] Scharmer, C. O. (2009) *Theory U, Leading from the Future as it Emerges*, Berrett-Koehler Publishers, Inc., San Francisco, CA, pp92–95.

[41] Day, C. (2002) *Spirit and Place*, Elsevier, Oxford, p9.

[42] Shelley, P. B. (1818 [1994]) 'Sonnet: lift not the painted veil', *The Works of P. B. Shelley*, Wordsworth Editions Ltd, Ware, p341.

[43] Scruton, R. (2012b) *The Face of God, The Gifford Lectures 2010*, Continuum, London, p68.

[44] Woodhead, L. (2012) 'Restoring religion to the public square', *The Tablet*, 28 January, pp6–7.

[45] Scruton, R. (2012b) *The Face of God, The Gifford Lectures 2010*, Continuum, London, pp68–72.

[46] Watts, A. W. (1957) *The Way of Zen*, Arkana, London, p72.

[47] Cottingham, J. (2005) *The Spiritual Dimension: Religion, Philosophy and Human Value*, Cambridge University Press, Cambridge, pp5, 140.

[48] King, U. (2009) *The Search for Spirituality: Our Global Quest for Meaning and Fulfilment*, Canterbury Press, Norwich, p4.

[49] Watts, A. W. (1957) *The Way of Zen*, Arkana, London, p58.

[50] Christianson, E. S. (2007) *Ecclesiastes Through the Centuries*, Wiley-Blackwell, Malden, MA, p70.

[51] For example: Plato's Phaedo, 64d–67b.

[52] Hawken, P. (2007) *Blessed Unrest: How the Largest Movement in the World Came into Being and Why No One Saw It Coming*, Viking, New York, pp184–188.

[53] Cottingham, J. (2005) *The Spiritual Dimension: Religion, Philosophy and Human Value*, Cambridge University Press, Cambridge, pp150–151.

[54] Scruton, R. (2012) *The Face of God, The Gifford Lectures 2010*, Continuum, London, pp73, 136.

[55] Palmer, M. (2012) 'Secretary General, Alliance of Religions and Conservation', interview, BBC Radio 4's *'Sunday'* programme, 26 February, available at www.arcworld.org, accessed 26 February 2012.

[56] Eagleton, T. (2009) *Reason, Faith and Revolution: Reflections on the God Debate*, Yale University Press, New Haven, CT, p39.

[57] Woodhead, L. (2012) 'Religion à la mode', *The Tablet*, 28 April 2012, pp8–9.

[58] Woodhead, L. (2012) 'Religion à la mode', *The Tablet*, 28 April 2012, pp8–9.

[59] Capra, F. (2012) 'Ecological Literacy', in *Resurgence*, The Resurgence Trust, Bideford, no. 272, pp42–43.

[60] Mathews, F. (2006) 'Beyond modernity and tradition: a third way for development', *Ethics & the Environment*, vol. 11, no. 2, pp85–113.

[61] Carey, G. (2011) *Submission to the European Court of Human Rights*, 11 September, available at www.glcarey.co.uk/Speeches/PressReleases/ECHR.html, accessed 27 April 2012.

[62] Jouanneau, D. (2011) *The Niqab and the French Social Pact*, French Diplomatie, available at www.diplomatie.gouv.fr/en/country-files/pakistan-504/france-and-pakistan/political-relations-5981/article/the-niqab-and-the-french-social, accessed 27 April 2012.

[63] BBC (2005) 'US Bans Commandments in courtroom', 27 June, available at http://news.bbc.co.uk/1/hi/world/americas/4627459.stm, accessed 10 June 2012.

[64] Dalai Lama (2011) *Beyond Religion: Ethics for a Whole World*, Rider/Ebury Publishing, London.

[65] Hick, J. (1999) *The Fifth Dimension: An Exploration of the Spiritual Realm*, One-world Publications, Oxford, p2.

[66] Schuon, F. (1984) *The Transcendent Unity of Religions*, Quest Books, Wheaton, IL.

[67] Lynch, G. (2007) *The New Spirituality: An Introduction to Progressive Belief in the Twenty-first Century*, I.B. Taurus, London, pp86–87.

153

[68] Scott, T. (2000) 'Understanding symbol', *Sacred Web: A Journal of Tradition and Modernity*, vol. 6, no. 2, available at www.sacredweb.com/online_articles/sw6_scott.html, accessed 18 April 2012, pp91–106.

[69] Chevalier, J. and Gheerbrant, A. (1992) *The Penguin Dictionary of Symbols*, trans. Buchan-Brown, J., Penguin Group, London, pp248, 504.

[70] Evans-Wentz, W. Y. (ed.) (2008) *The Tibetan Book of the Dead Or the After-Death Experiences on the Bardo Plane*, trans. Lama Kazi Dawa-Samdup, available at www.holybooks.com/wp-content/uploads/The-Tibetan-Book-of-the-Dead.pdf, accessed 19 July 2012, p21.

[71] Comte-Sponville, A. (2007) *The Book of Atheist Spirituality: An Elegant Argument for Spirituality without God*, trans. N. Huston, Bantam Books, London, p168.

[72] Eliade, M. (1964 [1989]) *Shamanism: Archaic Techniques of Ecstasy*, trans. Trask, W. R., Arkana, London, p340.

[73] For example: Genesis 28:17; 1 Samuel 9:18–19; Ezekiel 46:1–3.

[74] For example: Matthew 7:13; Luke 13:24.

[75] Herrington, C., Forsgren, K. A. and Benskin, E. (2002) *Arts of the Islamic World: A Teacher's Guide*, Smithsonian Freer Gallery of Art and Arthur M. Sackler Gallery, Smithsonian Institution, available at www.asia.si.edu/explore/teacherresources/islam.pdf, accessed 19 April 2012, p32.

[76] Scott, T. (2000) 'Understanding symbol', *Sacred Web: A Journal of Tradition and Modernity*, vol. 6, no. 2, available at www.sacredweb.com/online_articles/sw6_scott.html, accessed 18 April 2012, pp91–106.

[77] Nikhilananda, Swami (trans.) (1949) *The Upanishads*, Ramakrishna-Vivekananda Center, New York, available at www.vivekananda.net/PDFBooks/upanishads_nikhilananda.pdf, accessed 18 July 2012.

[78] Mascaró, J. (trans.) (1973) *The Dhammapada*, Penguin Group, London, p42.

[79] Paine, R. T. and Soper, A. (1981) *The Art and Architecture of Japan*, Yale University Press, New Haven, CT, p285.

[80] Eliade, M. (1964 [1989]) *Shamanism: Archaic Techniques of Ecstasy*, trans. Trask, W. R., Arkana, London, pp292–295.

[81] Chevalier, J. and Gheerbrant, A. (1992) *The Penguin Dictionary of Symbols*, trans. Buchan-Brown, J., Penguin Group, London, pp997.

[82] Oflaz, M. (2011) 'The effect of right and left brain dominance in language learning', *Procedia Social and Behavioural Sciences*, vol. 15, pp1507–1513.

[83] Oflaz, M. (2011) 'The effect of right and left brain dominance in language learning', *Procedia Social and Behavioural Sciences*, vol. 15, pp1507–1513.

[84] Mikels, J. A. and Reuter-Lorenz, P. A. (2004) 'Neural gate keeping: the role of interhemispheric interactions in resource allocation and selective filtering', *Neuropsychology*, vol. 18, no. 2, pp328–339.

[85] Edwards, B. (1979) *Drawing on the Right Side of the Brain: A Course in Enhancing Creativity and Artistic Confidence*, J. P. Tarcher, Inc., Los Angeles, CA, p25–43.

154

86 Feng, G. F. and English, J. (trans.) (1989) *Tao Te Ching, by Lao Tsu*, Vintage Books, New York, vs.1, p3.

87 Needleman, J. (1989) 'Introduction', in *Tao Te Ching*, trans. Feng, G. F and English, J., Vintage Books, New York, p vii.

88 Leonard, A. (2010) *The Story of Stuff*, Constable, London.

89 Strauss, C. and Fuad-Luke, A. (2008) 'The slow design principles: a new interrogative and reflexive tool for design research and practice', in Cipolla, C. and Paolo Peruccio, P. (eds), *Changing the Change Proceedings*, pp1440—1450, Changing the Change conference, Turin, Italy, June 2008, available at www.changingthechange.org/papers/ctc.pdf, accessed 20 July 2012.

90 Nikhilananda, Swami (trans.) (1949) *The Upanishads*, Ramakrishna-Vivekananda Center, New York, available at www.vivekananda.net/PDFBooks/upanishads_nikhilananda.pdf, accessed 18 July 2012, p185.

91 Hamill, S. (trans.) (1998) 'Introduction', in Bashō M. *Narrow Road to the Interior and Other Writings*, Shambhala Publications, Inc., Boston, MA, p xi.

92 Havemann, S. and Fellner, D. (2004) 'Generative parametric design of gothic window tracery', *Proceedings of International Conference on Shape Modeling and Applications 2004 (SMI'04)*, pp350–353, available at http://generative-modeling.org/GenerativeModeling/Documents/window-tracery-smi04-04.pdf, accessed 10 April 2012.

93 Gandhi, M. (1982) *The Words of Gandhi*, edited by R. Attenborough, Newmarket Press, New York, p75.

94 Walker, S. (2011) *The Spirit of Design: Objects, Environment and Meaning*, Earthscan, Abingdon, p112.

95 Murphy-O'Connor, C. quoted in Norton, T. (2008) 'Cardinal wants Piero in a church', *The Tablet*, 6 December.

96 Scruton, R. (2012b) *The Face of God, The Gifford Lectures 2010*, Continuum, London, p171.

97 Yuasa, N. (trans.) (1966) 'Introduction', in *The Narrow Road to the Deep North and Other Travel Sketches*, Penguin Books, London, p37.

155

7 A Form of Silence: design for doing no-thing

An earlier, summary version of this chapter was presented at the *Miracles and Management Conference*, 3rd Conference of Management, Spirituality and Religion, Lourdes, France, 16–19 May 2013.

1 Berg, M. V. (2012) *Trio Solisti Program*, Maverick Concerts, Sunday, 12 August, available at www.maverickconcerts.org/TRIOSOLISTI_2012.html, accessed 16 October 2012.

2 One series of these explorations can be characterized as: utilitarian, symbolic and religion-specific (see: Walker, S. (2011) *The Spirit of Design: Objects, Environment and Meaning*, Earthscan, Abingdon, pp185–205); another as: non-utilitarian, symbolic and religion-specific (see Chapter 3); and a third as: non-utilitarian, symbolic and trans-religious (see Chapter 6).

[3] Lansley, S. (1994) *After the Gold Rush: The Trouble with Affluence – 'Consumer Capitalism' and the Way Forward*, Century Business Books, London, pp16–17, 105.

[4] Chomsky, N. (2012a) 'How the Magna Carta became a Minor Carta, part 1', *Guardian*, 24 July 2012, available at www.guardian.co.uk/commentisfree/2012/jul/24/magna-carta-minor-carta-noam-chomsky?INTCMP=SRCH, accessed 25 July 2012.

[5] Chomsky, N. (2012b) 'How the Magna Carta became a Minor Carta, part 2', *Guardian*, 25 July 2012, available at www.guardian.co.uk/commentisfree/2012/jul/25/magna-carta-minor-carta-noam-chomsky?INTCMP=SRCH, accessed 25 July 2012.

[6] Lansley, S. (1994) *After the Gold Rush: The Trouble with Affluence – 'Consumer Capitalism' and the Way Forward*, Century Business Books, London, pp107–140.

[7] Skidelsky, R. and Skidelsky, E. (2012) *How Much is Enough: Money and the Good Life*, Other Press, New York, p183.

[8] Skidelsky, R. and Skidelsky, E. (2012) *How Much is Enough: Money and the Good Life*, Other Press, New York, pp180–218.

[9] Wilkinson, R. and Pickett, K. (2009) *The Spirit Level: Why More Equal Societies Almost Always Do Better*, Allen Lane, London, p45.

[10] Skidelsky, R. and Skidelsky, E. (2012) *How Much is Enough: Money and the Good Life*, Other Press, New York, p148.

[11] Turkle, S. (2011) *Alone Together: Why We Expect More From Technology and Less From Each Other*, Basic Books, New York, p227.

[12] Herzfeld, N. (2009) *Technology and Religion: Remaining Human in a Co-Created World*, Templeton Press, West Conshocken, PA, p89.

[13] Curtis, M. (2005b) *Distraction: Being Human in the Digital Age*, Futuretext Ltd, London, p63.

[14] Eagleton, T. (2007) *The Meaning of Life*, Oxford University Press, Oxford, p95.

[15] Tucker, M. E. (2003) *Worldly Wonder: Religions Enter their Ecological Phase*, Open Court, Chicago, IL, pp50–54.

[16] King, U. (2009) *The Search for Spirituality: Our Global Quest for Meaning and Fulfilment*, Canterbury Press, Norwich, pp31, 167.

[17] Watts, A. W. (1957) *The Way of Zen*, Arkana, London, pp12, 46–47.

[18] The New Testament of the Bible, The Gospel of Matthew 15:11.

[19] Woodhead, L. (2012a) 'Restoring religion to the public square', *The Tablet*, 28 January, pp6–7.

[20] Sulston, J., Bateson, P., Biggar, N., Fang, C., Cavenaghi, S., Cleland, J., Mauzé, J. C. A. R., Dasgupta, P., Eloundou-Enyegue, P. M., Fitter, A., Habte, D., Jackson, T., Mace, G., Owens, S., Porritt, J., Potts Bixby, M., Pretty, J., Ram, F., Short, R., Spencer, S., Xiaoying, Z. and Zulu, E. (2012) *People and the Planet*, The Royal Society, London, available at http://royalsociety.org/policy/projects/people-planet/report, accessed 26 April 2012, p8.

[21] Sachs, J. D. (2008) *Common Wealth: Economics for a Crowded Planet*, Penguin Books, London, pp73–74.

22 Sachs, J. D. (2008) *Common Wealth: Economics for a Crowded Planet*, Penguin Books, London, pp205–206.

23 Sulston, J., Bateson, P., Biggar, N., Fang, C., Cavenaghi, S., Cleland, J., Mauzé, J. C. A. R., Dasgupta, P., Eloundou-Enyegue, P. M., Fitter, A., Habte, D., Jackson, T., Mace, G., Owens, S., Porritt, J., Potts Bixby, M., Pretty, J., Ram, F., Short, R., Spencer, S., Xiaoying, Z. and Zulu, E. (2012) *People and the Planet*, The Royal Society, London, available at http://royalsociety.org/policy/projects/people-planet/report, accessed 26 April 2012, pp9, 69, 75.

24 ISO 14000 International Standard for Environmental Management, available at www.iso.org/iso/iso14000, accessed 30 October 2012.

25 WEEE (2007) Waste Electrical and Electronic Equipment Directive, available at www.environment-agency.gov.uk/business/topics/waste/32084.aspx, accessed 30 October 2012.

26 Eco-design Directive (2009) Directive 2009/125/EC of the European Parliament and of the Council of 21 October 2009, available at http://eur-lex.europa.eu/LexUriServ/LexUriServ.do?uri=OJ:L:2009:285:0010:0035:en:PDF, accessed 30 October 2012.

27 Gorz, A. (2010) *Ecologica*, trans. Turner, C., Seagull Books, London, pp65–66.

28 Porritt, J. (2007) *Capitalism as if the World Matters*, Earthscan, London, p92.

29 Nair, C. (2011) *Consumptionomics: Asia's Role in Reshaping Capitalism and Saving the Planet*, Infinite Ideas Ltd, Oxford, pp38–39.

30 Sulston, J., Bateson, P., Biggar, N., Fang, C., Cavenaghi, S., Cleland, J., Mauzé, J. C. A. R., Dasgupta, P., Eloundou-Enyegue, P. M., Fitter, A., Habte, D., Jackson, T., Mace, G., Owens, S., Porritt, J., Potts Bixby, M., Pretty, J., Ram, F., Short, R., Spencer, S., Xiaoying, Z. and Zulu, E. (2012) *People and the Planet*, The Royal Society, London, available at http://royalsociety.org/policy/projects/people-planet/report, accessed 26 April 2012, pp8–9.

31 Skidelsky, R. and Skidelsky, E. (2012) *How Much is Enough: Money and the Good Life*, Other Press, New York, p215.

32 Wilkinson, R. and Pickett, K. (2009) *The Spirit Level: Why More Equal Societies Almost Always Do Better*, Allen Lane, London, p232.

33 Saul, J. R. (2005) *The Collapse of Globalism, and the Reinvention of the World*, Viking, Toronto, ON, pp24–25.

34 Skidelsky, R. and Skidelsky, E. (2012) *How Much is Enough: Money and the Good Life*, Other Press, New York, pp186–187, 204–218.

35 Merton, T. (1969) *Contemplative Prayer*, Doubleday, New York, p86.

36 Crow, K. D. (2012) Principal Research Fellow, Islam and Modernity, International Institute of Advanced Islamic Studies, Kuala Lumpur, Malaysia, interviewed on *The Future is Halal*, BBC Radio 4, London, broadcast 5:00 p.m., 26 August.

37 Shuman, M. H. (1998) *Going Local: Creating Self-reliant Communities in a Global Age*, Routledge, New York, p6.

38 Transition Culture (2010) *'Localism' or 'Localisation'? Defining Our Terms*, 23 July, available at http://transitionculture.org/2010/07/30/localism-or-localisation-defining-our-terms, accessed 27 August 2012.

157

[39] Saul, J. R. (2005) *The Collapse of Globalism, and the Reinvention of the World*, Viking, Toronto, p31.

[40] Scruton, R. (2012a) *Green Philosophy: How to Think Seriously About the Planet*, Atlantic Books, London, p399.

[41] Scruton, R. (2012a) *Green Philosophy: How to Think Seriously About the Planet*, Atlantic Books, London, pp260–263, 411–413.

[42] Watts, A. W. (1957) *The Way of Zen*, Arkana, London, pp12–13.

[43] Williams, A. (trans.) (2006) *Rumi: Spiritual Verses – The First Book of the Masnavi-ye Ma'navi*, Penguin Books, London, p17.

[44] Merton, T. (1969) *Contemplative Prayer*, Doubleday, New York, pp47–50.

[45] Inwood, M. (1997) *Heidegger*, Oxford University Press, Oxford, pp93–96, 127.

[46] Heidegger, M. (1993) *Basic Writings: Revised and Expanded Edition*, edited by D. F. Krell, Routledge, London, p85.

[47] Merton, T. (1969) *Contemplative Prayer*, Doubleday, New York, pp57–73, 92.

[48] McGinn, B. (2006) *The Essential Writings of Christian Mysticism*, The Modern Library, New York, p534.

[49] Williams, A. (trans.) (2006) *Rumi: Spiritual Verses – The First Book of the Masnavi-ye Ma'navi*, Penguin Books, London, pp33–34.

[50] Tanahashi, K. (ed.) (1985) *Moon in a Dewdrop: Writings of Zen Master Dogen*, North Point Press, New York, pp70–89.

[51] Watts, A. W. (1957) *The Way of Zen*, Arkana, London, p86.

[52] Watts, A. W. (1957) *The Way of Zen*, Arkana, London, pp63–65.

[53] CDBU (2012) *Council for the Defence of British Universities*, available at http://cdbu.org.uk, accessed 9 November 2012.

[54] Csikszentmihalyi, M. (1990) *Flow: The Psychology of Optimal Experience*, HarperCollins, New York, p86.

[55] Merton, T. (1969) *Contemplative Prayer*, Doubleday, New York, pp90–91.

[56] Skidelsky, R. and Skidelsky, E. (2012) *How Much is Enough: Money and the Good Life*, Other Press, New York, pp185–186.

[57] Scruton, R. (2012a) *Green Philosophy: How to Think Seriously About the Planet*, Atlantic Books, London, p288.

[58] Yuasa, N. (trans.) (1966) 'Introduction', in *The Narrow Road to the Deep North and Other Travel Sketches*, Penguin Books, London, p37.

[59] Larson, K. (2012) *Where the Heart Beats: John Cage, Zen Buddhism and the Inner Life of Artists*, Penguin Press, New York, p177.

[60] Watts, A. W. (1957) *The Way of Zen*, Arkana, London, pp38–39.

[61] The New Testament of the Bible, The Gospel of Luke 12:22–23.

[62] Barrett, W. (ed.) (1956) 'Zen for the West', in *Zen Buddhism: Selected Writings of D. T. Suzuki*, Doubleday, New York, p xi.

[63] Heidegger, M. (1993) *Basic Writings: Revised and Expanded Edition*, edited by D. F. Krell, Routledge, London, p183.

[64] Gompertz, W. (2012) *What Are You Looking At? 150 Years of Modern Art in the Blink of an Eye*, Viking, London, pp170–176.

[65] Stangos, N. (1981) *Concepts of Modern Art*, Thames & Hudson, London, pp138–140.

[66] Watts, A. W. (1957) *The Way of Zen*, Arkana, London.

[67] Skidelsky, R. and Skidelsky, E. (2012) *How Much is Enough: Money and the Good Life*, Other Press, New York, pp187–190.

[68] Williams, R. J. (2011) 'Technê-Zen and the spiritual quality of global capitalism', *Critical Inquiry*, vol. 37, pp34, 53–54.

[69] Davison, A. (2001) *Technology and the Contested Meanings of Sustainability*, State University of New York Press, Albany, NY, pp22, 74.

[70] Heidegger, M. (1993) *Basic Writings: Revised and Expanded Edition*, edited by D. F. Krell, Routledge, London, pp340–341.

[71] Merton, T. (1969) *Contemplative Prayer*, Doubleday, New York, pp61–63.

[72] Merton, T. (1969) *Contemplative Prayer*, Doubleday, New York, pp61–63.

[73] Jones, J. (2012) 'Greenland's ice sheet melt: a sensational picture of a blunt fact', *Guardian*, London, 27 July, available at www.guardian.co.uk/commentisfree/2012/jul/27/greenland-ice-sheet-melt, accessed 1 August 2012.

[74] Harvey, F. (2012) 'Europe looks to open up Greenland for natural resources extraction', *Guardian*, London, 31 July, available at www.guardian.co.uk/environment/2012/jul/31/europe-greenland-natural-resources, accessed 1 August 2012.

[75] Skidelsky, R. and Skidelsky, E. (2012) *How Much is Enough: Money and the Good Life*, Other Press, New York, p215.

[76] Sennett, R. (2008) *The Craftsman*, Penguin Books, London, pp8, 27.

[77] Walker, S. (2011) *The Spirit of Design: Objects, Environment and Meaning*, Earthscan, Abingdon, p185.

[78] Larson, K. (2012) *Where the Heart Beats: John Cage, Zen Buddhism and the Inner Life of Artists*, Penguin Press, New York, p58.

[79] Feng, G. F. and English, J. (trans.) (1989) *Tao Te Ching, by Lao Tsu*, Vintage Books, New York, vs. 3, p5.

[80] Eagleton, T. (2009) *Reason, Faith and Revolution: Reflections on the God Debate*, Yale University Press, New Haven, CT, pp158–166.

[81] Sim, S. (2007) *Manifesto for Silence: Confronting the Politics and Culture of Noise*, Edinburgh University Press, Edinburgh, pp86, 101.

[82] Gay, P. (2007) *Modernism: The Lure of Heresy from Baudelaire to Beckett and Beyond*, Vintage Books, London, p163.

[83] Larson, K. (2012) *Where the Heart Beats: John Cage, Zen Buddhism and the Inner Life of Artists*, Penguin Press, New York, p275.

[84] As mentioned elsewhere in the text, 'a grain of sand' is in the opening line of Blake's poem, *Auguries of Innocence*; in addition, Archibald Belaney, commonly known as Grey Owl and often called Canada's first environmentalist, famously once said to an audience during one of his early twentieth-century speaking tours, 'I come to offer you, what? A single green leaf' (See: Dickson, L. (1938) *The Green Leaf: A Memorial to Grey Owl*, Lovat Dickson Ltd Publishers, London, facing p6); and thirteenth-century Zen master Eihei Dogen taught that even a tiny

dewdrop manifests the entirety of the universe (see: Tanahashi, K. (ed.) (1985) *Moon in a Dewdrop: Writings of Zen Master Dogen*, North Point Press, New York, p71).

85 Larson, K. (2012) *Where the Heart Beats: John Cage, Zen Buddhism and the Inner Life of Artists*, Penguin Press, New York, pp xv, 45.

86 Herzfeld, N. (2009) *Technology and Religion: Remaining Human in a Co-Created World*, Templeton Press, West Conshocken, PA, p138.

87 Williams, A. (trans.) (2006) *Rumi: Spiritual Verses – The First Book of the Masnavi-ye Ma'navi*, Penguin Books, London, p245.

88 Williams, A. (trans.) (2006) *Rumi: Spiritual Verses – The First Book of the Masnavi-ye Ma'navi*, Penguin Books, London, p58.

89 Cirlot, J. E. (1971) *A Dictionary of Symbols*, trans. Sage, J., 2nd edition, Routledge, London, p69.

90 For example: 'And the Word was made flesh, and dwelt among us', the New Testament of the Bible, the Gospel of John 1:14.

91 For example: 'Split a piece of wood; I am there. Lift up the stone, and you will find me there.' Meyer, M. (trans.) (1992) *The Gospel of Thomas*, HarperCollins, New York, vs. 53, 77, pp53, 71.

92 Wright, J. K. (2001) *Schoenberg, Wittgenstein, and the Vienna Circle: Epistemological Meta-Themes in Harmonie Theory, Aesthetics, and Logical Positivism*, PhD thesis, Faculty of Graduate Studies and Research, McGill University, Montreal, Quebec, Canada, available at http://digitool.library.mcgill.ca/R/?func=dbin-jump-full&object_id=38438&local_base=GEN01-MCG02, accessed 23 September 2012, p111.

93 Tanahashi, K. (ed.) (1985) *Moon in a Dewdrop: Writings of Zen Master Dogen*, North Point Press, New York, pp146–147.

94 Ruskin, J. (1859 [1908]) *The Two Paths*, Cassell & Company, Ltd, London, pp106–109.

95 Blake, W. (c.1803 [1994]) 'Auguries of Innocence', in *The Selected Poems of William Blake*, Wordsworth Editions Ltd, Ware, p135.

96 Williams, R. J. (2011) 'Technê-Zen and the spiritual quality of global capitalism', *Critical Inquiry*, vol. 37, p34.

97 Smith, H. (2001) *Why Religion Matters: The Fate of the Human Spirit in an Age of Disbelief*, HarperCollins, New York, p200.

98 Foster, R. J. (1980) *Celebration of Discipline: The Path to Spiritual Growth*, Hodder & Stoughton, London, p2.

8 A New Game: function, design and post-materialist form

1 Wilkinson, R. and Pickett, K. (2009) *The Spirit Level: Why More Equal Societies Almost Always Do Better*, Allen Lane, London, pp40, 70.

2 Berger, J. J. (2013) *Exploring Climate Change Disinformation*, EcoMENA, 15 April 2013, available at www.ecomena.org/tag/climate-change-debate, accessed 12 May 2013.

[3] Connor, S. (2013) 'Billionaires secretly fund attacks on climate science', *The Independent*, 24 January 2013, available at www.independent.co.uk/environment/climate-change/exclusive-billionaires-secretly-fund-attacks-on-climate-science-8466312.html, accessed 25 January 2013.

[4] Thoreau, H. D. (1854 [1983]) 'Walden', in Thoreau, H. D., *Walden and Civil Disobedience*, Penguin Books, London, p138.

[5] Schwarz, B. (2005) *The Paradox of Choice: Why More is Less*, HarperCollins, New York, pp54–56.

[6] Thoreau, H. D. (1854 [1983]) 'Walden', in Thoreau, H. D., *Walden and Civil Disobedience*, Penguin Group, New York, pp56–57.

[7] Michaels, F. S. (2011) *Monoculture: How One Story is Changing Everything*, Red Clover Press, Kamloops, BC, pp105–107.

[8] Lewis, C. S. (1947) *Miracles: A Preliminary Study*, HarperCollins, London, p63.

[9] Gompertz, W. (2012) *What Are You Looking At: 150 Years of Modern Art in the Blink of an Eye*, Viking, London, p138.

[10] Lewis, C. S. (1947) *Miracles: A Preliminary Study*, HarperCollins, London, p63.

[11] Lamy, P. (2013) 'World Trade Organisation's Pascal Lamy: capitalism must change', *Hardtalk*, BBC, 21 January, available at http://news.bbc.co.uk/1/hi/programmes/hardtalk/9786725.stm, accessed 4 March 2013.

[12] Longley, C. (2012) 'Virtue ethics fills a gaping hole in our explanation of what has gone wrong', *The Tablet*, 8 December 2012, p11.

[13] MacIntyre, A. (2007) *After Virtue*, 3rd edition, Bristol Classical Press, London, p148.

[14] Thomson, J. A. K. (1976) *The Ethics of Aristotle: The Nicomachean Ethics*, Penguin Books, London, p104.

[15] Henriot, P. J., DeBerri, E. P. and Schultheis, M. J. (1988) *Catholic Social Teaching: Our Best Kept Secret*, Orbis Books, Maryknoll, NY and the Center of Concern, Washington, DC, pp20–22.

[16] MacIntyre, A. (2007) *After Virtue*, 3rd edition, Bristol Classical Press, London, p149.

[17] Mishra, P. (2012) *From the Ruins of Empire: The Revolt against the West and the Remaking of Asia*, Allen Lane, London, pp306–309.

[18] Stewart, H. and Elliot, L. (2013) 'Nicholas Stern: "I got it wrong on climate change – it's far, far worse"', *Guardian*, 26 January, available at www.guardian.co.uk/environment/2013/jan/27/nicholas-stern-climate-change-davos, accessed 27 January 2013.

[19] Confino, J. (2012) 'Moments of revelation trigger the biggest transformations', *Guardian Professional*, 9 November 2012, available at www.guardian.co.uk/sustainable-business/epiphany-transform-corporate-sustainability, accessed 10 December 2012; also see: *Guardian Sustainable Business* interview available at www.guardian.co.uk/sustainable-business/video/interview-lynda-gratton-sustainability-leadership-video?intcmp=122, accessed 27 January 2013.

[20] *Journal of Management, Spirituality & Religion* (2012), available at www.tandfonline.com/toc/rmsr20/current, accessed 13 January 2013.

[21] Lewis, C. S. (1947) *Miracles: A Preliminary Study*, HarperCollins, London, p278.

[22] Weber, M. (1965) *The Sociology of Religion*, available at www.e-reading-lib. org/bookreader.php/145149/The_Sociology_of_Religion.pdf, accessed 25 January 2013, p157.

[23] Chesterton, G. K. (1908) *Orthodoxy*, Image Books, London, p66.

[24] Gill, S. (ed.) (2004) *William Wordsworth: Selected Poems*, Penguin Books Ltd, London, pp144–145.

[25] Gill, S. (ed.) (2004) *William Wordsworth: Selected Poems*, Penguin Books Ltd, London, pp24–25.

[26] Stryk, L. (trans.) (1985) 'Introduction' in *On Love and Barley: Haiku of Basho*, Penguin Books, London, p12.

[27] Hamill, S. (trans.) (2000) *Narrow Road to the Interior and Other Writings*, Shambhala Publications Inc., Boston, MA, pp117, 158.

[28] Stryk, L. (trans.) (1985) 'Introduction' in *On Love and Barley: Haiku of Basho*, Penguin Books, London, pp14–19.

[29] Yuasa, N. (trans.) (1966) 'Introduction' in *The Narrow Road to the Deep North and Other Travel Sketches*, Penguin Books, London, p37.

[30] Meyer, M. (trans.) (1992) *The Gospel of Thomas*, HarperCollins, New York.

[31] Meyer, M. (trans.) (1992) *The Gospel of Thomas*, HarperCollins, New York, p53.

[32] Needleman, J. (2005) 'Foreword' in LeLoup, J.-Y., *The Gospel of Thomas: The Gnostic Wisdom of Jesus*, trans. Rowe, J., Inner Traditions, Rochester, VT, p viii.

[33] Costa, C. D. N. (trans.) (2005) 'Hermotimus or on philosophical schools', in *Lucian: Selected Dialogues*, Oxford University Press, Oxford, p126.

[34] McGrath, A. (2003) *The Reenchantment of Nature: The Denial of Religion and the Ecological Crisis*, Doubleday/Galilee, New York, pp32–36.

[35] Short, W. (2008) 'Talk 7: the call of creatures (1210–1225)', *St. Francis of Assisi: A New Way of Being Christian*, audio lecture series, Now You Know Media, Rockville, MD.

[36] Sorrell, R. D. (1988) *St. Francis of Assisi and Nature: Tradition and Innovation in Western Christian Attitudes Toward the Environment*, Oxford University Press, Oxford, pp79–92, 145.

[37] Emerson, R. W. (1836 [1995]) 'Nature', in *Essays and Poems*, edited by C. Bigsby, Everyman, J. M. Dent, London, pp260–274.

[38] Heuer, K. (2006) *Being Caribou: Five Months on Foot with an Arctic Herd*, McClelland & Stewart Ltd, Toronto, ON, pp98–99.

[39] Heuer, K. (2006) *Being Caribou: Five Months on Foot with an Arctic Herd*, McClelland & Stewart Ltd, Toronto, ON, pp192–193.

[40] Walters, A. L. (1989) *The Spirit of Native America: Beauty and Mysticism in American Indian Art*, Chronicle Books, San Francisco, CA, pp35, 45.

[41] Lynch, G. (2007) *The New Spirituality: An Introduction to Progressive Belief in the Twenty-first Century*, I. B. Taurus, London, p53.

[42] King, U. (2009) *The Search for Spirituality: Our Global Quest for Meaning and Fulfilment*, Canterbury Press, Norwich, p143.

[43] Sparke, P. (2004) *An Introduction to Design and Culture: 1900 to the Present*, Routledge, London, p94.

[44] Sparke, P. (2004) *An Introduction to Design and Culture: 1900 to the Present*, Routledge, London, pp89–93.

[45] Dormer, P. (1990) *The Meanings of Modern Design*, Thames & Hudson, London, p19–20.

[46] Dormer, P. (1990) *The Meanings of Modern Design*, Thames & Hudson, London, pp19–20.

[47] Whitford, F. (1984) *Bauhaus*, Thames & Hudson, London, p9.

[48] Scheidig, W. (1966) *Weimar Crafts of the Bauhaus: 1919–1924/An Early Experiment in Industrial Design*, Reinhold Publishing Corporation, New York, p26.

[49] Raizman, D. (2010) *History of Modern Design*, Laurence King Publishing, London, pp199–200.

[50] Grunfeld, F. V. (1975) *Games of the World*, Swiss Committee for UNICEF, Zurich, p63.

[51] In addition to these meanings, priorities and values, which are embedded into the object at the design stage, over the course of its useful life an object may acquire a variety of other meanings, such as sentimental significance. Generally, these associative meanings lie outside the sphere of influence of the designer.

[52] Krasny, J. (2013) *The Ethics of 3D Printers: And the Guns They Can Produce*, INC., 15 May, available at www.inc.com/jill-krasny/ethics-of-3d-printers-guns.html, accessed 27 May 2013.

[53] Sierra Club (2008) *Bottled Water: Learning the Facts and Taking Action*, available at www.sierraclub.org/committees/cac/water/bottled_water/bottled_water.pdf, accessed 10 February 2013.

[54] Gelineau, K. (2009) 'Australians ban bottled water', *Huffington Post*, available at www.huffingtonpost.com/2009/07/09/australians-ban-bottled-w_n_228678.html, accessed 14 February 2013.

[55] *Huffington Post* (2013) 'Plastic bottle ban in Concord, Massachusetts goes into effect', *Huffington Post*, available at www.huffingtonpost.com/2013/01/02/plastic-bottles-banned-concord-massachusetts_n_2395824.html, accessed 14 February 2013.

[56] Fager, C. (2009) 'The top ten reasons (plus three) why bottled water is a blessing', *Friends Journal: Quaker Thought and Life Today*, 1 July, available at www.friendsjournal.org/bottled-water, accessed 10 February 2013.

[57] Aas, G. and Riedmiller, A. (1994) *Trees of Britain and Europe*, Collins, London, p182.

[58] Collins, W. and Dickens, C. (1857 [2011]) *The Lazy Tour of Two Idle Apprentices*, Hesperus Press Ltd, London, pp84–86.

[59] Williamson, P. (1999) *From Confinement to Community: The Moving Story of 'The Moor'*, P. Williamson, Lancaster, quoting an extract from the *Lancaster Guardian* newspaper article from 19 September 1857, p12.

163

[60] Kew Gardens (2013) *Kew Royal Botanical Gardens: Holm Oak*, available at http://apps.kew.org/trees/?page_id=91, accessed 4 March 2013.

[61] Kew Gardens (2013) *Kew Royal Botanical Gardens: Holm Oak*, available at http://apps.kew.org/trees/?page_id=91, accessed 4 March 2013.

[62] Wright, D. (trans.) (1964) *The Canterbury Tales: A Modern Prose Rendering*, FontanaPress, London, p47.

[63] Folkard, R. (1892) *Plant Lore, Legends, and Lyrics: Embracing the Myths, Traditions, Superstitions, and Folk-Lore of the Plant Kingdom*, Cornell University Internet Archive, available at http://archive.org/details/cu31924062766666, accessed 17 January 2013, pp385–386.

[64] Feng, G. F. and English, J. (trans.) (1989) *Tao Te Ching*, by Lao Tsu, Vintage Books, New York, vs. 76, p78.

[65] Haidt, J. (2012) *The Righteous Mind*, Allen Lane, London, pp xv, 11.

[66] Herzfeld, N. (2009) *Technology and Religion: Remaining Human in a Co-created World*, Templeton Press, West Conshohocken, PA, pp86, 91.

9 Epilogue

[1] Hern, M. (ed.) (2008) 'On education', by Leo Tolstoy in *Everywhere All the Time: A New Deschooling Reader*, AK Press, Oakland, CA, pp1–6.

[2] Merton, T. (1969) *Contemplative Prayer*, Doubleday, New York, p48.

[3] Griffith, T. (2000) *Plato: The Republic*, edited by Ferrari, G. R. F., Cambridge University Press, Cambridge, pp54–56.

[4] Longley, C. (2013a) 'The welfare measures amount to dictation about how people should live their lives', *The Tablet*, 6 April 2013, p11.

[5] Wolters, C. (trans.) (1972) *Richard Rolle: The Fire of Love*, Penguin Books, Hardmondsworth, p58.

[6] 1 Corinthians 8:1.

[7] Wolters, C. (trans.) (1972) *Richard Rolle: The Fire of Love*, Penguin Books, Hardmondsworth, pp58–59.

[8] The term 'transcategorical' is used by the theological philosopher John Hick to mean 'beyond the range of our human systems of concepts or mental categories'; see Hick, J. (2001) *Who or What is God?*, available at www.johnhick.org.uk/article1.html, accessed 19 February 2013, p3.

Sources of quotations at the beginning of each chapter

Ch. 1   Farid Ud-Din Attar (twelfth century [1984]) *The Conference of the Birds*, trans. Darbandi, A. and Davis, D., Penguin Books, London, lines 3645–3648, p188.

Ch. 2   Plato (fourth century BCE [2005]) *Phaedrus*, trans. Rowe, C., Penguin Group, London, vs. 246, p25.

Ch. 3   Arnold, M. (1867) 'Dover Beach', originally published in *New Poems*. In Arnold, M. (1994) *Dover Beach and Other Poems*, Dover Publications, New York, pp86–87.

Ch. 4   Camus, A. (1947) *The Plague*, trans. Gilbert, S., Penguin Group, London, p6.

Ch. 5   Longley, C. (2013b) 'The world may admire but not change: there is no call to conversion', *The Tablet*, 23 March, p5.

Ch. 6   Hesse, H. (1951) *Siddhartha*, trans. Rosner, H., New Directions Publishing, New York, p119.

Ch. 7   Conrad, J. (1904 [1996]) *Nostromo: A Tale of the Seaboard*, Wordsworth Editions Ltd, Ware, pp45–46.

Ch. 8   de la Mare, W. (1913 [2001]) 'A song of enchantment', *Peacock Pie: A Book of Rhymes*, Faber & Faber, London, pp102–103.

Ch. 9   Farid Ud-Din Attar (twelfth century [1984]) *The Conference of the Birds*, trans. Darbandi, A. and Davis, D., Penguin Books, London, lines 3744–3746, p193.

Bibliography

Aas, G. and Riedmiller, A. (1994) *Trees of Britain and Europe*, Collins, London.

Alexander, C. (1979) *The Timeless Way of Building*, Oxford University Press, New York.

Anderson, R. (2009) *Confessions of a Radical Industrialist*, Random House, London.

Armstrong, K. (1994) *Visions of God: Four Medieval Mystics and their Writings*, Bantam Books, New York.

Armstrong, K. (2002) *Islam: A Short History*, Phoenix Press, London.

Arnold, M. (1867 [1994]) 'Dover Beach', originally published in *New Poems*, in Arnold, M., *Dover Beach and Other Poems*, Dover Publications, New York.

Arnold, M. (2006 [1869]) *Culture and Anarchy*, Oxford University Press, Oxford.

Bakan, J. (2004) *The Corporation: The Pathological Pursuit of Profit and Power*, Constable & Robinson Ltd, London.

Barrett, W. (ed.) (1956) 'Zen for the West', in *Zen Buddhism: Selected Writings of D. T. Suzuki*, Doubleday, New York.

BBC (2005) 'US bans Commandments in courtroom', 27 June, available at http://news.bbc.co.uk/1/hi/world/americas/4627459.stm, accessed 10 June 2012.

Beattie, T. (2007) *The New Atheists: The Twilight of Reason & The War on Religion*, Darton, Longman & Todd Ltd, London.

Berg, M. V. (2012) *Trio Solisti Program*, Maverick Concerts, Sunday, 12 August, available at www.maverickconcerts.org/TRIOSOLISTI_2012.html, accessed 16 October 2012.

Berger, J. J. (2013) *Exploring Climate Change Disinformation*, EcoMENA, 15 April 2013, available at www.ecomena.org/tag/climate-change-debate, accessed 12 May 2013.

Berry, T. (2009) *The Sacred Universe*, edited by Mary Evelyn Tucker, Columbia University Press, New York.

Bhamra, T. and Lofthouse, V. (2007) *Design for Sustainability: A Practical Approach*, Gower, Aldershot.

Bianco, N. M. and Litz, F. T. (2010) *Reducing Greenhouse Gas Emission in the United States Using Existing Federal Authorities and State Action*, World Resources Institute, Washington, DC.

Blake, W. (c.1803 [1994]) 'Auguries of innocence', in *The Selected Poems of William Blake*, Wordsworth Editions Ltd, Ware.

Borgmann, A. (2000) 'Society in the postmodern era', *The Washington Quarterly*, Winter, available at www.twq.com/winter00/231Borgmann.pdf, accessed 26 April 2011.

Borgmann, A. (2001) 'Opaque and articulate design', *International Journal of Technology and Design Education*, vol. 11, pp5–11.

Borgmann, A. (2003) *Power Failure: Christianity in the Culture of Technology*, Brazos Press, Grand Rapids, MI.

Borgmann, A. (2006) *Real American Ethics*, University of Chicago Press, Chicago, IL.

Borgmann, A. (2010) 'I miss the hungry years', *The Montana Professor*, vol. 21, no. 1, pp4–7.

Branzi, A. (2009) *Grandi Legni* [exhibition catalogue essay], Design Gallery Milano and Nilufar, Milan.

Briggs, A. S. A. (ed.) (1962) 'Socialism', various writings in *William Morris: News From Nowhere and Selected Writings and Designs*, Penguin Group, London, pp158–180.

Buchanan, R. (1989) 'Declaration by design: rhetoric, argument, and demonstration in design practice', in Margolin, V. (ed.), *Design Discourse: History, Theory, Criticism*, University of Chicago Press, Chicago, IL, pp91–109.

Buchanan, R. (1995) 'Rhetoric, humanism and design', in Buchanan, R. and Margolin, V. (eds), *Discovering Design: Explorations in Design Studies*, University of Chicago Press, Chicago, IL.

Burns, B. (2010) 'Re-evaluating obsolescence and planning for it', in Cooper, T. (ed.), *Longer Lasting Products: Alternatives to the Throwaway Society*, Gower, Farnham, pp39–60.

Cain, S. (2013) *Quiet: The Power of Introverts in a World that Can't Stop Talking*, Penguin Books, London.

Camus, A. (1942 [2005]) *The Myth of Sisyphus*, Penguin Books, London.

Camus, A. (1947) *The Plague*, trans. Gilbert, S., Penguin Group, London.

Capra, F. (2012) 'Ecological literacy', in *Resurgence*, The Resurgence Trust, Bideford, UK.

Carey, G. (2011) *Submission to the European Court of Human Rights*, 11 September, available at www.glcarey.co.uk/Speeches/PressReleases/ECHR.html, accessed 27 April 2012.

Carey, G. and Carey, A. (2012) *We Don't Do God: The Marginalization of Public Faith*, Monarch Books, Oxford.

Carlson, D. and Richards, B. (2010) *David Report: Time to ReThink Design*, vol. 12, available at http://static.davidreport.com/pdf/371.pdf, accessed 20 May 2011.

Carr, N. (2010) *The Shallows: How the Internet is Changing the Way We Think, Read and Remember*, Atlantic Books, London.

CDBU (2012) *Council for the Defence of British Universities*, available at http://cdbu.org.uk, accessed 9 November 2012.

Chan, J., de Haan, E., Nordbrand, S. and Torstensson, A. (2008) *Silenced to Deliver: Mobile Phone Manufacturing in China and the Philippines*, SOMO and SwedWatch, Stockholm, Sweden, available at www.germanwatch.org/corp/it-chph08.pdf, accessed 30 March 2011.

Chesterton, G. K. (1908) *Orthodoxy*, Image Books, London.

Chevalier, J. and Gheerbrant, A. (1992) *The Penguin Dictionary of Symbols*, trans. Buchan-Brown, J., Penguin Group, London.

Chomsky, N. (2012a) 'How the Magna Carta became a Minor Carta, part 1', *Guardian*, London, 24 July, available at www.guardian.co.uk/commentisfree/2012/jul/24/magna-carta-minor-carta-noam-chomsky?INTCMP=SRCH, accessed 25 July 2012.

Chomsky, N. (2012b) 'How the Magna Carta became a Minor Carta, part 2', *Guardian*, London, 25 July, available at www.guardian.co.uk/commentisfree/2012/jul/25/magna-carta-minor-carta-noam-chomsky?INTCMP=SRCH, accessed 25 July 2012.

Christianson, E. S. (2007) *Ecclesiastes Through the Centuries*, Wiley-Blackwell, Malden, MA.

Cirlot, J. E. (1971) *A Dictionary of Symbols*, trans. Sage, J., 2nd edition, Routledge, London.

Collins, W. and Dickens, C. (1857 [2011]) *The Lazy Tour of Two Idle Apprentices*, Hesperus Press Ltd, London.

Comte-Sponville, A. (2007) *The Book of Atheist Spirituality: An Elegant Argument for Spirituality without God*, trans. Huston, N. Bantam Books, London.

Confino, J. (2012) 'Moments of revelation trigger the biggest transformations', *Guardian Professional*, 9 November 2012, available at www.guardian.

co.uk/sustainable-business/epiphany-transform-corporate-sustainability, accessed 10 December 2012.

Connor, S. (2013) 'Billionaires secretly fund attacks on climate science', *Independent*, 24 January, available at www.independent.co.uk/ environment/climate-change/exclusive-billionaires-secretly-fund-attacks-on-climate-science-8466312.html#, accessed 25 January 2013.

Conrad, J. (1904 [1996]) *Nostromo: A Tale of the Seaboard*, Wordsworth Editions Ltd, Ware.

Costa, C. D. N. (trans.) (2005) 'Hermotimus or on philosophical schools', in *Lucian: Selected Dialogues*, Oxford University Press, Oxford.

Cottingham, J. (2005) *The Spiritual Dimension: Religion, Philosophy and Human Value*, Cambridge University Press, Cambridge.

Crompton, T. (2010) *Common Cause: The Case for Working with our Cultural Values*, WWF-UK, available at http://assets.wwf.org.uk/downloads/ common_cause_report.pdf, accessed 14 June 2012.

Crow, K. D. (2012) Principal Research Fellow, Islam and Modernity, International Institute of Advanced Islamic Studies, Kuala Lumpur, Malaysia, interviewed on *The Future is Halal*, BBC Radio 4, London, broadcast 5:00 p.m., 26 August.

Csikszentmihalyi, M. (1990) *Flow: The Psychology of Optimal Experience*, HarperCollins, New York.

Curtis, M. (2005a) 'Distraction technologies', in *Distraction: Being Human in the Digital Age*, Futuretext Ltd, London, pp53–69.

Curtis, M. (2005b) *Distraction: Being Human in the Digital Age*, Futuretext Ltd, London.

Dalai Lama (2011) *Beyond Religion: Ethics for a Whole World*, Rider/Ebury Publishing, London.

Daly, H. E. (2007) *Ecological Economics and Sustainable Development: Selected Essays of Herman Daly*, Edward Elgar Publishing, Cheltenham.

Davison, A. (2001) *Technology and the Contested Meanings of Sustainability*, State University of New York Press, Albany, NY.

Davison, A. (2008) 'Ruling the future? Heretical reflections on technology and other secular religions of sustainability', *Worldviews*, vol. 12, pp146–162, available at http://ade.se/skola/ht10/infn14/articles/seminar4/ Davison%20-%20Ruling%20the%20Future.pdf, accessed 30 August 2011.

Day, C. (1998) *Art and Spirit: Spirit and Place – Consensus Design*, available at www.fantastic-machine.com/artandspirit/spirit-and-place/consensus. html, accessed 28 March 2011.

Day, C. (2002) *Spirit and Place*, Elsevier, Oxford.

de la Mare, W. (1913 [2001]) 'A song of enchantment', in *Peacock Pie: A Book of Rhymes*, Faber & Faber, London.

Dickens, C. (1854 [2003]) *Hard Times: For These Times*, Penguin Group, London.

Dickson, L. (1938) *The Green Leaf: A Memorial to Grey Owl*, Lovat Dickson Ltd Publishers, London.

Dormer, P. (1990) *The Meanings of Modern Design*, Thames & Hudson, London.

Duhigg, C. and Bradsher, K. (2012) 'How U.S. lost out in iPhone work', *New York Times*, 21 January, available at www.nytimes.com/2012/01/22/business/apple-america-and-a-squeezed-middle-class.html, accessed 22 January 2012.

Eagleton, T. (2007) *The Meaning of Life*, Oxford University Press, Oxford.

Eagleton, T. (2009) *Reason, Faith and Revolution: Reflections on the God Debate*, Yale University Press, New Haven, CT.

Eagleton, T. (2011) *Why Marx Was Right*, Yale University Press, New Haven, CT.

Easwaran, E. (trans.) (1985) *The Bhagavad Gita*, Vintage Books, New York.

Eco-design Directive (2009) Directive 2009/125/EC of the European Parliament and of the Council of 21 October 2009, available at http://eur-lex.europa.eu/LexUriServ/LexUriServ.do?uri=OJ:L:2009:285:0010:0035:en:PDF, accessed 30 October 2012.

Edwards, B. (1979) *Drawing on the Right Side of the Brain: A Course in Enhancing Creativity and Artistic Confidence*, J. P. Tarcher, Inc., Los Angeles, CA.

Ehrenfeld, J. R. (2008) *Sustainability by Design: A Subversive Strategy for Transforming Our Consumer Culture*, Yale University Press, New Haven, CT.

EIA (2011) *System Failure: The UK's Harmful Trade in Electronic Waste*, London: Environmental Investigation Agency, available at www.eia-international.org/files/news640-1.pdf, accessed 20 May 2011.

Eliade, M. (1964 [1989]) *Shamanism: Archaic Techniques of Ecstasy*, trans. Trask, W. R., Arkana, London.

Emerson, R. W. (1836 [1995]) 'Nature', in *Essays and Poems*, edited by C. Bigsby, Everyman, J. M. Dent, London, pp260–274.

Erlhoff, M. and Marshall, T. (eds) (2008) *Design Dictionary: Perspectives on Design Terminology*, Birkhäuser Verlag AG, Basel.

Evans-Wentz, W. Y. (ed.) (2008) *The Tibetan Book of the Dead Or the After-Death Experiences on the Bardo Plane*, trans. Lama Kazi Dawa-Samdup, available at www.holybooks.com/wp-content/uploads/The-Tibetan-Book-of-the-Dead.pdf, accessed 19 July 2012.

Fager, C. (2009) 'The top ten reasons (plus three) why bottled water is a blessing', *Friends Journal: Quaker Thought and Life Today*, 1 July 2009, available at www.friendsjournal.org/bottled-water, accessed 10 February 2013.

Farid Ud-Din Attar (twelfth century [1984] *The Conference of the Birds*, trans. Darbandi, A. and Davis, D., Penguin Books, London.

Feng, G. F. and English, J. (trans.) (1989) *Tao Te Ching, by Lao Tsu*, Vintage Books, New York.

Folkard, R. (1892) *Plant Lore, Legends, and Lyrics: Embracing the Myths, Traditions, Superstitions, and Folk-Lore of the Plant Kingdom*, Cornell

University Internet Archive, available at http://archive.org/details/
cu31924062766666, accessed 17 January 2013.

Foster, R. J. (1980) *Celebration of Discipline: The Path to Spiritual Growth*, Hodder & Stoughton, London.

Friedman, M. (1962 [1982]) *Capitalism and Freedom*, University of Chicago Press, Chicago, IL, available at www.4shared.com/document/GHk_gt9U/Friedman_Milton_Capitalism_and.html, accessed 10 September 2011.

Fry, T., Tonkinwise, C., Bremner, C., Fitzpatrick, L., Norton, L. and Lopera, D. (2011) *Future Tense: Design, Sustainability and the Urmadic University*, ABC National Radio, Australia, broadcast 4 August 2011, transcript available at www.abc.net.au/radionational/programs/futuretense/design-sustainability-and-the-urmadic-university/2928402, accessed 12 January 2012.

Fuad-Luke, A. (2009) *Design Activism: Beautiful Strangeness for a Sustainable World*, Earthscan, London.

Gandhi (1925) *The Collected Works of Mahatma Gandhi*, vol. 33, no. 25, September 1925–10 February 1926 (excerpt from *Young India*, 22 October 1925), available at www.gandhiserve.org/cwmg/VOL033.PDF, accessed 12 May 2011.

Gandhi, M. (1982) *The Words of Gandhi*, edited by R. Attenborough, Newmarket Press, New York.

Gay, P. (2007) *Modernism: The Lure of Heresy from Baudelaire to Beckett and Beyond*, Vintage Books, London.

Gelineau, K. (2009) 'Australians ban bottled water', *Huffington Post*, available at www.huffingtonpost.com/2009/07/09/australians-ban-bottled-w_n_228678.html, accessed 14 February 2013.

Gill, S. (ed.) (2004) *William Wordsworth: Selected Poems*, Penguin Books Ltd., London.

Gladwell, M. (2000) *The Tipping Point*, Abacus, London.

Gompertz, W. (2012) *What Are You Looking At? 150 Years of Modern Art in the Blink of an Eye*, Viking, London.

Gorz, A. (2010) *Ecologica*, trans. Turner C., Seagull Books, London.

Grayling, A. C. (2011) 'Epistle to the reader', foreword of *The Good Book: A Secular Bible*, Bloomsbury Publishing, London.

Griffith, T. (2000) *Plato: The Republic*, edited by Ferrari, G. R. F., Cambridge University Press, Cambridge.

Grunfeld, F. V. (1975) *Games of the World*, Swiss Committee for UNICEF, Zurich.

Habermas, J. (1980 [2010]) 'Modernity', in Leitch, V. B (ed.), *The Norton Anthology of Theory and Criticism*, 2nd edition, W. W. Norton & Co., London.

Haidt, J. (2012) *The Righteous Mind*, Allen Lane, London.

Hamill, S. (trans.) (1998) 'Introduction', in Bashō, M., *Narrow Road to the Interior and Other Writings*, Shambhala Publications, Inc., Boston, MA.

171

Hamill, S. (trans.) (2000) *Narrow Road to the Interior and Other Writings*, Shambhala Publications Inc., Boston, MA.

Harries, R. (1993) *Art and the Beauty of God*, Mombray, London.

Harrison, K. (2012) *End of Growth and Liberal Democracy*, lecture, Australian Centre for Sustainable Catchments, University of Southern Queensland, available at http://vimeo.com/41056934, accessed 17 May 2012.

Harvey, F. (2012) 'Europe looks to open up Greenland for natural resources extraction', *Guardian*, 31 July, available at www.guardian.co.uk/environment/2012/jul/31/europe-greenland-natural-resources, accessed 1 August 2012.

Havemann, S. and Fellner, D. (2004) 'Generative parametric design of gothic window tracery', *Proceedings of International Conference on Shape Modeling and Applications 2004 (SMI'04)*, available at http://generative-modeling.org/GenerativeModeling/Documents/window-tracery-smi04-04.pdf, accessed 10 April 2012.

Hawken, P. (2007) *Blessed Unrest: How the Largest Movement in the World Came into Being and Why No One Saw It Coming*, Viking, New York.

Heidegger, M. (1993) *Basic Writings: Revised and Expanded Edition*, edited by D. F. Krell, Routledge, London.

Henriot, P. J., DeBerri, E. P. and Schultheis, M. J. (1988) *Catholic Social Teaching: Our Best Kept Secret*, Orbis Books, Maryknoll, NY and the Center of Concern, Washington, DC.

Hern, M. (ed.) (2008) 'On education' by Leo Tolstoy in *Everywhere All the Time: A New Deschooling Reader*, AK Press, Oakland, CA.

Herrigel, E. (1953 [1999]) *Zen in the Art of Archery*, Vintage Books, New York.

Herrington, C., Forsgren, K. A. and Benskin, E. (2002) *Arts of the Islamic World: A Teacher's Guide*, Smithsonian Freer Gallery of Art and Arthur M. Sackler Gallery, Smithsonian Institution, available at www.asia.si.edu/explore/teacherresources/islam.pdf, accessed 19 April 2012.

Herzfeld, N. (2009) *Technology and Religion: Remaining Human in a Co-Created World*, Templeton Press, West Conshohocken, PA.

Heskett, J. (1987) *Industrial Design*, Thames & Hudson, London.

Hesse, H. (1951) *Siddhartha*, trans. Rosner, H., New Directions Publishing, New York.

Heuer, K. (2006) *Being Caribou: Five Months on Foot with an Arctic Herd*, McClelland & Stewart Ltd, Toronto, ON.

Hick, J. (1982) *God Has Many Names*, The Westminster Press, Philadelphia, PA.

Hick, J. (1989) *An Interpretation of Religion: Human Responses to the Transcendent*, Yale University Press, New Haven, CT.

Hick, J. (1999) *The Fifth Dimension: An Exploration of the Spiritual Realm*, Oneworld Publications, Oxford.

Hick, J. (2001) *Who or What is God?*, available at www.johnhick.org.uk/article1.html, accessed 19 February 2013, p3.

Hick, J. (2002) *Science/Religion*, a talk given at King Edward VI Camp Hill School, Birmingham, March 2002, available at www.johnhick.org.uk/jsite/index.php?option=com_content&view=article&id=52:sr&catid=37:articles&Itemid=58, accessed 19 February 2011.

Hick, J. (2004) 'The real and it's personae and impersonae', a revised version of an article in Tessier, L. (ed.) (1989) *Concepts of the Ultimate*, Macmillan, London, available at www.johnhick.org.uk/jsite/index.php?option=com_content&view=article&id=57:thereal&catid=37:articles&Itemid=58, accessed 19 February 2011.

Hill, K. (2008) *Legal Briefing on the Climate Change Bill: The Scientific Case for an 80% Target and the Proposed Review of the 2050 Target: Legal Briefing*, ClientEarth, London, available at www.clientearth.org/publications-all-documents, accessed 5 September 2012.

Hobsbawm, E. (1962) *The Age of Revolution 1789–1848*, Abacus, London.

Holloway, R. (2000) *Godless Morality*, Canongate, Edinburgh.

Horkheimer, M. and Adorno, T. W. (1947 [2010]) 'The culture industry: enlightenment as mass-deception', in Leitch, V. B. (ed.), *The Norton Anthology of Theory and Criticism*, 2nd edition, W. W. Norton, London, pp1110–1127.

Huffington Post (2013) 'Plastic bottle ban in Concord, Massachusetts goes into effect', *Huffington Post*, available at www.huffingtonpost.com/2013/01/02/plastic-bottles-banned-concord-massachusetts_n_2395824.html, accessed 14 February 2013.

Huitt, W. (2007) 'Maslow's hierarchy of needs', *Educational Psychology Interactive*, Valdosta State University, Valdosta, GA, available at www.edpsycinteractive.org/topics/regsys/maslow.html, accessed 30 August 2011.

Humphreys, C. (1949) *Zen Buddhism*, William Heinemann Ltd, London.

IDSA (2012) *Industrial Design: Defined*, Industrial Designers Society of America, available at www.idsa.org/content/content1/industrial-design-defined, accessed 10 February 2012.

IEA (2011) *Prospect of Limiting the Global Increase in Temperature to 2°C is Getting Bleaker*, International Energy Agency, 30 May, available at www.iea.org/index_info.asp?id=1959, accessed 11 January 2012.

Inayatullah, S. (2011) 'Spirituality as the fourth bottom line', available at www.metafuture.org/Articles/spirituality_bottom_line.htm, accessed 30 August 2011.

Inwood, M. (1997) *Heidegger*, Oxford University Press, Oxford.

ISO 14000 International Standard for Environmental Management, available at www.iso.org/iso/iso14000, accessed 30 October 2012.

Jackson, T. (2006) 'Consuming paradise? Towards a social and cultural psychology of sustainable consumption', in Jackson, T. (ed.), *Sustainable Consumption*, Earthscan, London, pp367–395.

Jackson, T. (2009) *Prosperity without Growth: Economics for a Finite Planet,* Earthscan, London.

Jessop, T. E. (1967) 'Nietzsche, Friedrich', in MacQuarrie, J. (ed.), *A Dictionary of Christian Ethics,* SCM Press Ltd, London, p233.

Johnston, W. (ed.) (2005) *The Cloud of Unknowing and the Book of Privy Counseling,* Doubleday, New York.

Jones, J. (2012) 'Greenland's ice sheet melt: a sensational picture of a blunt fact', *Guardian,* London, 27 July, available at www.guardian.co.uk/commentisfree/2012/jul/27/greenland-ice-sheet-melt, accessed 1 August 2012.

Jouanneau, D. (2011) *The Niqab and the French Social Pact,* French Diplomatie, available at www.diplomatie.gouv.fr/en/country-files/pakistan-504/france-and-pakistan/political-relations-5981/article/the-niqab-and-the-french-social, accessed 27 April 2012.

Journal of Management, Spirituality & Religion (2012), available at www.tandfonline.com/toc/rmsr20/current, accessed 13 January 2013.

Keble College (2012) *Keble Chapel Treasures: The Light of the World,* Oxford University, Oxford, available at www.keble.ox.ac.uk/about/chapel/chapel-history-and-treasures, accessed 24 May 2012.

Kelly, M. (2001) *The Divine Right of Capital,* Berret-Koehler, San Francisco, CA, quoted in Porritt, J. (2007) *Capitalism as if the World Matters,* Earthscan, London.

Kew Gardens (2013) *Kew Royal Botanical Gardens: Holm Oak,* available at http://apps.kew.org/trees/?page_id=91, accessed 4 March 2013.

King, U. (2009) *The Search for Spirituality: Our Global Quest for Meaning and Fulfilment,* Canterbury Press, Norwich.

Korten, D. C. (1999) *The Post-Corporate World: Life After Capitalism,* Berrett-Koehler Publishers, San Francisco, CA; and Kumarian Press, West Hartford, CT.

Krasny, J. (2013) *The Ethics of 3D Printers: And the Guns They Can Produce,* INC., 15 May, available at www.inc.com/jill-krasny/ethics-of-3d-printers-guns.html, accessed 27 May 2013.

Krueger, D. A. (2008) 'The ethics of global supply chains in China: convergences of East and West', *Journal of Business Ethics,* vol. 79, pp113–120.

Kumon, K. (2012) 'Overview of next-generation green data center', *Fujitsu Scientific & Technical Journal,* vol. 48, no. 2, pp177–183.

Lamy, P. (2013) 'World Trade Organisation's Pascal Lamy: capitalism must change', *Hardtalk,* BBC, 21 January, available at http://news.bbc.co.uk/1/hi/programmes/hardtalk/9786725.stm, accessed 4 March 2013.

Lanier, J. (2010) *You Are Not a Gadget: A Manifesto,* Penguin Books, London.

Lansley, S. (1994) *After the Gold Rush: The Trouble with Affluence – 'Consumer Capitalism' and the Way Forward,* Century Business Books, London.

Larson, K. (2012) *Where the Heart Beats: John Cage, Zen Buddhism and the Inner Life of Artists,* Penguin Press, New York.

174

Leonard, A. (2010) *The Story of Stuff*, Constable, London.

Lewis, C. S. (1947a) *Miracles: A Preliminary Study*, HarperCollins Publishers, London.

Lewis, C. S. (1947b) *The Abolition of Man*, HarperCollins Publishers, New York.

Lindsey, E. (2010) *Curating Humanity's Heritage*. TEDWomen, December, available at www.ted.com/talks/elizabeth_lindsey_curating_humanity_s_heritage.htm, posted February 2011, accessed 21 March 2011.

Longley, C. (2012) 'Virtue ethics fills a gaping hole in our explanation of what has gone wrong', *The Tablet*, 8 December, p11.

Longley, C. (2013a) 'The welfare measures amount to dictation about how people should live their lives', *The Tablet*, 6 April 2013.

Longley, C. (2013b) 'The world may admire but not change: there is no call to conversion', *The Tablet*, 23 March.

Lynch, G. (2007) *The New Spirituality: An Introduction to Progressive Belief in the Twenty-first Century*, I. B. Taurus, London.

MacIntyre, A. (2007) *After Virtue*, 3rd edition, Bristol Classical Press, London.

Manzini, E. and Jégou, F. (2003) *Sustainable Everyday: Scenarios for Urban Life*, Edizioni Ambiente, Milan.

Marx, K. and Engels, F. (1848 [2004]) *The Communist Manifesto*, Penguin Group, London.

Mascaró, J. (trans.) (1965) *The Upanishads*, Penguin Group, London.

Mascaró, J. (trans.) (1973) *The Dhammapada*, Penguin Group, London.

Mason, D. (1998) *Bomber Command: Recordings from the Second World War*, CD Liner Notes, Pavilion Records Ltd, Wadhurst, UK.

Mathews, F. (2006) 'Beyond modernity and tradition: a third way for development', *Ethics & the Environment*, vol. 11, no. 2, pp85–113.

McGinn, B. (2006) *The Essential Writings of Christian Mysticism*, The Modern Library, New York.

McGrath, A. (2003) *The Reenchantment of Nature: The Denial of Religion and the Ecological Crisis*, Doubleday/Galilee, New York.

Meroni, A. (ed.) (2007) *Creative Communities: People Inventing Sustainable Ways of Living*, Edizioni Poli.design, Milan.

Merton, T. (1967) *Mystics and Zen Masters*, Farrar, Straus & Giroux, New York.

Merton, T. (1969) *Contemplative Prayer*, Doubleday, New York.

Meyer, M. (trans.) (1992) *The Gospel of Thomas*, HarperCollins, New York.

Michaels, F. S. (2011) *Monoculture: How One Story is Changing Everything*, Red Clover Press, Kamloops, BC.

Mikels, J. A. and Reuter-Lorenz, P. A. (2004) 'Neural gate keeping: the role of interhemispheric interactions in resource allocation and selective filtering', *Neuropsychology*, vol. 18, no. 2, pp328–339.

Mishra, P. (2012) *From the Ruins of Empire: The Revolt against the West and the Remaking of Asia*, Allen Lane, London.

Nair, C. (2011a) *Consumptionomics: Asia's Role in Reshaping Capitalism and Saving the Planet*, Infinite Ideas Ltd, Oxford.

Nair, C. (2011b) Interview, *Business Daily*, BBC World Service Radio, 21 September.

Nasr, S. H. (1966 [1994]) *Ideals and Realities of Islam*, Aquarian/HarperCollins Publishers, London.

Needleman, J. (1989) 'Introduction', in *Tao Te Ching*, trans. Feng, G. F. and English, J., Vintage Books, New York.

Needleman, J. (1991) *Money and the Meaning of Life*, Doubleday, New York.

Needleman, J. (2005) 'Foreword' in LeLoup, J.-Y. *The Gospel of Thomas: The Gnostic Wisdom of Jesus*, trans. Rowe, J., Inner Traditions, Rochester, VT.

Nicoll, M. (1950 [1972]) *The New Man*, Penguin Books Inc., Baltimore, MD.

Nicoll, M. (1954) *The Mark*, Vincent Stuart Publishers, London.

Nietzsche, F. (1889 [2003]) *Twilight of the Idols and the Anti-Christ*, Penguin Group, London.

Nikhilananda, Swami (trans.) (1949) *The Upanishads*, Ramakrishna-Vivekananda Center, New York, available at www.vivekananda.net/PDFBooks/upanishads_nikhilananda.pdf, accessed 18 July 2012.

Northcott, M. S. (2007) *A Moral Climate: The Ethics of Global Warming*, Darton, Longman & Todd Ltd, London.

Norton, T. (2008) 'Cardinal wants Piero in a church', *The Tablet*, 6 December.

O'Neill, S. J., Boykoff, M., Niemeyer, S. and Day, S. A. (2013) 'On the use of imagery for climate change engagement', *Global Environmental Change*, available at SciVerse ScienceDirect, http://sciencepolicy.colorado.edu/admin/publication_files/2013.02.pdf, accessed 30 January 2013.

Oflaz, M. (2011) 'The effect of right and left brain dominance in language learning', *Procedia Social and Behavioural Sciences*, vol. 15, pp.1507–1513.

Orr, D. W. (2003) *Four Challenges of Sustainability*, School of Natural Resources – The University of Vermont, Spring Seminar Series 2003 – Ecological Economics, available at www.ratical.org/co-globalize/4CofS.html, accessed 17 May 2011.

Paine, R. T. and Soper, A. (1981) *The Art and Architecture of Japan*, Yale University Press, New Haven, CT.

Palmer, M. (2012) 'Secretary General, Alliance of Religions and Conservation', interview, BBC Radio 4's 'Sunday' programme, 26 February 2012, available at www.arcworld.org, accessed 26 February 2012.

Papanek, V. (1971 [1984]) *Design for the Real World: Human Ecology and Social Change*, 2nd edition, Thames & Hudson, London.

Papanek, V. (1995) *The Green Imperative: Ecology and Ethics in Design and Architecture*, Thames & Hudson, London.

Park, M. (2010) 'Defying obsolescence', in Cooper, T. (ed.), *Longer Lasting Products: Alternatives to the Throwaway Society*, Gower, Farnham, pp77–105.

Patton, L.L. (trans. and ed.) (2008) 'Introduction', in *The Bhagavad Gita*, Penguin Group, London.

Peattie, K. (2010) 'Rethinking marketing', in Cooper, T. (ed.), *Longer Lasting Products: Alternatives to the Throwaway Society*, Gower, Farnham, pp243–272.

People and the Planet, The Royal Society, London, available at http://royalsociety. org/policy/projects/people-planet/report, accessed 26 April 2012.

Perry, G. (2011) *The Tomb of the Unknown Craftsman*, The British Museum Press, London.

Peters, G. P., Minx, J. C., Weber, C. L. and Edenhoffer, O. (2011) 'Growth in emission transfers via international trade from 1990 to 2008', *Proceedings of the National Academy of Sciences of the United States of America (PNAS)*, open access article published online 25 April 2011, available at www.pnas.org/content/early/2011/04/19/1006388108, accessed 26 April 2011.

Plato (fourth century BCE [2005]) *Phaedrus*, trans. Rowe, C., Penguin Group, London.

Plato (fourth century BCE [2000]) *The Republic*, edited by Ferrari, G. R. F., trans. Griffith, T., Cambridge University Press, Cambridge.

Porritt, J. (2002) 'Sustainability without spirituality: a contradiction in terms?', *Conservation Biology*, vol. 16, no. 6, p1465.

Porritt, J. (2007) *Capitalism as if the World Matters*, Earthscan, London.

Power, T. M. (2000) 'Trapped in consumption: modern social structure and the entrenchment of the device', in Higgs, E., Light, A. and Strong, D. (eds), *Technology and the Good Life*, University of Chicago Press, Chicago, IL.

Princen, T. (2006) 'Consumption and its externalities: where economy meets ecology', in Jackson, T. (ed.), *Sustainable Consumption*, Earthscan, London.

RAF History (2005) *Bomber Command: Campaign Diary May 1942*, available at www.raf.mod.uk/bombercommand/may42.html, accessed 18 March 2011.

Raizman, D. (2010) *History of Modern Design*, Laurence King Publishing, London.

Raymond, R. (1986) *Out of the Fiery Furnace: The Impact of Metals on the History of Mankind*, Pennsylvania State University Press, University Park, PA.

Roadmap 2050 (2010) *Roadmap 2050: A Practical Guide to a Prosperous, Low-Carbon Europe: Technical Analysis*, vol. 1, April, McKinsey & Company, KEMA, The Energy Futures Lab at Imperial College London, Oxford Economics and the ECF, available at www.roadmap2050.eu/ attachments/files/Volume1_fullreport_PressPack.pdf, accessed 26 November 2012.

Rowell, M. (ed.) (1986) *Joan Miró: Selected Writings and Interviews*, Da Capo Press, Cambridge, MA.

Ruskin, J. (1857 [1907]) 'The political economy of art: addenda 5 – invention of new wants', in Rhys, E. (ed.), *Unto This Last and Other Essays on Art and Political Economy*, Everyman's Library, J. M. Dent & Sons Ltd, London.

Ruskin, J. (1859 [1908]) *The Two Paths*, Cassell and Company Ltd, London.

Ruskin, J. (1862–63 [1907]) 'Essays on the political economy, part 1: maintenance of life – wealth, money and riches', in Rhys, E. (ed.), *Unto This Last and other Essays on Art and Political Economy*, Everyman's Library, J. M. Dent & Sons Ltd, London.

Ruskin, J. (1884) *The Storm-Cloud of the Nineteenth Century*, two lectures delivered at the London Institution 4 and 11 February, available at www.archive.org/stream/thestormcloudoft20204gut/20204-8.txt, accessed 21 January 2012.

Sachs, J. D. (2008) *Common Wealth: Economics for a Crowded Planet*, Penguin Books, London.

SACOM (2011) 'Foxconn and Apple fail to fulfill promises: predicaments of workers after the suicides', report of Students and Scholars against Corporate Misbehaviour, Hong Kong, 6 May 2011, available at http://sacom.hk/wp-content/uploads/2011/05/2011-05-06_foxconn-and-apple-fail-to-fulfill-promises1.pdf, accessed 20 May 2011.

Saul, J. R. (2005) *The Collapse of Globalism, and the Reinvention of the World*, Viking, Toronto, ON.

Scharmer, C. O. (2009) *Theory U: Leading from the Future as it Emerges*, Berrett-Koehler Publishers, San Francisco, CA.

Scheidig, W. (1966) *Weimar Crafts of the Bauhaus: 1919–1924/An Early Experiment in Industrial Design*, Reinhold Publishing Corporation, New York.

Schmidt-Bleek, F. (2008) *FUTURE: Beyond Climatic Change*, position paper 08/01, Factor 10 Institute, available at www.factor10-institute.org/publications.html, accessed 5 September 2012.

Schumacher, E. F. (1973) *Small is Beautiful: A Study of Economics as if People Mattered*, Sphere Books Ltd, London.

Schumacher, E. F. (1977) *A Guide for the Perplexed*, Vintage Publishing, London.

Schuon, F. (1984) *The Transcendent Unity of Religions*, Quest Books, Wheaton, IL.

Schwarz, B. (2005) *The Paradox of Choice: Why More is Less*, Harper Collins, New York.

Scott, T. (2000) 'Understanding symbol', *Sacred Web: A Journal of Tradition and Modernity*, vol. 6, no. 2, available at www.sacredweb.com/online_articles/sw6_scott.html, accessed 18 April 2012, pp91–106.

Scruton, R. (2009) *Beauty*, Oxford University Press, Oxford.

Scruton, R. (2012) *Green Philosophy: How to Think Seriously about the Planet*, Atlantic Books, London.

Scruton, R. (2012) *The Face of God, The Gifford Lectures 2010*, Continuum, London.

Senge, P., Smith, B., Kruschwitz, N., Laur, J. and Schley, S. (2008) *The Necessary Revolution: How Individuals and Organizations are Working Together to Create a Sustainable World*, Nicholas Brealey Publishing, London.

Sennett, R. (2008) *The Craftsman*, Penguin Books, London.

Sheldrake, R. (2013) 'The science delusion', *Resurgence & Ecologist*, May/June no. 278.

Shelley, P. B. (1818 [1994]) 'Sonnet: lift not the painted veil', *The Works of P. B. Shelley*, Wordsworth Editions Ltd, Ware.

Short, W. (2008) 'Talk 7: the call of creatures (1210–1225)', *St. Francis of Assisi: A New Way of being Christian*, audio lecture series, Now You Know Media, Rockville, MD.

Shuman, M. H. (1998) *Going Local: Creating Self-reliant Communities in a Global Age*, Routledge, New York.

Sierra Club (2008) *Bottled Water: Learning the Facts and Taking Action*, available at www.sierraclub.org/committees/cac/water/bottled_water/bottled_water.pdf, accessed 10 February 2013.

Sim, S. (2007) *Manifesto for Silence: Confronting the Politics and Culture of Noise*, Edinburgh University Press, Edinburgh.

Simon, M. (2010) 'Product life cycle management through IT', in Cooper, T. (ed.), *Longer Lasting Products: Alternatives to the Throwaway Society*, Gower, Farnham, pp351–366.

Skidelsky, R. and Skidelsky E. (2012) *How Much is Enough: Money and the Good Life*, Other Press, New York.

Smith, H. (1991) *The World's Religions* (revised edition), HarperSanFrancisco, New York.

Smith, H. (1996 [2005]) 'Foreword' in Johnston, W. (ed.), *The Cloud of Unknowing and the Book of Privy Counseling*, Image Books, Doubleday, New York.

Smith, H. (2001) *Why Religion Matters: The Fate of the Human Spirit in an Age of Disbelief*, HarperCollins, New York.

Smith-Spark, L. (2007) 'Apple iPhone draws diverse queue', *BBC News*, 29 June, available at http://news.bbc.co.uk/1/hi/technology/6254986.stm, accessed 17 January 2012.

Sorrell, R. D. (1988) *St. Francis of Assisi and Nature: Tradition and Innovation in Western Christian Attitudes Toward the Environment*, Oxford University Press, Oxford.

Sparke, P. (1986) *An Introduction to Design and Culture in the 20th Century*, Allen & Unwin, London.

Sparke, P. (2004) *An Introduction to Design and Culture: 1900 to the Present*, 2nd edition, Routledge, London.

Stahel, W. (2010) 'Durability, function and performance', in Cooper, T. (ed.), *Longer Lasting Products: Alternatives to the Throwaway Society*, Gower, Farnham, pp157–176.

Stangos, N. (1981) *Concepts of Modern Art*, Thames & Hudson, London.

179

Steele, T. J. (1984) *Santos and Saints: The Religious Folk Art of Hispanic New Mexico*, Ancient City Press, Santa Fe.

Stevens, D. (2007) *Rural*, Mermaid Turbulence, Leitrim, Ireland.

Stevenson, R. L. (1888 [1988]) 'The lantern bearers', in *The Lantern Bearers and Other Essays*, edited by Treglown, J., Cooper Square Press, New York.

Stewart, H. and Elliot, L. (2013) 'Nicholas Stern: "I got it wrong on climate change – it's far, far worse"', *Guardian*, 26 January, available at www.guardian.co.uk/environment/2013/jan/27/nicholas-stern-climate-change-davos, accessed Sunday 27 January 2013.

Strauss, C. and Fuad-Luke, A. (2008) 'The slow design principles: a new interrogative and reflexive tool for design research and practice', in Cipolla, C. and Paolo Peruccio, P. (eds), *Changing the Change Proceedings*, pp1440–1450, Changing the Change conference, Turin, Italy, June 2008, available at www.changingthechange.org/papers/ctc.pdf, accessed 20 July 2012.

Stryk, L. (trans.) (1985) 'Introduction', in *On Love and Barley: Haiku of Basho*, Penguin Books, London.

Sulston, J., Bateson, P., Biggar, N., Fang, C., Cavenaghi, S., Cleland, J., Mauzé, J. C. A. R., Dasgupta, P., Eloundou-Enyegue, P. M., Fitter, A., Habte, D., Jackson, T., Mace, G., Owens, S., Porritt, J., Potts Bixby, M., Pretty, J., Ram, F., Short, R., Spencer, S., Xiaoying, Z. and Zulu, E. (2012) *People and the Planet*, The Royal Society, London, available at http://royalsociety.org/policy/projects/people-planet/report, accessed 26 April 2012.

Swann, C. (2002) 'Action research and the practice of design', *Design Issues*, vol. 18, no. 2, pp49–61.

Tanahashi, K. (ed.) (1985) *Moon in a Dewdrop: Writings of Zen Master Dogen*, North Point Press, New York.

Tarnas, T. (1991) *The Passion of the Western Mind*, Harmony Books, New York.

Tate Britain (2012) *Walter Richard Sickert, Ennui, c.1914*, available at www.tate.org.uk/art/artworks/sickert-ennui-n03846, accessed 24 May 2012.

Taylor, C. (1991) *The Malaise of Modernity*, Anansi, Concord, ON.

Taylor, C. (2007) *A Secular Age*, The Belknap Press of Harvard University Press, Cambridge, MA.

Thomson, J. A. K. (1976) *The Ethics of Aristotle: The Nicomachean Ethics*, Penguin Books, London.

Thoreau, H. D. (1854 [1983]) 'Walden', in Thoreau, H. D., *Walden and Civil Disobedience*, Penguin Group, New York, pp45–382.

Tillich, P. (1952 [2000]) *The Courage to Be.* 2nd edition, Yale University Press, New Haven, CT.

Transition Culture (2010) *'Localism' or 'Localisation'? Defining Our Terms*, 23 July, available at http://transitionculture.org/2010/07/30/localism-or-localisation-defining-our-terms, accessed 27 August 2012.

180

Tucker, M. E. (2003) *Worldly Wonder: Religions Enter their Ecological Phase*, Open Court, Chicago, IL.

Tucker, S. (1998) 'ChristStory nightingale page', *ChristStory Christian Bestiary*, available at ww2.netnitco.net/users/legend01/nighting.htm, accessed 19 March 2011.

Turkle, S. (2011) *Alone Together: Why We Expect More from Technology and Less from Each Other*, Basic Books, New York.

Uddin, M. and Rahman, A. A. (2012) 'Energy efficiency and low carbon enabler green IT framework for data centers considering green metrics', *Renewable and Sustainable Energy Reviews*, vol. 16, no. 2, pp4078–4094.

Van der Ryn, S. and Cowan, S. (1996) *Ecological Design*, Island Press, Washington, DC.

Van Wieren, G. (2008) 'Ecological restoration as public spiritual practice', *Worldviews*, vol. 12, pp237–254, available at www.uvm.edu/rsenr/greenforestry/LIBRARYFILES/restoration.pdf, accessed 30 August 2011.

Walker, S. (2009) 'The spirit of design: notes from the shakuhachi flute', *International Journal of Sustainable Design*, vol. 1, no. 2, pp130–144.

Walker, S. (2011) *The Spirit of Design: Objects, Environment and Meaning*, Earthscan, Abingdon.

Walker, S. and Giard, J. (eds) (2013) *The Handbook of Design for Sustainability*, Bloomsbury Academic, London.

Walters, A. L. (1989) *The Spirit of Native America: Beauty and Mysticism in American Indian Art*, Chronicle Books, San Francisco.

Ware, K. (1987) 'The theology and spirituality of the icon', in *From Byzantium to El Greco: Greek Frescoes and Icons*, Royal Academy of Arts, London.

Watts, A. W. (1957) *The Way of Zen*, Arkana, London.

Weber, M. (1965) *The Sociology of Religion*, available at www.e-reading-lib.org/bookreader.php/145149/The_Sociology_of_Religion.pdf, accessed 25 January 2013.

WEEE (2007) Waste Electrical and Electronic Equipment Directive, available at www.environment-agency.gov.uk/business/topics/waste/32084.aspx, accessed 30 October 2012.

Whitford, F. (1984) *Bauhaus*, Thames & Hudson Ltd, London.

Wilkinson, R. and Pickett, K. (2009) *The Spirit Level: Why More Equal Societies Almost Always Do Better*, Allen Lane, London.

Williams, A. (trans.) (2006) *Rumi: Spiritual Verses – The First Book of the Masnavi-ye Ma'navi*, Penguin Books, London.

Williams, R. J. (2011) 'Technê-Zen and the spiritual quality of global capitalism', *Critical Inquiry*, vol. 37, pp17–70.

Williamson, P. (1999) *From Confinement to Community: The Moving Story of 'The Moor'*, P. Williamson, Lancaster, quoting an extract from the *Lancaster Guardian* newspaper article from 19 September 1857.

Wilson, A. N. (2011) *Dante in Love*, Atlantic Books, London.

181

Wittgenstein, L. (1921a [1961]) *Tractatus Logico-Philosophicus*, trans. Pears, D. F. and McGuinness, B. F., Routledge, London.

Wittgenstein, L. (1921b) *Tractatus Logico-Philosophicus*, Proposition 7, trans. Ogden, C. K., available at www.kfs.org/~jonathan/witt/tlph.html, accessed 17 May 2011.

Wolters, C. (trans.) (1972) *Richard Rolle: The Fire of Love*, Penguin Books, Hardmondsworth.

Woodhead, L. (2012a) 'Restoring religion to the public square', *The Tablet*, 28 January.

Woodhead, L. (2012b) 'Religion à la mode', *The Tablet*, 28 April.

Wright, D. (trans.) (1964) *The Canterbury Tales: A Modern Prose Rendering*, FontanaPress, London.

Wright, J. K. (2001) *Schoenberg, Wittgenstein, and the Vienna Circle: Epistemological Meta-Themes in Harmonie Theory, Aesthetics, and Logical Positivism*, PhD thesis, Faculty of Graduate Studies and Research, McGill University, Montreal, Quebec, Canada, available at http://digitool.library.mcgill.ca/R/?func=dbin-jump-full&object_id=38438&local_base=GEN01-MCG02, accessed 23 September 2012.

Yamakage, M. (2006) *The Essence of Shinto: Japan's Spiritual Heart*, Kodansha International, Tokyo.

Yuasa, N. (trans.) (1966) 'Introduction', in *The Narrow Road to the Deep North and Other Travel Sketches*, Penguin Books, London.

Index

Figures are shown by a page reference in *italics*, and tables are in **bold**.

185